8/14

# The Art of Scouting

## Seven Decades Chasing Hopes and Dreams in Major League Baseball

"Art Stewart has done it all: Stadium clean-up kid, sandlot baseball manager, professional scout, Major League executive and hilarious storyteller. For example, one of Art's tricks was to hide me from competing scouts by pitching me exclusively against the Joliet and Statesville, Illinois penitentiary teams. The next trick was to making it out of there. And eventually I made it to the Yankees. Thanks, Art."

**Jim Bouton,** 20-game winner for the New York Yankees and best-selling author of Ball Four

"Eat a good meal and sit down for a while, because you're going to hear a lot of great stories. He's an encyclopedia of great stories and facts. His memory is incredible. He's just a wonderful source of entertainment, stories, knowledge and information."

**Denny Matthews,** Ford Frick Award winner from the Hall of Fame and voice of the Kansas City Royals from the team's inception in 1969

"Art Stewart represents the greatest era in the baseball scouting profession. His expertise, experiences, and stories as a baseball man are to be cherished. He is simply loved and respected by all who know and work with him."

**Dayton Moore,** general manager Kansas City Royals

"Art is a legend in baseball. He's passionate about the game, and hasn't lost that passion. He's rare. You don't see people involved in the game often with that length of service, and stay as involved as he does. He can talk baseball forever. He's that rare individual who will never tire of it, and bring up great points and great discussions, from a historical or contemporary perspective."

**Dave Dombrowski,** general manager of the 1997 World Champion Florida Marlins and Detroit Tigers GM since 2002

"Passion, loyalty, integrity, work ethic, competiveness, friendship. This would be the scouting report on Art Stewart. Having signed 70 major leaguers and traveling millions of miles evaluating thousands of players, whom is more qualified to tell the scouts' story?"

**Pat Gillick,** Hall of Fame general manager for the Toronto Blue Jays, Baltimore Orioles, Seattle Mariners and Philadelphia Phillies

"Three of the most influential men who really put the Royals on the map are Ewing Kauffman, George Brett and Art Stewart. Art is like a doctor at the Mayo Clinic, at the top of his field, but also like your grandfather, someone you just want to sit with and listen to his stories. Henry Ford brought to life the automobile, and Art Stewart brought to life scouting. The proof of that is in his stories, his connections, his life."

**Mike Sweeney,** five-time All-Star and
2007 winner of the Hutch Award

"Art is a pioneer. He believes what he sees, what those eyes tell him. He has a real gut feel for it, and a real passion for people. He's just a tremendous, tremendous person and obviously a very talented baseball man. I've always had the utmost respect for him. He's one of the originals."

**Jim Leyland,** three-time MLB manager of the year
and world champion with the 1997 Florida Marlins

"Art is among the greatest who've been part of our game. He has a wonderful smartness about who can play and how they should play. He learned so much from so many great experiences, and has a terrific personality so he's always around people who want to share their knowledge and love for the game. And the thing that puts him over the top is longevity, because he's accumulated all of this over decades and can pass it along in a book about our modern game."

**Tony LaRussa,** Hall of Fame manager and three-time world
champion with the Oakland A's and St. Louis Cardinals

"Art Stewart is an icon in the scouting world. Art is the ultimate pro. His focus during games, complete concentration, and knowing when to approach coaches and players after the game is a model for scouts young and old. Times have changed around him, but Art excels under any circumstance. His book is educational and entertaining on all levels."

**Roland Hemond,** three-time MLB Executive of the
Year winner and the first person other than the namesake
to win the Buck O'Neil Lifetime Achievement Award

"Art was always there for me from day one when I signed with the Royals and he took me to Memphis to start my baseball career. I've never seen anyone who loved the game more. He gave his life to it. His wife, Donna, was like a second mother to me and I could always hear her voice even if there were 40,000 people in the stadium.."

**Bo Jackson,** Royals All-Star, NFL Pro Bowler, Heisman Trophy
winner and ESPN Sports Science's greatest athlete of all-time

"His passion and his fervor and love of baseball is so obvious. This is his life, his dedication. He brings an energy that is beyond measure. He is a goer, a digger, he gets information about where the players are and who they are. What stands out to me is his passion, energy, vigor and complete, total-body-experience dedication to baseball. His wife, too. You'd see Donna with her radar gun and stopwatch, they were a real baseball family. A baseball couple. And he still has the same passion today. For a guy to be working 60-some years with no diminished light in the eye or interest or reverence for the game, every breath he takes in and out is about finding players and keeping the pipeline filled."

> **John Schuerholz,** Atlanta Braves president and two-time World
> Champion general manager with the Braves and Kansas City Royals

"I first met him in 1970, because Mr. K wanted to know what kind of prospects he had in the Baseball Academy. When you go through the years, and you see the players he had contact with, the guys he found and signed, those players look at Art like a father figure after a while. He's been in the game so long, and remembers everything about them. You don't get that from a lot of people. That tells me he didn't just sign guys. He took a personal interest in who they were."

> **Frank White,** nine-time Gold Glove winner and one of
> only three Kansas City Royals with their number retired

"I scouted against Art. We had the same area and he was one of the veteran scouts even back then that you're competing against and you knew Art was always a threat. He was one of those guys, if you saw him at the park you knew it would be a battle to get that player. A guy scouting as long as he has, that's almost unreal. He is a well-rounded, efficient scout who could close deals. And that's the trick. If he was at the game you went to, you knew you had some issues. The Bo Jackson thing didn't happen by chance, you know."

> **Terry Ryan,** two-time executive of the year and
> former general manager of the Minneosta Twins

"I've known Art since I was 16 years old. He's been with the Royals almost since their first day, and his opinion has been important for the team, and the game of baseball. When I think about Art, I think of love and passion. The only thing he wants to do is make a difference in people's lives, whether they're baseball players or otherwise. He's always making certain he can do the best he can to put a smile on your face."

> **Ron Washington,** winningest manager in Texas Rangers
> history and two-time American League champion

# The Art of Scouting

## Seven Decades Chasing Hopes and Dreams in Major League Baseball

# Art Stewart

## with Sam Mellinger

Requests for permission should be addressed to: Ascend Books, LLC, Attn: Rights and
Permissions Department, 12710 Pflumm Road, Suite 200, Olathe, KS. 66062

10 9 8 7 6 5 4 3 2 1

ISBN: print book  978-0-9912756-1-8
ISBN: e-book  978-0-9912756-2-5

Library of Congress Cataloging-in-Publications Data Available Upon Request
Publisher: Bob Snodgrass
Editor:  Jim Bradford
Publication Coordinator: Christine Drummond
Sales and Marketing: Lenny Cohen and Dylan Tucker
Dust Jacket and Book Design: Rob Peters

All photos courtesy of Art Stewart unless otherwise indicated.

Every reasonable attempt has been made to determine the ownership of copyright.
Please notify the publisher of any erroneous credits or omissions, and corrections will
be made to subsequent editions/future printings. The goal of Ascend Books is to publish
quality works. With that goal in mind, we are proud to offer this book to our readers.
Please note however, that the story, the experiences and the words are those of the authors
alone.
Printed in the United States of America

www.ascendbooks.com

# Table of Contents

# SPECIAL THANKS TO:

# Dedication

To Donna, my wife of 47 years, our daughter Dawn
and grandsons David and Mark, and to major league
scouts past and present.

# Foreword
# by George Brett

*P*eople tend to think of Ewing Kauffman or Frank White or myself when they think of the Royals, but every man who's worked for this organization thinks of Art Stewart just as often and just as quickly.

Art is the longest tenured Royals employee in baseball operations.

I'm no. 2, even if you count my three years in the minor leagues, 21 as a player, and now 21 more in the front office.

Put it this way: Art was with the Royals before I was, and I've known him so long I can't even remember the first time I met him. But I'll bet you it was in instructional league right after I was drafted, when I had my head down, scared out of my mind that I couldn't make it, desperate to impress men like him.

Art is everywhere, even after more than 60 years in this game. There are rare guys who stick around a really long time like Art, but they're usually not as active. Not as vocal. Not as passionate.

If you're ever around me, or Bret Saberhagen, or Mike Sweeney, or Joe Randa, any number of the players Art either helped bring to the Royals or raise through the system, it will make our day when we see him. Chances are it'll make your day if you meet him, too.

He's the most positive guy I've ever met in my life. Every year is *the* year, and every player is *the* player. That type of energy and outlook is infectious. Every time you're around him, you get pumped up about the Royals. He's just that kind of guy. Every game he goes to, he'll find something good that someone did and point that out.

But you know what else about Art? He'll call you out when you're not giving the effort you should. His background, and his passion make him the perfect guy to do it, too.

It's because he's everywhere. He's at every game, timing every guy down to first base, putting his radar gun on every guy's fastball and curveball and changeup. He knows when you're slacking off. He's like the eye in the sky for us. It can be 40 degrees and raining, and Art is in the first row watching. It can be 100 degrees and humid, and Art is in the first row watching.

In the summer of 2013, when I was the hitting coach, he was in the coaches' room after every game to tell pitching coach Dave Eiland how good or bad the guy's breaking stuff was that night, where his velocity was in the first inning, the third inning, the seventh inning, everything you could want.

There isn't one person who's been involved with the Royals over the years who can't tell you about Art Stewart, and if they were involved before she passed away in 2008, they probably know all about Art's first wife Donna, too.

Me, I remember Donna yelling and screaming at me in the batters box when I'm swinging at bad pitches: "George, be more patient! Be patient!"

She was as much a part of the Royals as he was. She had her own stopwatch, and ran the radar gun at times. Come to think of it, I should've asked her to read Art's notes. When they were watching games together, you could see Donna holding the radar gun and Art running the stopwatch and then getting his blue pen to write something here and then his red pen to write something there and when it's over, I'm telling you, I couldn't tell what any of it means. But that scorebook sings to Art. I know Donna could read it, too, because there wasn't anything one of them did that the other wasn't doing, too.

I played more than 20 years in the big leagues, and I've been retired more than 20 years and Art has been in professional baseball longer than I've been alive. That doesn't happen by accident, and remember that Art didn't have a great big league career or legacy to draw on to earn credibility.

There aren't a lot of guys who've been in baseball that long, ever, but the ones who last that long usually had a long career to make connections. Art's career has been making those connections, and earning the respect he has by hard work.

You think about a guy who's been in professional baseball more than 60 years without playing or managing, and that's got to be someone who's not afraid to work and put miles in his car to drive out to watch two nothing high school teams in the middle of nowhere with the hope of finding one good player that nobody else knows about.

Art has done that, and most of the time there's nothing there. But he keeps going back, because the next time there might be something there. And if it happens like that, Art has a prospect to tell his big league club about — and he's got a story to tell the rest of us about.

That's the kind of thing you hear about when you talk to Art. You hear about finding Rick Reichardt in the middle of nowhere and following him all the way until they basically created a draft for him. You hear about him sneaking into a house and overhearing some other scout's offer, then outbidding him. You hear about him charming cops out of speeding tickets, and convincing a farmer on the side of the road in Alligator Alley to siphon gas for his rental car.

Art's drive and relentless desire to find the next great player are an important part of why the Royals were winners so quickly, and for so long. The Royals Academy that helped Frank White and Ron Washington and others to the big leagues was fueled by Art.

Bo Jackson didn't get to the Royals by accident. We were at the bottom of the draft in 1986, the year after winning the World Series, and the Royals still found eight big leaguers in the draft with Art as the scouting director. That hardly ever happens. There are so many stories like that, and we all know the Royals fell on hard times after Mr. Kauffman died but that's not Art's fault. There were years in the draft where we just didn't have the money to draft the best players. We all play within our boundaries.

Now that the Royals are back spending what it takes to sign the best talent available, Art is part of that group that built the farm system into one of the best in baseball. Just like he did with the Royals in the 1970s and 1980s, and just like he did with the Yankees before that.

I don't know where the Royals would be without Art, but I know you couldn't have a more loyal guy. You couldn't have a guy with a longer history in the game, and more stories about living inside the game for more than six decades.

I'm looking forward to reliving so many of them in this book, and hearing new ones, too.

## Chapter

# 1

# Donna Wakely and the two great loves of my life

**W**e were all there for Ethan Blackaby. That name probably doesn't mean anything to you. He only made it 15 games in the big leagues, for the Braves. But back in July of 1960 he was a big prospect. He ended up getting $45,000 to sign.

More importantly, he's the reason I met this beautiful young lady named Donna Wakely at the state semi-pro tournament at Wing Park in Elgin, Ill.

Starting that night, for 47 years, Donna and baseball were the most constant parts of my life — my two greatest loves.

• • •

Donna walked in and everybody noticed her. I don't distract easily at baseball games. It's my office, my job, and you never know when something subtle will happen on the field that will tell you about someone.

But Donna, she caught my eye.

I was sitting five rows or so back, behind home plate. Donna walks in with a friend and sits in the front row. Nick Kamzic is there, scouting for the Angels, and Nick is a talker. Always talking. Good at it, too, including with the ladies. He's started talking to her about his job and his team and, well, she let him know exactly what she thought..

"There's only one club in baseball," she told Nick. "And that's the New York Yankees."

Nick is shut down, so he points back at me.

"The Yankees scout is right up there," he says to her.

Then, to me, "Hey Artie, here's a good Yankee fan!"

So she comes back and sits next to me and we start talking and she knew all about the Yankees. Every player, every moment. Before we ever met, we shared a love for baseball and the Yankees. Her grandfather brought her up to be a Yankee fan from the time she was a little girl. She knew all about Lou Gehrig and Babe Ruth and Joe DiMaggio and the team we had that year with Roger Maris, Mickey Mantle and Whitey Ford.

What a fan. Turns out she came to this state tournament every year. Around the sixth or seventh inning, I test her.

"Who's the best player out here?"

She doesn't pause a second.

"That centerfielder out there," she says, pointing to Blackaby. "He can run well, and he has a good swing."

I'm thinking, "Oh, my. Another scout."

It was almost like love at first sight. And, of course, her knowledge and love of baseball and the Yankees helped, without a doubt.

We got married, and one of the first things we did together was decorate our den in Yankee stuff. She even custom-ordered a big rug from Puerto Rico. Yep, that Yankee logo met you first thing when you walked into the room.

• • •

Donna was tough. Oh, man, was she tough. You have to be tough to make in baseball, and to be a scout's wife. She came on the road with me a lot, but there are still a lot of nights you're alone. You have to be confident, independent.

Donna was all of those things and more.

She was fearless, too. We were on a scouting trip together one year in Rockford, Ill., and when we were in the parking lot before the game the car in front of us got side-swiped. Everyone there could hear the collision, but the driver just kept on going. He sped off.

You know what Donna did? She grabbed her purse, pulled out her lipstick, and used it to write down the license plate number of the guy who drove off.

16

She found a cop, gave him the number, and they found the guy. Turned out to be a high school kid who went to the game.

As it turns out, the car he hit belonged to a Phillies scout.

Baseball is a small world.

• • •

We really only had one disagreement, and it was in 1969, when I left the Yankees.

It was a tough decision, and we'll get into that later, but I knew it was the right thing. The Yankees had changed ownership, and it really wasn't the same. It was much more corporate, and I'd heard so many good things about the environment Ewing Kauffman was starting in Kansas City. What they were talking about with the Royals was what I fell in love with about the Yankees.

But Donna didn't see it that way. She wasn't happy.

"How could you leave the Yankees?"

"How could you leave the pinstripes?"

She didn't accept it at all. She was still rooting for the Yankees, even after I started working for the Royals.

It went on like this for more than a year, and neither of us budged. The Yankees were her team, and the Royals were my team. I'm telling you, it's really the only disagreement we ever had.

That started to change, gradually. The Royals started winning quickly, quicker than any expansion team in history. We won 85 games in our

*Photo Courtesy of Kansas City Royals*

This is Donna with one of Frank White's Gold Gloves. Frank was always one of her favorites, both because of his glove and that he came out of the Academy. She was like my co-scout for nearly five decades of marriage, helping me with the stopwatch and never being shy with her opinions. The players got to know Donna right along with me. Bo Jackson said he could always pick Donna's voice out of the thousands at Royals Stadium.

third year, 88 in the fifth year, 91 in the seventh year and went to the ALCS the next season.

So after a year or so, she started to see all the talent on the field and listened to me about all the talent we had in the farm system. That first year we drafted Paul Splittorff, then Al Cowens and in 1971 we got George Brett in the second round.

Donna gradually came around. One turning point was an awards dinner we had my first year, in 1970. They had it at the Muelbach Hotel, and I was so humbled when I won the scouting award named after Mr. Kauffman. I could tell that Donna was impressed. That plaque still hangs in my den.

I told you Donna knew the game, so she was impressed with what we were doing. I went on the road to see a farm club, I think it was Omaha, and I came home and I'll never forget walking in the den.

The Yankee rug was gone, and the whole room was redone in Royals blue and gold. The curtains, the walls, the pictures, everything. There was a new rug, done in Royals' colors.

That's when I knew I finally won her over as a Royal.

Of course, I guess you could say the team won her over.

That's how it always was with Donna. Our lives revolved around each other, and around baseball.

• • •

Bo Jackson always said that out of thousands of voices in the ballpark, he could always pick out Donna's.

They had such a good relationship. They just

*Here we are at a writers' dinner in 1962. That's me on the left, the old Cubs manager Leo Durocher on the right, and Nick Kamzic in the middle. Nick was not only my best friend, and the best man in our wedding, but he also introduced Donna and me. It happened at a baseball game, of course. Donna told Nick she was a Yankee fan, and Nick pointed her my way. The rest was history.*

took a liking to each other. I think Bo could tell that Donna's interest and intentions were genuine, and Donna saw a special blend of ability, confidence and drive in Bo.

I'll never forget that last spring, after the football injury that basically ended Bo's career in both sports. He'd be in the whirlpool at the Residence Inn in Baseball City, Fla., and Donna would come in and talk with him. She'd encourage him. Bo needed that, and he never forgot it. Even later, when he came back and played for the White Sox, he'd find her before games against us and he and Donna would go on talking and laughing like lifelong friends.

She got to know all our players well. She was more than a wife to me, really. She became like a partner on the job. She was a big asset for not just me, but the Royals.

I remember being in Des Moines to see our Omaha club play the Iowa Cubs. Joe Randa was with the Omaha team at the time, still waiting for his shot in the big leagues. His wife was there. She was worried. She wondered if Joe would get that shot, worried about what kind of career he'd have, what the big league life would be like. And she gravitated toward Donna for answers.

Donna could explain things in a way that I and other scouts couldn't. She knew the game so well, but still came from a different place. The wives, especially, appreciated that. She helped Johnny Damon's wife a lot, too. They became close. And Bo's wife, Linda.

She could understand it so well because she understood it.

Heck, understand it? She was part of it.

• • •

Donna probably watched more baseball games than just about anyone who wasn't paid to do it. She went on the road with me, and she went to home games with me. We went to games together when we were young, and when we weren't as young. She came to games when she was pregnant with our daughter. That summer, when the sun was shining bright, was one of the few times we didn't sit together.

Late at night, after a long day at the ballpark, she'd have some snacks ready before we went to bed. Early in the morning, she'd gather stories from around the country on different prospects for me to read.

She helped me scout. She made me better. I signed a player at Comiskey Park once, without the White Sox even knowing we were in the building. Donna came with me, and took the player's stepmother out shopping while we got the deal done. That player turned out to be Fritz Peterson, who became an all-star with the Yankees.

Donna and I always made a good team. Everybody knew Donna. I'd be at the ballpark, and if she wasn't around, guys would ask about her.

Dayton Moore, who, of course, is our general manager now, never forgot meeting Donna. This goes all the way back to the 1980s. Donna was with me at the Seven State Regional Tournament in South Dakota. Dayton was this little, good-looking second baseman. He made some nice plays, handled the bat OK.

His team played against Greg Olson, the pitcher who went on to win the Rookie of the Year with the Orioles in 1989 with that great curveball. Dayton played really well in that game, and he was only a junior, so I made a point to meet him after the game. I asked him to fill out an information card so we could keep tabs on him.

So, years and years later, this is when Dayton was still working for the Braves and making a name for himself there. He finds me one day.

"You probably don't remember this," he says. "But you were the first scout to ever give me an information card to fill out. And you know how a player feels when a major league team talks to him. I'll never forget that, and what that felt like."

He paused for a second.

"And I'll never forget Donna being with you."

• • •

She really did know the game. She could tell when a guy was playing through pain, could tell when a guy had the good breaking ball working, and could tell when the hitter missed his pitch.

She loved the game as much as I did, and wasn't afraid to point out what she saw.

I'll give you an example. We're at this amateur tournament in Eau Claire, Wisc. It's a big tournament with a lot of talent, the kind of event where there's more pro prospects than any one team could sign.

There was this first baseman there, a power hitter. I didn't warm up to him that much. He was heavy, didn't move too well.

"Gee," I tell Donna, "I don't know about that body. I don't know if he can make it with that body."

"Yeah, but Art," she says, "Look at the way he's swinging the bat. Oh, I think he's going to have some power. I wouldn't worry about that body."

I still didn't like him that much, but I'll be darned if that next June, Rosie Gillhouse didn't get up in the draft room and make a case for this kid.

We ended up drafting him in the 15th round. His name was Ken Phelps, and he took that big body 11 years in the big leagues, hitting 24 or more homers four times.

I'll tell you something else, too: Donna would let me know when she was right. She didn't let me forget.

Like I say, she was a real asset to not just me but the Royals. After the World Series in 1985, all the wives got these pendants with the top of the championship rings on them. Donna deserved hers, and more. Our daughter Dawn wears it to this day.

Meeting Donna, it was absolutely fate.

Fate and baseball.

• • •

We were playing Toronto at home, late in the 2007 season. I was scouting the game, and Donna was with me, the same way she was with me a few thousand times before.

"After 47 years," she said, "these seats must be getting to my back."

The next day, she felt even worse. When she didn't feel up for the

This is Dayton and me before a game at Kauffman Stadium. Sometimes he still brings up the first time we met. I'd forgotten about this, but I had him fill out an information card when he was in high school. I was the first big league scout to talk to Dayton, and a player never forgets that. Dayton always said, "I remember you had Donna with you, too." She made a lot of scouting trips with me.

*Photo Courtesy of Kansas City Royals*

game, I knew something was wrong. We took her to the hospital. The doctors found some lesions in her back. Those were treatable. Then they found cancer in her breast. Advanced cancer. She did all the treatment. They put a rod in her leg, and she never complained. Not even once. She was always so tough.

By February of the next year, we knew what was happening. She lost consciousness one day. Dawn and I talked to her anyway. After a while, she opened her eyes. I know she saw us. I think she even smiled, just a little bit.

And that was it.

Donna lived long enough to hear they were inducting me to the Royals Hall of Fame, but not long enough to see it.

That's OK. I know she saw it. And she knows it was for both of us.

*Photo Courtesy of Kansas City Royals*

*I always said being married to Donna was like being married to another scout. She loved the game as much as I did, and when we were watching games, we were both working. She knew the game, and was never shy about telling me what she thought. She was usually right, too.*

# Chapter
# 2

# Bo Jackson and the greatest scouting story of my life

*T*he greatest pure scouting story of my seven decades in baseball turned out to give us the greatest pure athlete I've ever seen.

This kid had everything. A once-in-a-lifetime physical talent. Superstardom. Trust. Lies. Corruption. detective work, psychological work, patience, urgency, luck and a story that shook up not just Major League Baseball but the NFL and American sports.

You know about Bo Jackson. You've probably seen "The Throw." You've seen him run over Brian Bosworth and you've heard the stories about how men who've spent their entire lives in each sport swear he'd be in the Hall of Fame of both football and baseball if not for the injuries.

So you know a lot of the popular stories about Bo Jackson.

But do you know the real story of why he even tried professional baseball in the first place, and why he tried it with the Kansas City Royals?

• • •

The first time I heard Bo Jackson's name was the spring of 1980. He was a sophomore at McAdory High School in Bessemer, Ala., and Kenny Gonzales, our scout in the area called me with wonder in his voice.

"I saw this player down here," he says. "I don't know if he's a boy or a man."

Kenny was hooked from the very beginning. This kid had everything. It was like a movie, like a story someone would make up. I've never seen anything like it since, and I never saw anything like it before.

He pitched sometimes, and it was just unfair. Sometimes, when he was really feeling it, his whole defense would sit down on the field with their gloves on the ground, daring the batter just to make contact. He was 9-0 or something like that as a pitcher, throwing 95 and 96 mph off the mound.

When he played, he just broke the game. He was too good, too powerful, too athletic. The high school fields looked like little league parks. Bo tied the national high school record with 20 home runs his senior year, and he did it in only 25 games. He missed about seven because he was competing in track meets, and, of course, he set all kinds of records in those track meets, too. The 60-yard dash, the 100-yard dash, the 120-yard hurdles.

I'll tell you how fast he is. He ran the 60 in 6.15 seconds, and that's the fastest I've ever seen in baseball. Willie Wilson was a 6.3, to give you an idea. Heck, Deion Sanders was a 6.3. Bo Jackson was just on a different level.

He ended up with 90 stolen bases in 91 attempts in high school. Many years later, after we signed him, I said to Bo, "I need to know who the heck that catcher was because we're going to sign him, too!"

Bo laughed. It turns out he stumbled twice before he could get going. He stumbled on his jump, took off, then stumbled again.

Ken Gonzales, far left, with me and Hugh Walker, who played briefly for the Royals before going into player development and scouting. Ken was the lead scout in the pursuit and eventual signing of Bo Jackson. Ken really got to know Bo and his family, which paid off when we passed on him in the draft three times before drafting him in 1986.

"And the guy only got me by a hair," he said.

Bo was like his generation's Mickey Mantle in a lot of ways. Some of the stories about Mickey sounded like they had to be made up. The 500-foot home runs from each side of the plate, the way he was the most powerful and fastest son of a gun in the big leagues at the same time. Mickey liked to have a good time, everybody knew that, and everybody knew the stories about how he'd be out until all hours of the night and then make it for a day game and hit two home runs.

I was there for a lot of Mickey's time with the Yankees, so I know all those stories are true, just like I know they sound made up to a lot of people. I think that's how it is with Bo a little bit. How could a guy hit 32 home runs in the big leagues, be the MVP of the All-Star game, and then walk onto a football field and be one of the best running backs in the NFL?

How could he hit these long home runs, and run flat over these linebackers, run a 4.12 40-yard dash at the combine — they won't count that as official because it was handheld — without ever lifting a weight?

I know this all sounds exaggerated, and there are times we scouts get overly excited about a player. I might not have believed some of this if I hadn't seen it myself.

I've done this for seven decades, and I've never seen anything like this guy.

Of course, seeing the talent is one thing. Signing the talent is quite another thing, and that was especially true with Bo.

• • •

Florence Bond was a big, buxom woman with a loud laugh and a big smile — and an even bigger heart. She was Bo's mother, and she was so proud of her boy. Not just because of sports, either.

They had a bond like glue, even as Bo sometimes got in some boys-will-be-boys type of trouble as a kid. Bo could be a stubborn boy who wanted things his own way, but he never disrespected his mother. She controlled him with a tough love you had to admire.

Kenny knew how Bo felt about his mom, and about how close they were. So every time he went to Bessemer, Ala., Kenny stayed at the Ramada Inn where Florence worked as a maid. He found out when she took her coffee break, and he planned his day around it. He would sit with her, eat with her, take her for coffee and talk.

They both knew why he was there, but Kenny didn't make a hard sell. You never want to do that in the beginning, but I don't think Kenny ever went for the hard sell. He was such a genuine guy, and Florence saw that early. Kenny was honest with her, and he asked questions, and he listened. Eventually, it's a really close relationship.

People sometimes think you have to be smooth or funny or make big promises to break through with top-level athletes and their families, but I don't think it works like that. There are enough people around doing all that, saying what they can provide, what they can offer, and flashing shiny things. Sometimes what sticks out to the kid and his parents is someone who *asks* what they want, someone who isn't blowing smoke, and won't make false promises.

That was the approach I've always tried to take, and the approach I've always wanted our scouts to take. Kenny was one of the best.

By the time his senior year comes around, of course Bo is known across the country. College football coaches are all over him, and every club in baseball was on to him. The Royals were no different. Kenny had close to an 80 report on him, which is as good as you can get. You don't fill out more than a few 80 reports in a decade, and Kenny made it clear to both Bo and Florence that we would love to draft him.

*Photo Courtesy of Kansas City Royals*

Here is where that relationship became so useful. Bo had a scholarship to Alabama, and a scholarship to Auburn. Both schools said he could play both sports. Kenny could've made his pitch about the signing bonus and how that would help Bo and his family. They could've used the money, too.

But Kenny was one of the few who really took the time to get to know Florence, and she told him before the draft that Bo promised he would go to college if he got the chance.

She had eight children, and none of them went to

*I like this picture because it's symbolic of the role we scouts have in the game. Bo is here in the on-deck circle, warming up and the focus of the picture, like he should be. And that's me in the background, taking notes, keeping score, doing the work of a scout.*

college. If Bo could be the first, that was very important to the family.

"He's definitely going to college," she told Kenny. "Tell the Royals not to draft him."

That was enough for us, and if anyone had any doubts before the draft we knew the information was good when the Yankees took him in the second round and their scout couldn't even get into the house. George Steinbrenner was so upset about it, he fired the scout.

So Bo goes to college, and Kenny stays close to Florence.

• • •

Bo just kept getting better in college. You never know how these things will work out. Baseball history is filled with high school phenoms who turned down professional baseball and never got another chance.

But this guy, this guy just couldn't miss.

He missed his sophomore season of baseball with a shoulder injury he suffered in football, but after that he was Superman again. He really grew into a top-level football prospect. He went for more than 1,000 yards and scored 14 touchdowns as a sophomore. He ran for 256 yards against Alabama. I know Bo took special pride in that game, because when Alabama recruited him they told him he probably wouldn't play much until his junior year. Bo loved proving people wrong, and when he won the MVP of the Sugar Bowl you knew the NFL was going to offer him a lot of money.

The thing was, Bo was taking to baseball, too. He had a dominant junior season — .401 with a .500 on-base percentage, 17 home runs, and 43 RBIs in 42 games. Somewhere along the way he qualified for the NCAA nationals in track as a sprinter.

As much as we thought of him out of high school, our scouting judgments were even higher after his improvement in college.

And this being his junior year, he's eligible for the draft again. This is the kind of player you don't get the opportunity to draft very often.

So Kenny sits down with Florence.

"He promised me he'd finish his education," she tells him. "You could come in and offer a million dollars and he wouldn't take it."

Just like three years earlier, that was good enough for us. The trust paid off for us then, and we knew it would again. Kenny had the insight and the trust that nobody else had.

The Angels took Bo anyway. They sent Reggie Jackson to meet him with some front office guys, and they actually did offer a million dollars.

Bo turned it down.

And Kenny stayed close with Florence.

• • •

Bo's senior year, he was sensational. He rushed for 1,786 yards — 6.4 yards per carry. At the time, nobody had ever been that good in the SEC. He won the Heisman Trophy.

They hold the ceremony in New York, you know, and to this day he swears he never let that trophy out of his sight. He took it to the room with him after the ceremony, and he drove back to Alabama with it strapped into the back seat with a seat belt.

By this time, Bo is a certified national star and we're beginning to worry about whether he'll even want to play baseball. I mean, he's going to be the No. 1 pick in the whole damn NFL draft. They can offer him more money, more prestige and he won't have to ride busses in the minor leagues.

We're worried.

But he's telling everybody he still wants to play baseball, that he loves both sports, so now he's playing his senior year at Auburn. His numbers aren't great, but it's early, and he hit a home run at Georgia that they still say is the longest they've ever seen there. People in that stadium swear it was 550 feet or something. Dead center, out of the stadium. Just a monster home run, one of those Bo Jackson legends you always hear about.

The Pirates have the first pick in the draft that year, and they're practically living with Bo. They're watching every game, every practice. We just won the World Series the year before, so we're picking 24th. At this point, I don't know how the heck we're going to get the kid. The Angels had five picks in the first round that year, including two before us. I'm starting to think we've wasted a lot of time scouting a kid we'll never even spend a draft pick on.

But then we got very lucky, a string of events that we had no control over broke our way, starting on March 21, 1986.

The Tampa Bay Buccaneers had the first pick in the NFL draft that year, and their owner, Hugh Culverhouse, sent a plane to fly Bo from

Auburn to Tampa. Bo thought it was basically a recruiting trip. He wasn't playing football anymore, and everyone knew the Bucs wanted to draft him, so this was a chance for him to get to know the franchise.

Well, getting on that plane also made him ineligible for the rest of his baseball career at Auburn. The NCAA no longer considered him an amateur athlete.

And that changed Bo, because he was so damn mad. He was convinced that Culverhouse did this on purpose, that the plan was to keep him from playing baseball so he'd have no choice but to take the money in football. Culverhouse's move changed history, but not in the way he thought.

Bo swore he wouldn't play for the Bucs after that. Culverhouse didn't believe him. They drafted him first overall, and offered a $7.6 million contract.

But I told you, Bo is a different guy. Florence told Kenny that Bo would never sign with Tampa Bay because of what they did. Bo wants to play baseball even more now.

I'm starting to feel a little more optimistic.

• • •

So now it's the weekend before the baseball draft, and the phone rings in general manager John Schuerholz's office. It's Richard Woods, Bo's agent.

"Bo would like to visit Kansas City," Woods says. "He'd like to see the players, see the stadium. But he doesn't want to work out."

John calls and tells me.

"I think we're being used," he says. "I think we're being used for leverage they can use in football."

*The greatest scouting story of my lifetime was how Kenny Gonzales helped bring Bo Jackson into the Royals system. For a time, Bo was the biggest thing in baseball and he was doing it in a Royals uniform because of great scouting.*

Photo Courtesy of Kansas City Royals

29

"John," I say. "All I can tell you is that Kenny Gonzales has spent seven years on Bo Jackson, and knows him and his family better than anyone. They treat him like a member of the family. We have to believe in Kenny."

John agrees, and we bring him in. I knew he'd arrived before I even saw him. Linda Smith, our great manager of scouting operations for so many years, called me in the office.

"Art," she says, "Standing in front of me is the biggest man I've ever seen. He looks like Adonis."

I knew it was Bo.

• • •

At first, we're just talking baseball. We're talking about Bo's career, and the Royals team that year. It's fairly casual, but John is a very stern, serious guy. He looks Bo in the eyes and the mood in the room changes.

"Bo," he says. "Do you really want to play baseball?"

Bo didn't flinch.

"Yes, I do," he says. "That's why I'm here."

So John sends us all down to give Bo a tour of the clubhouse, and meet the players, watch batting practice.

We get out to the field for batting practice, and Bo is just watching. You might remember our teams back then. We were really good, but we didn't have much power.

"Hey Art," Bo says. "Not a lot of these guys hitting the ball out of the park, huh? This looks easy."

Then we're watching infield, and you might remember our team back then, we didn't have a lot of good arms in the outfield. Darryl Motley was in right field, and he was maybe average. Lonnie Smith was in left and he was below average. Willie Wilson was in center, and he was well below average.

"Hey Art," Bo says, "These guys don't throw so good. I could throw better than that."

I look right back at him.

"We know that, Bo," I say. "We've got you for an 80 arm."

We go through the clubhouse and Bo is meeting some of the guys. Bret Saberhagen, George Brett, Buddy Black, Hal McRae, Frank White.

They all say hello. Everyone is nice as can be, but then as Bo is walking out of the clubhouse, George shouts from across the room, "Good luck in football, Bo!"

Bo stops in his tracks, storms back, and for a second there I think he's going to take a swing at George. Instead, he points a finger right at him.

"Don't you bet on it," he says.

We get back upstairs, and I tell Bo there's only one thing about this whole situation that bothers me. We were doing our homework, not just with Kenny, but trying to keep track of what was being written and said about him. So, I tell him what bothers me is that I've read stories that say he doesn't want to make all the bus trips in the minor leagues.

"I didn't say that," he says. "What I said was I don't want to be riding busses for two or three years. That's what I said."

I liked that answer, and I liked how he handled George saying that thing in the clubhouse. Bo met for a little bit with owners Ewing Kauffman, and Avron Fogelman, and you know that left a good impression on Bo. So, we had the goodbye, drove him to the hotel, Bo flies back from Kansas City the next morning and we don't hear anything else.

All he told us in the direct conversations is that he wanted to play baseball. But you can interpret that a lot of different ways. Does he want to play baseball until he gets a better football situation? Does he want to play baseball, but not as badly as he wants to play football?

The draft is a few days later, and a couple hours before it starts, Schuerholz's phone rings. It's Richard Woods, the agent.

"Bo says if he plays major league baseball, he wants to play for the Kansas City Royals."

That's it. *If* he plays major league baseball. He *wants* it to be for us.

Naturally, John and ownership are still skeptical because we didn't get a commitment.

Honestly, as much as I loved Kenny, I was on the fence about it, too. I was the scouting director, and what happens if we take him first and he plays football anyway? Then we look bad.

"It's your decision," John tells me.

31

• • •

So now we're in the draft room. Kenny's information has been spot-on every step of the way, and he's saying that Bo will never play for the Bucs, might not play football at all, and wants to play baseball — especially if it's for us.

"Do you think anybody else knows what you know?" I ask.

"Definitely not," Kenny says.

Now, the way I saw it, the Angels had those five first-round picks, including two before we even had a pick. They took him the year before. We can't do anything about that. You can't trade picks. If the Angels know what we know, they're going to take him with one of those picks.

We get through the first round, and Bo Jackson isn't taken.

Now we have a chance.

The scouting report on Bo Jackson, filed by Ken Gonzales before the 1986 draft. Nobody knew whether Bo would want to play baseball. Two telling parts of Ken's report: "His major weakness is football…" and "Franchise type player; can do it all; a complete type player."

The second round goes by, and still nobody takes Bo. Third round, nobody takes Bo.

When it comes to the fourth round, and our pick comes up, I've made my decision.

"Gentlemen," I say, "if we blow the fourth-round draft pick with Bo Jackson, the franchise is not going to fold."

They did the draft on a conference call back then. So when it's time for our pick, I lean into the phone and I say: "The Royals select Vincent Edward Jackson, outfielder, Auburn University, better known as Bo."

You could've heard a pin drop on the call.

32

We got him signed for $1 million, and a $100,000 signing bonus. It's the first time the Royals ever gave a major league contract to an amateur player. Bo Jackson is a Royal, turning down millions from pro football, because Kenny Gonzales was right.

. . .

Now comes the press conference. This is June 21, 1986. Bo hasn't played a baseball game in three months. Actually, I don't think he's picked up a bat in three months.

But the media attention on this thing was so big we couldn't do it in a normal press room. We had to move it to that big banquet room we used to have down the left field line. The day of the press conference, John made sure Kenny could be there.

There's a home game that night, but the press is much more interested in Bo. It was like a World Series. You had reporters from Canada, Puerto Rico, all over North America. There are cameras everywhere, and I'm glad, because here's one of the greatest things I've ever seen in scouting.

They have this little reception line for Bo and his mother. Mr. and Mrs. Kauffman are there. So are Mr. and Mrs. Fogleman. Everyone is there. I told you that Florence was a bigger lady, but Kenny's a big guy himself. He's 6-foot-1 or so, more than 200 pounds, and you have to picture this. We're all shaking hands with the owners when Bo's mom walks in, sees Kenny, comes out of the line and right there in front of ownership gives him this big hug, lifting Kenny clear off the floor and kisses him right there on the cheek.

She's so happy to see Kenny, and thanks him for everything that he's done. As a scout, you couldn't create a more perfect scene.

Mr. K. looks at Fogleman.

"I realize what scouting's all about now," he says.

I can't tell you the feeling that gives you when ownership recognizes scouting like that. It was as nice as seeing Bo play for the first time.

. . .

The press conference goes smoothly, but one thing we didn't talk about beforehand was what would happen immediately after. I told you

Bo hadn't played in a few months, so we had in mind that he'd take some time to get in shape and work his way back into it.

But at the end of the press conference, one of the writers asks Bo what he's going to do now.

"Well," Bo says, "I'm going to go take batting practice."

Our mouths drop. This is our major draft pick. We don't want him to look bad in front of all these reporters. We didn't even want him to work out until the next day, but after he said that in front of all these reporters, what could we do?

Bo gets a uniform, and grabs a bat, and bunts a couple to get ready. Now, you know the crown scoreboard at our ballpark? It's a new scoreboard, but it's in the same place as the one we had back in '86, and with the first swing he's taken in months, *boom*, Bo hits the base of that damn scoreboard.

Avron Fogleman was an avid collector. He spent $10,000 for a Christy Mathewson ball. He had this big collection, and he's standing next to George Toma, our groundskeeper at the time, and he says, "George, have somebody get that ball!"

Well, no sooner had those words left his mouth than Bo hits another one, right off the scoreboard again, only a bit higher.

"George," Avron shouts. "Get that one for Mr. Kauffman!"

I never saw anything like this. Bo is making Royals Stadium look like a band box. He's hitting balls all over the place. One went over the waterfalls in right field, opposite field for Bo. George Brett, Frank White, they're all just sitting down on the field, watching the thing like kids.

That was the day that Buck O'Neil said those famous words about the ball hitting Bo's bat.

"I've only heard that sound three times. Babe Ruth, Josh Gibson, and now Bo Jackson."

• • •

I didn't want Bo Jackson to start at Class Double A. I thought that was too high for a guy with Bo's experience. But they sent him there, because Fogleman owned the Memphis Chicks. He wanted Bo close.

The Chicks typically drew about 6,000 for a special event. Well, for the opening night of Bo, they had almost 11,000 people there. Standing

34

room only. ESPN cut in for his first at bat. He's overmatched at this level, at least he should be when you compare his experience in college to the experience of the guys he's playing against.

His first at bat, he takes strike one right down the middle. Then he gets one outside, and the third pitch he smokes it right up the middle for a base hit in his first professional at bat.

I was with him down there about a week, and he did start to struggle. After a week or so, they would put a little box on the front page of the sports section with his average. He started out about .150, but every park he goes to, they're all filled to capacity. They're all sold out. When Bo was dragging, the president of the league said, "Art, he's struggling a little bit, you should send him back for another year." He was joking, but he could've used the attendance.

So Bo is starting slow, but if you know Bo, you know that he's one of the greatest competitors you'll ever see. You're not going to keep him down long. You start checking the papers after a while, and that barometer they have, it's up to .200, now it's .215, .250, .275 and by August it's up to .300 and he's hitting some of the longest home runs in the Southern League. His first professional home run came on a swing where he broke his bat, and this is just the kind of thing that Bo did.

One night, a scout of ours calls in late at night. It's John Boles.

"I just saw one of the longest home runs of my life," he says.

It was in Memphis, at old McCarver Stadium. They have stands behind the fence, and offices behind the stands. Bo hit one that was rising as it left the stadium. It went over the fence, over the stands and over the offices. They found the ball on a football field behind the stadium. It was in the middle of the field. Just unbelievable.

His professional experience is June 21 to Sept. 1, not even 2-and-a-half months. That's all he has, and the Royals bring him up. Now, Bo isn't the first to be in that situation. He's one of the exceptions, but even those other exceptions — great, great talents like Al Kaline and Robin Yount and guys like that — growing up they play baseball, baseball, baseball. Bo was this great football player who also ran track.

He basically did baseball in his spare time, and with nothing more than just raw talent. And now, he's got to learn to play baseball in the major leagues.

• • •

His first game is against the Chicago White Sox, and the guy pitching against us is Steve Carlton, one of the all-time greats.

Bo's first time up, he hits a routine bouncer to second base. Tim Hulett is playing second base for the Sox at the time. He takes a step, maybe two, to his right and makes the throw. You see that play a thousand times every season and it's always an out. But the damndest thing: Bo is across the bag before the throw's there. Like a jet. Us scouts, we look at our stopwatches, and we're all ashamed. We think we got him wrong.

Finally, one speaks up.

"I'll just say what I got," he says. "3.6."

That's what I had, too. And everyone else had the same thing.

Willie Wilson's best time from the left side was 3.6.

• • •

There were so many moments like that. So many moments you can never forget. His first home run is still the longest ever hit in a regular season game in our stadium. It was off Mike Moore, who made an All-Star team with the A's, and it was one of the hardest balls you'd ever see hit.

Straight out to leftfield, about where the Hall of Fame building is now, but back then it was a grassy hill with some flag poles. Bo hit it all the way up that hill, past the flags. Buck O'Neil was sitting across the aisle from me.

"I'm losing track of it, Art!" he says. "It's leaving the universe!"

The next spring, he hit one just as far, off Oil Can Boyd. He hit it over the scoreboard and way out there to where the traffic was coming in. That thing was 560, and he hit a ton of those.

George put it best: "You had to watch Bo every minute, because you may see something you never saw in your life."

It was a freak show. There was a game in New York, and you can imagine how the press there was hyping it up. Bo always tried to play it down with his words, but he legitimized that hype with his actions. He wanted to tell people he was just another player, but if you knew him, you knew that he wanted to show people he was special with his play.

That game in New York, he hit a home run to center in his first at bat. Second time up, he hit one to right field that they measured 464 feet. That's where guys like Ruth, Gehrig and Mantle used to hit it, but they were all from the left side. Bo did it from the right side.

The Yankees were trying to pitch around him the third time up, but they didn't throw it outside enough and Bo hit his third home run. He got hurt later in that game and couldn't go for four home runs, but in his first game back after the injury, he homered.

"There is something about Bo," John told reporters back then. "Call it mystical or magical."

In the first month of Bo's first full season in the big leagues, he had a game against the Tigers where he hit two home runs, including a grand slam, and stole a base. He drove in seven that day. He broke his bat on the grand slam.

There was the time he called timeout at the plate, realized the ump didn't give it to him, and jumped back in and hit a home run. He used to take some BP swings left handed every once in a while, and he usually hit those out of the stadium, too. He led off the 1989 All-Star game with a home run.

There was the night he ran up the wall in Baltimore. You never saw anything like it. He ran down a fly ball, and then ran up the wall like a damn spider. He must've been six or seven feet off the ground.

Everyone remembers "The Throw." They called it that on the front page of the sports section the next day. This was in 1989, in Seattle, when Bo was at the height of his powers. We went into extra innings, and Harold Reynolds is at first base. He's the fastest guy the Mariners have, and he's running on the pitch. There's no way he's not going to score. Reynolds is running hard, but he can't see that Bo ran the ball down in the corner, took it off the wall, turned and threw a clothesline to the plate to nail Reynolds.

"When Reynolds hit it, it's game over," Bob Boone told me later. "I'm walking off the field. Then I think, 'Holy smokes, the ball's coming.'"

• • •

The thing about Bo, he was one of those rare guys who amazed people inside the sport as much as outside. You don't get that very often. These big leaguers, they've seen it all. They've not only seen Felix Hernandez's fastball exploding on the inside corner, they've been in the batters box trying to get a hit off it. They've not only seen Miguel Cabrera hit the ball 450 feet into the opposite field seats, they've had a perfect slider low and outside the zone yanked for a home run.

These guys are hard to impress.

And they were all impressed with Bo's raw ability.

"You know," Frank White said many years later to a reporter, "I really did play baseball with Superman."

• • •

Bo was so proud of his association with Auburn. When he heard there was this really good prospect there, this big, agile, powerful first baseman named Frank Thomas, Bo took immediate interest.

I was going up to the Cape Cod League to scout the talent there, and Thomas was going to be there, so I told Bo. I just figured he'd want to say hi or something. But Bo goes into his locker and picks out one of those big black bats he used, signs it, and wants me to give it to Frank.

So I hop the plane for the Cape. They're having the All-Star game when I get there, and of course Frank is on the team. I go up to him to introduce myself. This is the day before the All-Star game. They were having the home run derby, just like they do in the big leagues. I give him the bat, and Frank's eyes get so big. He idolizes Bo. That's a star player, from his college, and now he has one of his game-quality bats.

*Bo with his wife and children before a father-son game in Kansas City. Bo's wife, Linda, told me that Bo planned on quitting football after the season that ended with the severe hip injury that effectively cut his career in both sports.*

"I'm going to use this in the home run derby," Frank says.

So a few hours later, they're having the home run derby, and Frank is hitting bombs all over the place. There are trees behind the field, and Frank is hitting them over the trees. He wins the home run derby, and the field that included Mo Vaughn.

The next day, before the All-Star game, I go up to Frank and congratulate him on the derby. I nod my head toward the bat.

"You should have a couple hits in that for the All-Star game," I say.

"No way," he says. "I would never use that bat in a game. I don't want to break it."

Frank really thought the world of Bo. He couldn't even use that bat.

• • •

Off the field, Bo was just as much of a specimen. He was the strongest guy in baseball, no question. He broke the Cybex machine in our weight room.

Bo loved to hunt, but he didn't do it with a gun. He did it with a bow and arrow. One day, he walks into the clubhouse and puts a target up on one end of the room. You should've seen the guys scattering out of there.

They say the average hunter pulls about 150 pounds on the bow, but of course Bo is way above that. He's at 235 pounds, and he's putting on a demonstration — just bullseye after bullseye, splitting them.

He's doing this a lot, so I know he's got to be up to something. I ask him about it toward the end of the season.

"I'm going with some friends," he says. "We're going to find that rare white mountain lion down in New Mexico."

Well, I forget all about that, but when spring training came around I see this big head of a mountain lion mounted over his locker.

"Bo," I yell, "You got it!"

"Right between the eyes, Art."

• • •

It really is a shame that he couldn't stay healthy. There's no doubt in my mind he could've been one of our game's greatest players if he put all his attention on baseball. And of course, he already was one of the best running backs in the NFL doing it basically in his spare time.

Bo's time with the Royals were some of the most exciting seasons in our history. We still haven't gotten back to the attendance of those years. The Royals were an event with Bo.

For so long, it was "George Brett and the Royals." Well, for a few years there, it was, "Bo Jackson and the Royals," and nobody was happier about that than George. He was happy for the biggest group of reporters on road trips to be around Bo's locker, not his, and George loves the game, so he enjoyed seeing what Bo would do next as much as anyone.

Bo and I stay in touch to this day. I don't know how many people know this, but his wife told me that Bo had decided he wasn't going to play football after the season he ended up hurting his hip. I asked him once, don't you feel like you've been cheated?

"No, Art," he said. He then went on to talk about overcoming a speech impediment, and being able to spend more time helping kids who struggle with that. Even now, he travels all over helping kids with speech impediments, obesity, all kinds of things. And he has more time for hunting and his family, things he really loves. It's like we feel worse about the injury than he does, because we wanted to see what was possible.

We all remember Bo for different reasons. I'll always remember him as the star of the greatest scouting story in my career.

# Chapter
# 3

# The shortstop from El Segundo who changed the Royals forever

*Y*ou know, we really thought Roy Branch was going to be the next Bob Gibson. Honest to goodness, that's the kind of arm and ability he had.

Roy was a hard-throwing right-handed pitcher out of St. Louis, then at Southern Illinois University. There were times you watched him and you knew the hitters didn't stand a chance. You see that with a lot of dominating amateurs, of course, but one of the differences with Roy was that the hitters knew they didn't have a chance, too.

Then, just before the draft in 1971, Roy had an arm injury on a tryout with the Cardinals. We had him at the top of our draft board, but you never know with pitchers and arm injuries so we had to be careful. We made other plans.

Tom Ferrick was one of our national cross checkers at the time, and he had his kid out in California he liked, but still had rated as a fringe prospect. But Ferrick and Gilhousen went out to see the kid one more time — mostly to see the opposing pitcher, a kid named Roy Thomas, but also get eyes on this other kid. The other kid went 4-for-4 and hit one off the wall.

Ferrick and Gilhousen came back to our draft meetings much more impressed, to the point that they saw the kid as a viable option if Branch's arm injury was serious or one of the teams drafting ahead of us took him.

"If it doesn't work out with Branch," Ferrick said, "I definitely would take that young shortstop out of El Segundo."

That's how he said it, too. "That young shortstop out of El Segundo."

Well, we were comfortable with Branch's arm so we ended up taking him fifth overall that year. But that "young shortstop out of El Segundo" was still there when we picked in the second round.

And that's how the Kansas City Royals ended up with George Brett.

Later, George told people his first reaction to being drafted by us was, "Where the hell is Kansas City? And who the hell are the Kansas City Royals?"

Nobody could've known it would turn into such a great situation, for both sides.

• • •

The first time I saw George play was the fall of 1971, in instructional league. You know how inexact scouting can be, well, before the draft we said he had a *chance* to turn into a good hitter. Isn't that something? One of the best hitters in big league history, the only man to win a batting title in three different decades, finishes his career with 3,154 hits and before the draft we said he had a *chance* to turn into a good hitter.

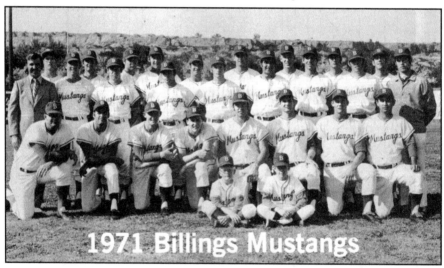

*Can you pick out the Hall of Famer? That's George Brett, in the kneeling row, second from the right, with his teammates on the 1971 Billings team. That was George's first professional season, when he was still trying to swing like Carl Yastrezemski, which was never going to work because he wasn't strong enough. But the thing you could tell even back then was that George was the most competitive guy on the field, no matter what field.*

Nobody else knew any better, either, or else he wouldn't have been there in the second round (incidentally, the Phillies took Mike Schmidt with the very next pick).

But what I saw in instructional league back then was even at just 18 years old, you could tell this was an all-out, hard-nosed player. That part of it goes overlooked a lot of times, because we all get distracted by raw talent, but it can be as important as any tool because at its most extreme it means the player is going to do everything he can to maximize his potential.

And I'm telling you, George was the most extreme.

He just played the game with all the desire you'd want to see anybody play with. That's what impressed me, and that's what impressed so many others. George was a good athlete. Not a great athlete, but a good one. He had a good arm, was a shade above average running to first. He was raw in the field, but he worked so damn hard at it. To this day, his work ethic is one of the best I've ever seen.

Things moved pretty quickly for George, though. We sent him to Billings, Mont., for rookie ball. George was our shortstop then, just because he was a good athlete. The third baseman there was a guy named Joe Zdeb out of Main Township High School in Parkridge, Ill. I got him in the fourth round in 1971. He was an all-state running back and had a full ride to the University of Missouri, and two teachers for parents, so we really had to work hard to get him to play.

Well, about two weeks into the season, there's this smoker hit right at Joe. The ball takes a bad hop and hits Joe, right in the teeth. There's blood everywhere. Joe's mouth is all messed up, and he has to miss about two weeks. So, our rookie team had an opening.

And that's how George Brett ended up at third base for us.

Incidentally, Joe made it to the big leagues — mostly as an outfielder. I still see him around Kansas City. He's a financial advisor.

• • •

George was a good enough athlete that he made his way through the minor leagues at a decent pace. He went from rookie ball to Class A in the California League. Then from Class A all the way to Triple A in Omaha. We had him playing one step from the big leagues when he was

19 years old, so we knew there was some talent there, but again, nobody could've seen what would happen.

George still had the swing he grew up with, which he modeled after Carl Yastrzemski. That was fine enough when he was a kid, because George really looked up to Yaz, but it wasn't going to make him a great professional hitter. He wasn't strong enough to pull it off, with the bat held high. He just didn't have the upper body strength.

I remember seeing him in Omaha, the season he ended up debuting for us in 1973, and by that time you could tell he would be a big leaguer. You knew he was the guy who would eventually replace Paul Schall for us at third base, but still, you didn't know how good he would be.

The truth is, George had no idea, either. He was just never all that highly thought of. He wasn't the best player on his own high school team, and didn't have any scholarship offers to Division I schools. Heck, he wasn't even the best player in his own *family*. By the time George was an eighth- or ninth-grader, his older brother Ken was pitching in the World Series for the Boston Red Sox. There are still some people who say Ken Brett is the best high school athlete in Los Angeles history. Ken was a great basketball and football player, and was picked fourth overall by the Red Sox as a pitcher — and there were teams who thought he was an even better outfielder.

But George was just trying to find his legs in the big leagues, and in the beginning, it really wasn't going well. He was hitting .205 with not much power into June of his first full big league season when Charley Lau, our hitting coach at the time, approached him and they began a working relationship that would change them both forever.

George will tell you he didn't have any choice but to give in to whatever Charley taught him, but there was more to it than that. George had that great work ethic, I told you, and all he ever wanted to do was play baseball. He was an easy sign out of high school because pro ball was always his dream and, well, now that he was in the big leagues he was going to do whatever it took to stay there.

So he and Charley tore apart his swing and built it back from the ground up. Charley used video — the same stuff he'd use with our Baseball Academy kids — and fast-frame photography to show George exactly what he wanted. The weight shift; the arms back; the quick, smooth swing with the perfect amount of uppercut.

The way that George took to Charley, and the way that Charley's ideas unlocked George's ability, it's not too much of an exaggeration to say that changed baseball history. George recovered that first full season in 1974 to hit .282. The next year, when he hit .308 and led the league in hits and triples, is the season that George says he turned a corner with his confidence.

After that 1975 season, Hal McRae, who was a veteran on the club then, told George he was in big trouble. George asked why.

"You hit .300 and you're only 22 years old," Hal said. "Now they're going to expect you to do that ever year."

"Christ, Hal," George said. "I expect to hit .300 every year now, too."

He was no longer *trying* to be a good hitter.

At that point, he *knew* he was a good hitter. He went from being afraid the other team would bring in that tough lefty in the late innings, to hoping they brought him in so he could hit a line drive in a gap somewhere.

You never saw a more confident player after that.

George didn't just hit .300 the year after he and Hal had that exchange. He hit .333, and won the batting title. He won two more batting titles, and finished one of the greatest careers in baseball history as a .305 hitter.

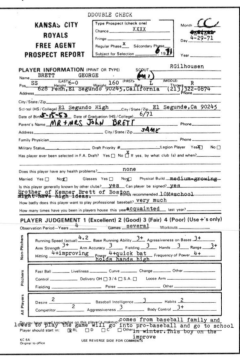

*This is Rosey Gilhousen's scouting report on George, filed shortly before the 1971 draft. Brett wasn't widely considered a top prospect at the time (he didn't have a Division I college scholarship offer when we drafted him), but Gilhousen's report foreshadowed George's move to third base, change in batting stance and physical growth.*

And he did it all for the Royals because we sent scouts back to take a few more looks at him, and those scouts had the confidence to change their evaluations from fringe prospect to high prospect.

• • •

Everyone has a story about the day they became a big leaguer, and George is no different.

He was at the apartment he shared with some of the other guys in Omaha, grilling burgers for lunch. They had a game that night. We used to put all the guys up in an apartment complex at 84th and Q in Omaha. George was staying with Mark Littell, who's as country a guy as you'll ever meet, and Buck Martinez — a catcher who went on to be a manager and broadcaster.

Harry Mahlmberg was the manager in Omaha at the time, and he went over to knock on their door. He walks into the apartment and says, "Congratulations, you're going to the big leagues!"

George and Buck were convinced Mahlmberg was talking to Littell. He was pitching really well at the time.

Mahlmberg said, no, and pointed at George: *You!*

Paul Schaal was our third baseman in Kansas City at the time, and the night before he sprained his ankle. We needed someone to meet the team in Chicago. George never hit .300 or even 10 home runs in the minor leagues. But we needed him.

And that's the day George made his big league debut.

Nobody could've guessed how long he'd stay.

• • •

The baseball world is so different now. We've been fortunate enough to draft and develop some very good players, from Johnny Damon to Carlos Beltran to Zack Greinke and others. We all know what the business of baseball is like, and there came a point where we had to trade all of those guys and others away.

That's part of what makes George Brett so special in Kansas City. I mean, don't get me wrong, he was a better player than Beltran or Damon or anyone else the Royals have ever had. He's one of the best 10 or 20 players in baseball history, as far as I'm concerned.

But he's also special because he stayed in Kansas City his entire career.

George was a California kid, born and raised. He always wanted to be a pro ballplayer, and was one of the easiest signings we've ever had. His graduating class in high school took a trip to Disneyland to celebrate, but George wanted no part of that. He hopped on the first plane we could get him on to start his professional career.

But he also told me he cried when that plane took off. The unknown was scary to him, and he was leaving California.

George became a Kansas Citian, gradually. After that first year when he hit so well, when he hit .308 in 1975, when he told Hal he had to expect to hit that well ever year, George got some advice from his other brother, Ken.

Ken told George he'd be in the big leagues a long time. Get to know the city, he told George. Make friends outside of baseball.

So George decided to live here in the offseason. At first, he was in this apartment in Raytown but bought a house in Blue Springs. Paul Splittorff was a real estate agent in the offseason, and that's where all the guys were living.

Well, a restaurant in town catered the postgame meal one day. It was a place that George recognized from back in California. He called the number and got directions. Turns out the place was in Westport. George had never been to Westport. He took one of the guys a few days later, and the way he tells the story, he's driving through there and he sees bar, restaurant, restaurant bar and thinks, "This is me, this is where I need to be."

He sold his house in Blue Springs and moved to Fairway.

He hasn't lived far from there ever since.

• • •

The times are so different now. The emphasis is greater than ever to develop your own players, and then to evaluate which ones are worth long-term contracts and then get those done.

One of the best successes we've had in recent years is not only identifying Sal Perez and helping him develop, but then signing him to a deal that both sides were comfortable with to keep him in Kansas City through 2019. If Sal keeps playing like he is now, we wouldn't be able to afford him on the free agent market.

It was different when George was coming up. How often in the modern world of baseball do you see a Hall of Fame player stay with his original, small-market team? Heck, how often do you see a Hall of Fame player stay with any one team? It doesn't happen often. Derek Jeter and Mariano Rivera with the Yankees. Chipper Jones with the Braves.

But we were able to keep George for all 21 of his seasons — he didn't even do that end-of-the-career thing where he played for another team the way Willie Mays and some others have over the years — because we were able to always be the best situation for George.

We kept winning, more than bigger markets like Boston or his hometown Angels. And we could match the Yankees in payroll spending. There were years we had the highest payroll in baseball.

People don't like to hear this, but as much as George loved playing for us it might've been different if he was playing in today's environment. A reporter asked George about this in 2013, when he came back to be our hitting coach.

"Back then," George said, "if the Royals were going to offer me $10 million and the Yankees were going to offer me $30 million, what do you think I would have done? I probably would have left."

The Royals and George were so good for each other. He ended up in the middle of most of our best moments, from the huge home run off Gossage that clinched the American League Championship Series in 1980 to that monster Game 3 in the 1985 ALCS.

I don't know when it happened, exactly, but at some point relatively early in his career George went from being that California kid who wanted to spend his afternoons surfing to a Kansas City man who really appreciated what he had here.

That's how we built those teams in the 1970s and 1980s. We kept guys like George, Frank White and Willie Wilson around for a lot of years with what people called "lifetime contracts." As a baseball organization, it really provided a level of stability. And for our fans, they knew who to expect at the ballpark, and it really opened up a close relationship.

And why wouldn't George want to stay in that situation?

He was a hero in Kansas City. Still is. We had a team that won, and he was always among the highest paid players in the game. Maybe he could've gone somewhere else for a little bit more money, but he would've been giving up something, too.

Fortunately for both sides, we never got to that point.

• • •

Some of the memories I have of George are the same that any Royals fan might have. Hitting that ball off Goose Gossage into the third deck of Yankee Stadium to put us in the World Series in 1980. That's probably the most vivid.

We were down in the stands watching when that happened, a few rows behind George Steinbrenner, the late, great Yankees owner. He got up and left after George's home run. Just walked out. He was so damn mad.

I remember him going over .400 in September of 1980. I can see that like it happened this morning. Tipping his helmet to the standing ovation. When I saw that, the reason it was so special for me is I was fortunate enough to see the last guy who hit .400 in person — the great Ted Williams in 1941. Ted Williams is still the greatest hitter I've ever seen, but George is one of the few you can put in the conversation.

I was so fortunate to see him grow with the Royals. That was my second draft with the club, when we got George. I became scouting director in 1985, the year George carried us to the World Series. To this day, I don't know if I've ever seen one player do more to help his team win a game — especially an important game — as George did in Game 3 of the ALCS that year.

People sometimes forget about that game because of the World Series, but that was unbelievable. We were down two games to none, and at that point, there were a lot of people around baseball who thought the Royals would only be good enough to *almost* win. We were an older team by 1985. You didn't know how many more chances we'd have. Hal was at the end of it, Frank White was 34, George was 32. Willie Wilson was about to turn 30. It was such a critical point for us.

And before that game, George told his teammates, "Climb on my back."

In the first inning, George homered. In the third inning, he made this spectacular play on Lloyd Moseby and threw Damaso Garcia out at the plate to keep us up by one. In his second at bat, he hit one off the top of the wall for a double, tagged up to make it to third, and then tagged up to score on a fly ball. We got down 5-3, but in the sixth, George homered with Wilson on and the score was tied. Then in the eighth, he singled and made it all the way around to score the winning run on some incredible base running. Turned out to be the game-winning run.

Of course, we went on to beat the Blue Jays in seven games, and then beat the Cardinals in the seventh game of the World Series that year, too. It's the greatest feeling possible in baseball.

Absolutely incredible. I'm not sure how many players have done more for a team than George did for us. We all owe so much to him.

• • •

George came back into uniform in 2013 to be our hitting coach for a bit, and it really was a nice shot in the arm for us. Our guys were really down at the time, and Dayton Moore basically just asked George to "rescue us, mentally."

Coincidence or not, we really started winning after George (and Pedro Grifol) took over as hitting coaches and I wasn't all that surprised when George gave it up after a while.

*This is from George Brett's last big league game, against the Rangers, in Arlington. George and Nolan Ryan, who was also retiring that year, exchange lineup cards before the game.*

Photo Courtesy of Texas Rangers

He has a lot of things going on, and being a hitting coach wasn't something he ever aspired to do. He does a lot for us behind the scenes, from working with the guys in spring training to throwing batting practice some days, to advising Dayton on personnel matters, to appearing in the community and even hitting the road to work with some of our minor leaguers during the season.

I remember one year, he gave Mark Teahen some pointers in Omaha and the next year Teahen was our player of the year in Kansas City.

I'll never forget talking to George after one trip out to the West coast to see a player. We sent him out there as a scout of sorts, to check on a few guys and tell us what he thought.

I talked to him when he came back and I still have what he said written down at home, and underlined.

"That's when I realized how important it is to have good scouting reports on young players," he said. "I don't know how you guys do it."

• • •

In the end, the biggest thing I'll always remember about George is that work ethic. That desire. A lot of guys have ability, but not many of them have ability *and* that kind of desire that just won't quit.

I talk to young players a lot. Amateur teams, our minor

*Photo Courtesy of Texas Rangers*

*This is George warming up in the on-deck circle before his last at bat. I always liked what he told reporters when they asked what he wanted from his last at bat. He told them he wanted to hit the ball back to the pitcher and run like hell down to first base, because he wanted his last moment on the field to be all-out, like the rest of his career.*

league clubs. I try to get this point across, that to become truly great you have to work at it and want it more than anything in your life.

The best way I know to make the point is something that George said. He played his last big league game in Arlington, against the Rangers in 1993. The reporters asked how he'd like his last at-bat to go, and everyone's waiting around for him to talk about a home run or a game-winner in the ninth inning.

"I want to hit a ball back to the pitcher and run as hard as I can to first base," he said.

That's a player who breezed into the Hall of Fame on his first try, right along with Nolan Ryan and Robin Yount (who George named one of his sons after, incidentally) in one of the greatest Hall of Fame classes ever. He is one of the best players in baseball history, saying he wants his last at bat in the big leagues to be a little comebacker to the pitcher so he can run as fast as he can down the line to show people that's how the game should be played.

That's George Brett to me. That's how I'll remember him.

He had baseball ability. But he became great because he worked so hard at it.

# Chapter
# 4

# How trades happen

*T*he worst trade in baseball history might be when the Cubs sent Lou Brock to the Cardinals for Ernie Borglio.

Brock was 25 at the time, and in the Cubs' defense, he really hadn't done much for them. He was in his third season, and he obviously had a lot of speed, but he struck out in bunches and had trouble getting on base.

There were other players involved in the trade. Jack Spring and Paul Toth were middle relievers, really just fringe big leaguers. They went with Brock to the Cardinals. Doug Clemens was a spare outfielder, and Bobby Shantz was an experienced but aging relief pitcher. They went to the Cubs with Borglio.

The Cubs thought they were getting a frontline big league starter in Borglio. He won 18 games for the Cardinals the year before, and 21 in 1960 — finished third in the Cy Young voting that year.

But once he got to Chicago, he was all but finished. He lasted only two more bad seasons and then he was out of the big leagues for good.

Brock turned into a star almost immediately after the trade. He hit .251 with the Cubs for the first two months of 1964, then .348 for the Cardinals the last four months. It was amazing. That speed showed up on the basepaths. Brock led the league in stolen bases eight of nine seasons for the Cardinals. He was the all-time base stealer when he retired, a record that stood until Ricky Henderson came along. Brock was so good with St. Louis that he made the Hall of Fame.

The trade has haunted the Cubs ever since. You hear people mention it with the billy goat curse and everything else. What made the trade even worse for the Cubs is that they made it with their rival, a team in their own division. So one minute they're trading away an underperforming player, and then for the next 16 years they're watching a Hall of Famer beat their brains in.

The way that trade played out, it's one reason teams don't make deals within their own division. It's in the back of their minds, that any sort of failure will be amplified in the eyes of their fans because they'll see the other player so often.

The Brock trade is the nightmare scenario for general managers.

The goal of everybody when they enter trade talks is to find a deal that works for both sides, something where each side gets players they want.

I'll give you good example.

• • •

Before the 2013 season, we felt pretty good about where we stood in a lot of places.

It has to be about developing our own players for us, and we felt good about Eric Hosmer's chances of bouncing back from a disappointing season, great about where Salvador Perez was, and saw a lot of talent around the field — Alex Gordon in leftfield, Lorenzo Cain in center, Alcides Escobar at shortstop and Mike Moustakas at third base.

Since Dayton came on, we've been consistent about building around pitching and defense. That's why Perez is so important to us, and why we really needed a shortstop who could field like Escobar in the Greinke trade. Everyone knows the money situation in baseball. We're not going to have a big-time home run guy unless we develop him ourselves. We can't afford an ace starting pitcher on the free agent market.

But we can build a good defense, and most measurements had us with the best defense in baseball in 2013.

Before that season, we had Wil Myers in Triple A and he was impressing a lot of people. He has such a loose, natural swing. The ball just jumps off his bat. He can be a little cocky, and sometimes that rubs people the wrong way, but he has the sort of innate confidence you like to see in a power hitter.

When we had him in for a workout, before he ever started his professional career, he was going to take batting practice. He came out on the field, and noticed the fountains weren't on. There was no game that day, there was no reason to have them on, but Wil wanted the fountains on.

"I want to hit some balls in there," he said.

That's just how he is. He gets it from his father, I think. Once, I asked Eric Myers why his son's name only has one L.

"Well, to be honest, he started out with two," Eric says. "But I needed one of them to beat his hind parts for most of his younger years."

I don't know how many times Eric has used that line, but each time, it comes with a hearty laugh. That's just the way that family is. There's an easy confidence there that translates well to the batters box.

Wil had a huge year in 2012. He played most of it in Omaha, with our Triple-A club, and he hit .314 with 37 home runs and 109 RBIs in 134 games. Now, Omaha's new stadium is a bit of a bandbox, especially to leftfield for right-handed pull hitters. But if you look at the list of guys who've hit that many home runs at the age of 21, it's an impressive list. *Baseball America* named Wil its minor league player of the year.

Now, at the time we had Jeff Francoeur in rightfield and a big empty spot at the top of our rotation. Nobody would disagree that Myers is more talented than Francoeur, but he can be an adventure in the outfield and for a team that's always wanted to build around pitching and defense we had to be open for a deal that would help our rotation.

Everyone could see the pieces matched up with the Rays. They're like us in that they need to be careful about every dollar they spend, and James Shields was into his final two years of arbitration. Salaries in those years aren't quite what they are for free agents, but they're close enough that a team like the Rays — especially when Evan Longoria makes a lot of money, and David Price was getting more expensive — has to pick its spots.

So we're there in our suite at the winter meetings in Nashville, and one of the biggest concerns on our side was that we didn't want to deplete our minor league system. We'd worked so hard to build it back up. When Dayton came on, there really wasn't much there beyond Billy Butler and Alex Gordon. But with Dayton's leadership, and David Glass spending on amateur talent, we built it back to what *Baseball America* called the best farm system they'd seen in 25 years.

As much as we wanted a frontline starting pitcher in a trade, we couldn't leave our farm system empty.

We didn't want to give up Myers. Power hitters are important, too, and with the way baseball's salary structure is, he was going to be very cheap for up to four years. But because of those factors and others, you also know that his trade value will never be higher.

So Dayton got the whiteboard out, and he writes down all of our best prospects. And then he started taking names out.

If we trade Myers, we still have Bubba Starling and Jorge Bonifacio as outfielders. If we trade Mike Montgomery and Jake Odorizzi, who debuted with us toward the end of the 2012 season, we still have Kyle Zimmer, Yordano Ventura, Danny Duffy, Chris Dwyer and John Lamb. We also put Patrick Leonard in the deal, and we didn't want to give him up, but he was behind Cheslor Cuthbert on our own depth chart. Plus, Adalberto Mondesi is coming fast.

If nothing else, we knew we'd still have more in the system than we had when Dayton took over and we went back to emphasizing player development.

Really, that was a turning point for a lot of us.

We didn't want to give up Myers — not to mention those other guys — but getting a proven, reliable, durable guy like Shields for the top of the rotation was just too much to pass up. We were also getting Wade Davis in the deal, who we knew could be good in the bullpen but still has a chance to be in a rotation.

One thing to think about, we re-signed Jeremy Guthrie and traded for Ervin Santana earlier in the offseason. So when we traded for Shields and Davis, it meant that the top two guys in our rotation from the year before were now competing for our fifth spot.

Another key point we talked about is that we had to start winning. It's time. And one of the ways you win is that you bring in winners. You have guys who are used to winning, who know what it takes. That's one of the reasons we've put so much thought into how we bring guys up through the system. We wanted Moustakas and Hosmer and Duffy and all those guys together in Wilmington and again at Northwest

Arkansas. We want them to get to know each other, sure, but we also want them to win. We want them to win together.

We really believe that can help translate once you get to the big leagues, but it also helps if you can give them a model to follow, someone who's done what they're trying to do in the big leagues. Shields is a great model for our young guys. He was overlooked out of high school, taken in the 16th round. Worked and worked and kept at it, spent six years in the minor leagues, and his rookie year the Rays lost 101 games. But he kept getting better, never missed a start, threw more than 200 innings for six straight seasons.

He was there when they went from last place to the World Series in one year. He's the only Rays pitcher to win a World Series game. Pitched on playoff teams. He's exactly what we want our guys to turn into, so we hope that being around him will help them see what it takes and help push our younger players around even if we can't keep Shields long-term.

It takes a team. It takes your whole 25-man roster and then some to have a good season, but I'll tell you this: We don't think it's a coincidence that the Royals won their most games since 1989 in Shields' first year.

• • •

One other thing about these trades. You never know when a deal is going to get ripped from you.

When we were talking with the Rays, we didn't know they were also deep into talking with the Tigers and Diamondbacks. We didn't know that until later, when those stories started spreading.

We found out later that the Rays were close to sending Shields and Davis to the Diamondbacks. Arizona would've sent Justin Upton to Texas, and the Rays would've got a package of prospects from both clubs in return.

We still don't know exactly why that deal fell through, but it wasn't going to happen after the Diamondbacks signed Brandon McCarthy.

You can second-guess every trade in baseball. You hate to give up talent from your own system, but that's the only way you're going to get something in return. You can wait until everything's in place. Like one of our scouts likes to say, that's like waiting until you're financially set before having kids. Good luck.

You'll never do it.

We just decided it was time. We were building something here, and we owed it to the guys in that clubhouse and to ourselves to be aggressive.

For so long, the Royals have been a team that had to trade our homegrown guys when they got too expensive. Now we're a team that at least sometimes can trade for those guys.

• • •

One thing people might not realize is how much work goes into a trade. It wasn't always like this, which may be why people sometimes think a trade just sort of happens quickly. But most of the time it takes months and months and sometimes years of work. You scout a guy, you ask questions, you follow him, you run all his statistics through every equation you have.

The margin for error is so much smaller with a trade today. All that work that goes into it today, well, in the old days a lot of times it was just a scout going to see a player one time and putting in a suggestion. Hard to believe now, but that's all it took sometimes.

When we traded for Nori Aoki prior to the 2014 season, to be our rightfielder and leadoff hitter, that was a trade we tried to make about six months earlier. We just couldn't get the pieces to line up. When Will Smith finished the year so strong, the Brewers took him in exchange for Aoki.

But it used to be that a trade could just happen in a conversation. If you've ever heard stories about two general managers sitting down at the hotel bar and working out a trade over a few scotches, well, that really did happen in the old days.

Today, it's just so different. The general managers are constantly thinking about different scenarios. Every day, they're giving their numbers guys different assignments or having their scouts put extra eyes on certain prospects or big leaguers. There's so much more information, so many more opinions for the GM to consider.

One thing that happens now that wasn't always the case is you ask your own big leaguers for their opinion. Players have more input now than they ever have before. That's a good thing, I think. This game has always been about the players first, whether executives wanted to admit that or not.

So, if we're thinking about trading for a guy, and we have a middle reliever who spent three years with him at a previous stop, we'd be foolish not to ask for an opinion. To be completely blunt, this became more prevalent in the early 2000s, because we wanted to know who might be on performance enhancers and who was doing it the honest way. That's the kind of information players have that you really can't get anywhere else. If you trade for a guy, you don't want to find out that extra velocity or power was from the juice and you certainly don't want to see him suspended for a failed test.

The players are usually pretty honest, too. And it doesn't have to be about drugs. Sometimes a guy has a bad year because of problems at home. Sometimes he's battling an injury or sickness that he only tells a few other players about. Sometimes a guy tends to only focus when there's a contract on the line, or maybe the pitching coach had him close his front shoulder and that's what unlocked the extra velocity.

These are the kinds of things you can sometimes learn from players. With the amount of money at stake in these trades, you have to pick up every bit of information.

Years ago, you didn't necessarily do all of this.

Years ago, it was so different.

• • •

The hottest place for trades is always the winter meetings. It developed this way over time. The winter meetings used to be something like an industry get-together, where you'd talk about the issues we all faced, maybe see some friends. It was sort of informal.

Nobody can say for sure when the winter meetings started. Baseball's history goes back so far. A lot of things are sort of fuzzy. They still fight over who invented the game, or who threw the first curveball, or even whether Babe Ruth really called his shot.

But there are a lot of people who say the winter meetings really became something baseball worked around back in 1911. That was before my time, but they say that Charles Murphy, the old Cubs owner, got it in his head that Cardinals manager Roger Bresnahan was somehow trying to steal one of his players.

Murphy had a short temper, so right there in the lobby of the hotel he cussed Bresnahan up one wall and down the other. There's always been a lot of emotion in our great game, but even by those standards, that was really something. When I got into pro baseball some 30 years after that, there were still some old-timers you'd see talk about the day Murphy gave it to Bresnahan. When that happened, it was a sign that the winter meetings were a place for action. There are so many baseball people in the same place, eventually, the conversation is bound to turn to what your roster looks like and my roster and, hey, who do you want for that shortstop?

And you know what else? When Murphy undressed Bresnahan like that, right there in front of everyone who happened to be in the hotel lobby, people really wanted to see what would happen at the next winter meetings.

But it's not all verbal warfare, of course. In between the fireworks, there tends to be silence. The winter meetings can be long and tedious. It can be hard to know when someone just wants to chat, when someone is killing time, and when someone is trying to find a way to bring up a trade. You can only tell the same old stories so many times.

That's OK. Part of scouting is reading people, and that extends beyond just the ball field. You have to read people's intentions. You have to know when they're bluffing, and when they're offering you this second baseman but really the whole point is that they want your centerfielder.

I'll tell you the key to the whole thing. People laugh at me for this, but when you go to these winter meetings you have to find time to sit down. When you stand around, make sure it's on carpet. You stand around for four days on those hard tile floors in the lobbies and meeting rooms. It's tough on your feet and legs. That's a mistake everyone makes once.

• • •

Well, one man who always found a way to spice up the winter meetings was Bill Veeck. He was such a character. He rubbed some people the wrong way, but I always admired how innovative he was.

He was the one who had the idea of planting ivy on the walls at Wrigley Field. When he owned the Indians, he signed Larry Doby and integrated the American League, and traded away the players who had a problem with it. He was always a promoter. He's the one who hired Max Patkin, who they called the "Clown Prince of Baseball," as a coach to basically entertain the crowd between pitches.

He signed Eddie Gaedel, who couldn't have even been 5-feet tall, and gave him elf shoes and "1/8" for his jersey number and put him in a game to pinch hit. He used to have games where he'd let the fans make managerial decisions, voting with signs they'd hold up in the outfield. Veeck was the first one to set fireworks out of a scoreboard, and he's the one who convinced Harry Caray to sing during the seventh inning stretch.

So, leave it to Veeck to innovate the winter meetings, too.

Back in 1975, they had the winter meetings at the Diplomat Hotel in Hollywood, Fla. The future of Veeck's White Sox were really in doubt at that point. There was an investment group out of Seattle that put in a bid for the team, and Veeck was fighting them off. He was desperate to improve the club from a fifth-place finish the year before, so even by his standards, he was ready to start slinging.

He traded Jim Kaat and Mike Buskey to the Phillies for Alan Bannister, Dick Ruthven and Roy Thomas. And that was only the beginning. Veeck set up this big table with all of these red phones. He sat behind the table, and had a sign made up that everyone could see: *OPEN FOR BUSINESS.*

Nobody knew what to make of it. A lot of the old-timers thought it was bush league, but at some point, those phones were just ringing off the hook. They called it the White Sox hotline. Someone was constantly on the phone, and as soon as they hang up, it rang again. This went on for 14 hours, non-stop. Veeck is really cheesing it up, when he sees someone from another team walk by, he'd say into the phone, "I don't know, he's one of our best players but if you want to make an offer..."

What nobody knew at the time was that Veeck had Buck Peden, his PR man, up in the room. Buck was the one calling down, the one making those phones ring so much. It was all a stunt, but nobody knew it at the time. Like most of the things Veeck did, this one worked.

They traded for Buddy Bradford, Greg Terlecky, Larvell Blanks, Ralph Garr, Jack Brohamer and Clay Carroll — in four different trades.

Veeck had the attention of the sport, which is what he really wanted in the first place. They didn't win any more games the next year, but in 1977 they won 90, which was their best finish in 12 years.

I don't know if people keep track of these things, but that has to be the busiest day any team ever had at the winter meetings.

. . .

John Schuerholz might've been the most thorough person you'd ever meet when it came to making a trade. In a way, he was part of that transition from the old days of working out a trade over a few drinks to the new days of spreadsheets and multiple reports and months of planning.

He thought about everything, including how people in the organization would react to a trade.

In 1987, we were there in our suite with the door closed and we're trying to get Floyd Bannister from the White Sox. He was a talented left-handed pitcher, the first overall pick back in 1976, and we wanted him for our rotation.

Larry Himes was the White Sox general manager at the time, and he was willing to give up Bannister but only for the right price. Himes wanted to get younger.

So we go back and forth a few times over the course of a few days and we finally settle on a deal.

We got Bannister and a young backup catcher named Dave Cochrane. The White Sox got a bunch of young guys we'd drafted and developed: Chuck Mount, a Kansas City kid we'd just taken in the draft the year before; John Davis, a young right-handed pitcher who only gave up 29 hits in 43 2/3 innings for us that season; Greg Hibbard, another guy fresh out of the draft; and Melido Perez, a kid who signed out of the Dominican who made it to our big league team when he was only 21 years old.

You can imagine how that went over with our player development people. You work with these young guys all year, and it becomes more than just a job. You smile at their successes, and you cry with their failures. You're tied to the performances of these guys in a very real way, both professionally and personally, so when you put your heart and sweat and blood into helping these guys it hurts when they're traded away.

John knew all of that. He knew the minor league coaches weren't going to like it, so he wrote a letter to all the scouts and player development folks in our organization, telling them how reluctant he was to give up all those players. He congratulated the scouts and coaches, telling them they did such a good job with this group that the big league club was able to get a 16-game winner in the deal.

That's really the way you have to look at it when you're in this game. All of us, from scouting high school kids to coaching guys in Omaha, our ultimate goal is to help the big league team.

It's the most fun when you can help the big league team by giving them a George Brett or a Frank White or a Carlos Beltran, but sometimes part of the job is helping train pieces that the front office can use in trades.

That was smart for John to write that letter. Once they read it, our guys understood where he was coming from.

The trade made our big league team better, which means the trade had to be made.

• • •

Back in 1991, they had the winter meetings at the Fountain Bleu Hotel in Miami. That's a swanky place. They have stars in and out of there all the time.

Right there on South Beach. It's kind of funny when the winter meetings are at a place like that, because most of us, we're old baseball lifers. We'd rather be at a ballgame with a stopwatch in our hands than some club with an overpriced cocktail.

Anyway, the Fountain Bleu is built in this crescent shape. Like a moon. The wings where the rooms are sort of swing around the pool. As it happened, our suite was on about the 19th floor and where they had us, we could walk out on the balcony and look across the way where the Mets were.

You might remember where we were as a team then. We won 82 games the year before, and only finished sixth in the AL West. By then, Kevin Appier was in the big leagues and he was just as good as Guy Hansen thought when we drafted him. He was proving us right giving that big bonus, and by then President Joe Burke could joke about telling us, "He better be able to pitch."

But we needed some pop in the lineup, and with Appier, Mike Boddicker, Mark Gubicza and Tom Gordon, we thought we could absorb giving up Bret Saberhagen — who was the most valuable of the bunch for a trade.

Fairly quickly, the Mets materialized as a trade partner that made sense. They were enticed by Saberhagen's talent — he was only three years removed from his second Cy Young Award, and made the All-Star team the year before — and had some hitters to offer.

We were going back and forth, back and forth, and at some point, we realized we could see the Mets across the little courtyard. It was impossible not to notice. We'd come out to our balcony to talk things over, and then look across and see the Mets' executives out on their balcony. And we're all talking about the same thing.

This goes on for two or three days. In any trade, there are times when you don't think it's going to get done but this situation was a little different because we could look across the way and see Buddy Kerr, one of their high-level scouts at the time, or someone else. You'd catch their eye and kind of signal to them, a thumbs up or something, like, "We're making progress, we're going to get there."

Eventually, we made that deal. We got Greg Jeffries, who then was one of the better young hitters in the American League, Kevin McReynolds, who had some pop, and Keith Miller, who could play all over the diamond.

That was a hard trade for me, personally. We got Sabes in the 19th round in 1982. He made the big leagues when he was just 21 years old, won the Cy Young Award and was our best pitcher in the World Series in 1985. Just a few months before the trade, I was sitting in my regular seat at Royals Stadium watching him throw a no-hitter against the White Sox.

As it turned out, in that particular trade, neither team got what it was hoping for. Saberhagen was good for the Mets, but not as good as he was for us. They traded him to the Rockies a few years later, he got hurt, and then finished his career with the Red Sox. Jeffries never hit in the American League quite like he did in the National League.

But I'll always remember that trade for the way it went down, the way you could see the other side talking about the same deal, in real time.

I'd never seen it before in all my years, and haven't seen it since.

# Chapter
# 5

# Bob Feller, straw hats and Peggy Move Up

*I* snuck into the attic of the house on Eddy Street. This was in the mid-1930s. I was 8 or 9 years old. Consequences of the Great Depression were still in the air. My mother and I lived on the north side of Chicago, and I don't know if it was boredom or curiosity or a desire to learn more about my father who had died when I was 4, but I went into the attic.

It wasn't finished up there. You had to be careful to walk on the beams, or else you'd fall right through the ceiling and into the main part of the house. But I saw an old trunk up there, black with gold trim. Dust all over the place. My father's stuff. I had to know what was in there.

I made my way across the beams and opened the top. Electronics, mostly. Dad was an engineer for RCA. They were working on television, even back then. I found some old magazines. Books. And then the grand treasure...

A baseball mitt.

It was brown and worn and barely held together by leather straps, but in my eyes, it was gorgeous. I'd been playing baseball with some kids in the neighborhood, but not with something like this on my hand. I put it on, pounded it a few times.

I couldn't wait to get to the park.

• • •

We played all the time. Every day. We didn't have organized leagues in those days. No travel teams. So depending on the day, there were four or five or six of us who'd meet in Kilbourn Park for a game we called Peggy Move-Up.

We did this every day. Mom would pack my lunch, and I'd walk about two miles to the park. We got there in the morning, and we'd have batting practice, just like we imagined the big leaguers did. Then we started playing.

We would've played real baseball, of course, but we didn't have enough kids. So we did what we could. The way it worked, the batter would set up in front of the backstop. You had a pitcher, a shortstop, a first baseman, and depending on how many guys you had that day, an outfielder or two and another infielder. You would bat until you made your three outs. If you got a double, you'd go back to the plate and if you got a base hit, that's a run. You might score one run, three runs, no runs. And then you'd rotate.

Whoever had the most runs won.

This thing was down to a science. We'd have our BP, play for a few hours, stop for lunch, and then play until the streetlights came on.

It's all I ever wanted to do. I was an OK student. I should've been better. It's just that my mind was always on baseball. When I wasn't playing, I was reading about it or listening to a game on the radio. Sometimes, I'd draw pictures of what I thought a stadium looked like.

My mom saw all this, of course. I was born on Feb. 6,

THURSDAY, JULY 20, 1944. ★ PAGE 23

TITLE CONFAB—Favorite in the Daily News-American Legion junior baseball tournament, now in the final Cook County round, is the Kilbourn Park club, sponsored by the Portage Park Legion Post 183. Here Organizer-Coach-Sparkplug-Shortstop Art Stewart of the Kilbourn Yanks (second from left) discusses strategy with three of his aces, Hurler Dick Kluck (left), Catcher Al Molina (second from right), and First Baseman Leroy Hirsch.     (Daily News photo.)

*I guess I was a leader from an early age. This is me at 17 years old, second from the left, the summer before my senior year at Schurz High School in Chicago, talking with some teammates on my American Legion team. The team was named for Kilbourn Park, where we often met to play a pickup baseball game we called Peggy Move Up.*

which happened to be Babe Ruth's birthday and in 1927 — the year the Bambino hit 60 home runs. Mom brought this up often.

"You're going to end up in professional baseball," my mom would say. "I think that could be your destiny."

• • •

The date is tattooed in my memory forever: Aug. 18, 1939. You don't forget your first big league ballgame. You don't forget falling deeper in love with the great game.

My uncle lived on the south side of Chicago, and we'd go over there on weekends. He knew what a baseball fan I was, even though I really didn't root for any particular team, and he agreed to take me to a game. My first game is at old Commiskey Park. It's the second night game they ever had there. Lights were just coming into use in baseball, and the White Sox were playing the Indians in front of 46,000 people.

I remember the lineup like it was yesterday. Bob Feller walks on the mound. Lou Boudreau, the great Hall of Famer, is at short. Ray Mack is at second, and big Al Trosky at first. The third baseman is Kenny Keltner, who stopped Joe Dimaggio's 56-game hitting streak with the great play in 1941.

I can tell you the whole White Sox lineup, too. Joe Kuhel, who grew up in Kansas City, he was a magician on the side and a magician with the glove at first base. You couldn't believe how fancy he was over there. Jackie Hays was at second base, he went blind later in life. Lucious Luke Appling was at short, the Hall of Famer who played that position until he was 40 years old. They used to ask how he could keep playing such a demanding position for so long, and he said he hunted every day in the offseason down in Georgia to keep his legs strong.

The bleachers are packed, and you can tell this is a special game. Feller is going against Eddie Smith, who is unknown in baseball history, but I'll never forget him. Blond guy, kind of an Eddie Lopat guy, could change speeds with that real good command. Well, Eddie battled with Feller for 11 innings. It's nothing-nothing. Eddie's getting by, but Feller is just dominating. I remember his pitches, they looked like aspirin tablets under the lights. Back then, he was throwing his curveball as fast as guys throw their fastball today.

You can imagine a 12-year-old at his first game, and this is the one. It was like a dream.

Well, in the bottom of the 11$^{th}$, Appling comes up and he fouls off 13 of Feller's great fastballs and breaking balls. Finally, he gets a walk. And then little Mike Kreevich, he couldn't have been more than 5-foot-7, gets a hold of Feller's fastball and hits over the centerfielder's head. It was 440 to dead center in old Comiskey Park, so Appling came around to score and the place is just going nuts.

Those straw hats that men used to wear in those days, they come flying out of the seats by the thousands. What a sight for a 12-year-old boy.

I didn't have a team I rooted for before that day. But I walked out of that park a White Sox fan for life.

At least until I joined professional baseball.

• • •

There were other ways we found to get into big league baseball games. I grew up about three miles from Wrigley Field, and we found out that the groundskeeper there was giving out free tickets.

What you had to do was show up after a game was over, and they'd give you a gunnysack and point you to a section of the stadium. That was the section you had to clean. You'd clean it out, sweep up all the cups and napkins and popcorn and peanut shells. This was harder than you'd think. But once you were done, someone would come over and inspect your section and give you a free ticket for Saturdays and Sundays to watch the big leaguers play.

You could see the game for nothing, if you were willing to work.

My best memory of Wrigley Field came in 1945. Me and my friends went to see what is still the last World Series for the Cubs. This was my senior year of high school, and we saved up enough money to buy bleacher tickets. I think they were $2, maybe $2.25. We get in line the day before the game, and there are about 300 people ahead of us. That's good enough that we know we're getting into the game, but not good enough to have our pick of seats.

Well, around 6 of 7 o'clock at night, one of my friends says there's supposed to be a big storm coming. Might be pretty rough. But we really want to see this game — we couldn't watch it on television — so he goes to a grocery store and gets these big cardboard boxes. When the rain started, we opened the boxes up and caught some shelter.

People all around us — and, most importantly, in front of us — were getting out of there so we moved right up in line with only 50 or so ahead of us. We were among the first ones through the gate when they opened at 11 the next morning.

I had no way of knowing that was the first of dozens and dozens of World Series games I'd be lucky enough to see.

• • •

I played at Schurz High, on Milwaukee Ave. on the north side. They made me the first freshman to ever play varsity, and by the time I was a junior and senior, I was team captain.

The best moment came when we beat Lane Tech, the big power in the area, on a hidden ball trick with their best hitter up in the last inning. You should've seen their legendary coach, Percy Moore. He went berserk.

Baseball never slowed down for me. Even when I wasn't playing, I wanted to be around the game. So going into my junior year, I found out they were putting people on hourly wages to work in the parks. We played our home games at a city park, and the field was just terrible, so I signed up for that field, made 50 cents an hour, and got to make sure our field was nice.

There were always two older gentlemen at our games, at least that I noticed. One sat down the left field line, and the other liked to sit in the stands down in right field. Both very well dressed. Suit, tie. You couldn't miss them. After our last game my senior year, one of them comes up to me.

"My name is George Sisler," he says. "I used to play first base for the Browns…"

I couldn't help myself. I shouldn't have interrupted the man, but I couldn't help it.

"What an honor, Mr. Sisler," I say. "I know exactly who you are."

This is a Hall of Fame player. Sisler hit .400 in the big leagues twice, including .420 in 1922 when he won the MVP. It was an honor just to talk to this man.

And then he starts complimenting me. He's scouting for the Dodgers then. He says he likes the way I play the game, likes my arm.

"Nobody has more hustle and holler than you," I remember him saying. "And you can run like a son of a bitch."

He said he wasn't sure if I could hit enough, but since I played the middle infield they wanted to give me a chance. They were offering a professional contract. This was my dream. They offered me $150 a month. I thanked Mr. Sisler, and told him I needed to talk it over with my mom.

Well, I get home that night and we're talking about the Dodgers offer and the phone rings.

"This is George Moriarty," the man says. "You probably don't know who I am."

I know exactly who he is.

I remember reading your name, Mr. Moriarty." I say. "You were the third baseman with Ty Cobb on the Tigers."

*I made a name for myself on the Chicago baseball scene by building a team I called the Chicago Yankees. I relied on the income from the team — both in sponsorships and side bets they'd make with a willing opposition — so much that I turned down a pro contract out of high school. Running the Chicago Yankees meant I was scouting before I even realized it, and it helped smooth my transition to the real Yankees.*

"How the hell did you know that?"

"I read a lot of baseball books."

Moriarty, a scout with the Tigers was the other guy at all those high school games. And he offers me a contract, same money as the Dodgers' offer. I thank him, and tell him I need to talk to my mom.

Well, this was my dream. Professional baseball. But our situation was a little bit different. I was playing semipro games then, and we made $25 per game and would bet so we could double our money. My mom is scrubbing floors and taking in laundry so we can stay in the house. It sounds strange now, but I was making more money in semipro games and working for the park than the pro contracts would pay.

My mom wanted me to do what I wanted to do, but after going through the figures, I just couldn't.

I wasn't into thinking negatively, but if I didn't advance or got released we could lose the house.

So instead of joining professional baseball as a player, I decided to start my own semipro team.

• • •

We called ourselves the Chicago Yankees. I wasn't going to the trouble of starting and organizing a team if we weren't going all out, trying to win.

So I thought back to those high school teams, and remembered the best players from the teams we played. I called them up and talked them into coming over and playing for us. We had all the best players, and we're winning city championship after city championship.

At one point, from 1948 to 1952, we had 24 players go into professional baseball from those teams.

I even got to meet the great Rogers Hornsby. He came to watch us play. Thinking back, I wish I'd gotten him to sign a ball. They're going for about $15,000 now. I remember Rogers never went to a movie. He never saw a movie his whole life, because he thought it would hurt his eyes. He went to the horse track instead. He was a great horse bettor.

Rogers had the great line. They asked him what he does in the baseball offseason.

"I just sit and look out the window and wait for spring," he said.

We had so many guys who were going into professional baseball, after a few years, the Yankees approached me about scouting. It was two of their scouts, Fred Hasselman and Lou Maguolo. But I still wanted to play. You always want to play as long as you can. Besides, I didn't know anything about scouting. I told Fred this, and he asked how I put together my team.

"I just find the best players and get them to play for me.," I said.

"That's scouting," Fred said.

He was right. I didn't even know it, but I was already scouting. So the Yankees gave me a different offer. They gave me a contract, and paid me a little bit, and I didn't even have to go out looking for guys. They just wanted me to give them a heads up if I saw a guy who could play pro ball on the other team, or with our team.

Gee, what did I have to lose?

*This is me in a uniform worn by Phil Rizzuto. The sponsor for our team dried up, and I worried we'd have to fold before someone with the Yankees caught wind and sent a set of the big league team's uniforms. I took the uniform of Rizzuto, the 5-foot-6 shortstop who helped win seven World Series and was inducted into the Baseball Hall of Fame.*

Cook's Sporting Goods was our sponsor, but they dropped us for a while because times were rough. I thought that might be it for our team, because without a sponsor we had no uniforms and without uniforms how could you play?

I called the Yankees to see if there was anything they could do for us. Our old uniforms were worn out. We'd put them into shreds over three or four years. Maguolo tells me he'll try.

A few weeks later, a truck pulls up to our house over there on Eddy Street and drops off these great big old boxes. I open them, and it was the most amazing sight. I'm pulling out Yankee uniforms. The real thing, the ones the guys wore in games. Joe Dimaggio. Whitey Ford. Phil Rizzuto. Gene Woodling. Yogi Berra. Vic Raschi. Eddie Lopat. Can you imagine what those would go for today? I wouldn't have to work in baseball if I had all that money.

And they just gave us the uniforms, with the real pinstripes. Sent us some socks, too. The only thing they asked is that we take the Yankee logo off. So I take the uniforms into Cook's, and I ask them to take the "NY" off and put a "CY." Cook's gave us hats, too, with the "CY" logo.

We used those uniforms about three years, until we wore them out. I wore Rizzuto's uniform, and I wish to this day I'd have kept it.

We looked like real Yankees. I'm telling you, we probably won some games just walking into the park with those uniforms.

After a few years of going like this, Hasselman left the Yankees for the White Sox. That's when I became full-time for the Yankees.

That's how I got started in seven decades of this scouting business. More than 60 years ago.

• • •

We all have big decisions in life. We all face forks in the road, where we could go one way but we choose another path that alters everything we do and see after that.

One of my biggest forks in the road was that decision after high school about whether to play pro ball. It was such an honor for George Sisler and George Moriarty — guys I'd read about doing so well in the big leagues — to think enough of my baseball talent and drive to offer contracts.

Some of my friends thought I was nuts to turn that down. You only get one chance to try professional baseball. There were times I wondered about that, too. Could I have made it? How far up the ladder of professional baseball would I have gone?

If I signed with the Tigers or Dodgers, if nothing else, I would've been in different organizations. My path would've been completely new, with different friendships and contacts and experiences.

Scouting myself as a player, honestly, I don't think I could've made the big leagues. I was small, and I didn't have much power. I don't think I could've hit enough, not when you get to the point where you're seeing the real good fastballs and breaking balls. Maybe I could've reached up to Double A, Triple A, just because of my fielding and how hard I worked. But I don't think I had big league talent.

As it turned out, the whole thing was a blessing. I know in my heart I made the right decision. Not just because it allowed me to help my mom and support her and keep the house. But it put me down the path of scouting, and here I am more than 60 years later still in Major League Baseball.

*One of my favorite parts of my baseball career is getting to know some of the players I grew up watching. My first big league game was at old Comiskey Park, where Bob Feller's Indians lost in extra innings in the stadium's second-ever night game. Many years later, after I told him that story, Feller gave me this personalized, autographed picture.*

I made it to the major leagues, I just made it in a different role. And it's a role that brought me more longevity than being a player, and the kinds of friendships and experiences I wouldn't trade for anything in the world.

• • •

One of the most rewarding parts of this baseball life has been the opportunity to get to know the game so well, and the people who make it so great.

Ted Williams is the greatest hitter I've ever seen, better than anybody who's come along since and that's no slight on guys like Hank Aaron, Pete Rose, Willie Mays, George Brett and Miguel Cabrera. But Ted was just different. His eyesight was out of this world. You might've heard old stories about how umpires would defer to his judgment and be so hesitant to call a strike on him. That's not an exaggeration. That's true.

Well, Ted is a guy I got to know on a personal level through this great game. The same thing with Joe DiMaggio, Mickey Mantle, Bob Feller and so many others.

I told Feller once about that first game I saw, on Aug. 18, 1939. He remembered the game, too, and we laughed a little about the memory. Well, I didn't think much of it, but many years later we ran into each other at a tournament in Wisconsin. We start talking, and after a while he reaches into his bag and hands me a picture of him as a young man in his Indians uniform. He autographed it.

*To Art:*
*Who saw his first game Aug. 18, 1939*
*Sincerely,*
*Bob Feller*

# 6

# Gun shots and bad cookies

*O*ne of the biggest changes over the years is the emphasis on scouting internationally. In some ways, what we did with the Royals Academy in Baseball City, Fla. in the 1970s was a precursor for what we and other teams put so much more time and effort into later in Latin America.

When I became scouting director in 1984, we only had three visas among our scouts. It just wasn't something we emphasized as much as we should have. That's the way it was back then. Toronto was heavy internationally, and it paid off with guys like Tony Fernandez, the shortstop, who started on their second World Series championship teams in the 1990s. But back in the early to mid '80s, there were really only two or three other clubs who went hard internationally.

So when I became scouting director, that was one of the things I wanted to work hard to change. There are only so many pools of talent, and if you're not in all of them, you're missing out.

Especially in Latin America, there's just so much talent there. It's always been like that. There are more big leaguers from the Dominican Republic than any other country in the world, except for the United States. And remember that this is a country of less than 10 million people. This would basically be like if 10 percent of big league baseball players came from Chicago or Los Angeles.

You go down there, and there's baseball talent everywhere you look.

You're just not fully engaged in developing talent if you're not fully engaged in Latin America.

• • •

John Schuerholz, the Royals GM at the time, gave us the go-ahead to ramp up our presence in Latin America. We already had a good scout there living in Santiago, Dominican Republic, named Luis Silverio. Luis later became a big league coach for us, after coming up through our system as a player.

He made it to the big leagues, briefly, in 1978 before an injury derailed him. Damdest thing, too. He hit a ball in the gap, and he's coming in for a triple but the third base coach is going back and forth about whether to slide or come in standing up. Luis got crossed, and he ended up hurting his knee. He tried to come back, but was just never the same player.

Silverio was a great guy to help get us started there. He grew up in a small village near Santiago, so the lay of the land was natural for him. He had contacts all over the country. Mostly from his own days of being a star player there in the Dominican, but also friends and family. He has 14 siblings.

*Here we are at the dedication of our academy in the Dominican Republic. The guy to my left was the Vice President of the Dominican. On the far left is Dan Glass, our club president. To my immediate right is Luis Silverio, whose career was cut short by a knee injury, but really led our academy from the ground up.*

Luis' story is the story of a lot of guys we scout and sign out of Latin America. The Dominican, especially, is a very poor country. Luis' father was a farmer, and he says the family might have $200 at the end of a growing season to buy food and presents and everything. They'd get a pair of pants, maybe some shoes, and that was enough.

Maybe you've heard stories about kids in the street, playing stickball. Those are all true. You won't see anything like it in the States. They'd take an old broom handle, or maybe a branch from a tree if it was the right size, and make a ball out of a rolled up wad of tape. If you saw kids with gloves, a lot of times they're just old milk cartons.

They played in the fields after the tobacco season, and played from sun up to sun down if they didn't have to work. Baseball was and is more than a game to a lot of kids in the Dominican. It's a way of life, and it's a way to a better life.

We wanted to show Dan Glass, who is now our club president, the international program. It was back in the mid '90s, and we were on a plane to go show him around. Dan was going to have a bigger part of the international program, so we really wanted to show him a good face there. Well, we're on the plane, one of these little puddle-jumpers, and the back just opens up. There's magazines, cups, papers, everything just flying out of the back.

We're all scared to death. It's all we can do to hang out and keep from flying out with the paper cups. It felt just like it looks in the movies. The air is rushing out the back, and you know that if you don't stay in your seat that's going to be it for you. The pilot comes on, gives us a little warning to hold tight, and then makes this dramatic, severe turn to get the door closed. I've never been so happy to get off a plane.

Dan was so impressed with the Dominican program. He fell in love with the country, the kids and the work we were doing there. It was topped off by our kids playing a team in the Yankees system. We beat the Yankees that day, and the kids felt like they won the World Series. Dan wanted to buy them dinner, and as it happened there was a Burger King on the way back. We all ate those burgers like a steak dinner at the Ritz.

It was important for us that Dan see what we were doing, and see what we were working with. On his return, he talked to his father and team owner David Glass, and it resulted in us getting a beautiful building down there to headquarter the program right across from the ballpark. The club was nice enough to name the building after me.

Coming from America, you realize how good we have it here. You never forget your first trip to the Dominican. The people there are great, especially when they find out you're there because of baseball. They love baseball as much as we do, so we always have a nice, common language to speak. But the poverty there — it'll break your heart. They're living under grass roofs, on dirt floors. You wonder how they make it.

It's about a 22-mile drive from Santiago to Salcedo where we eventually set up, and one of the things that sticks out on the way is how many baseball games you see. Kids, everywhere, playing baseball and they do it with such a natural joy. As much as the poverty is hard to stomach, it's so nice to see them rally around the great game. They play with smiles on their faces. Even the ones who make it to the big leagues, and have all the money they could ever imagine, they have a well-earned reputation for playing with a certain swagger, joy and emotion that we don't always have with American players.

You can sign guys for $1,000 and they're thrilled. You go into their house, and you see how they're living. Some of the places are like straw huts, with dirt floors and a pot belly stove. If it's true that Dominican players want it more than anyone else, you can see why.

Baseball is the Dominican's deep love. It's in the DNA down there, like something in the water makes these kids love and appreciate the great game. Maybe it *is* something in the water, because a lot of these kids have other worldly power and exploding fastballs.

You hear a lot now about how there are more performance enhancing drugs in Latin America than other places, and that might be true. The rules there are just different. The culture is different, too. But I know this: Before steroids were widely used anywhere, there was always such a high concentration of baseball talent in Latin America — and especially the Dominican.

One of the things that made Luis especially good for us is that he was 17 years old when we signed him and sent him to the Royals Academy in Florida. That was his first time in the United States, and I think it really made an impression. I think he remembered how we had it organized, with the fields close to where the players stayed, and all the coaches we had to work with guys there and even the emphasis on education. Luis remembered all of that.

That was a good thing, because we really wanted our presence in Latin America to mirror what we'd done with the academy in Florida.

• • •

We let Luis get the whole thing organized. He knew the area and the people better than any of us.

So he was the one who hired some bird dogs, and he was the one who talked to the city officials in Santiago to secure a home park where we could train. Back then, the rule was that you could have 30 to 35 players training in your complex, but after 30 days you had to either sign them to a contract or release them. For 30 days, you could put them up with a place to stay, feed them, give them whatever they needed for baseball, but after that time period, you had to sign them or let them go.

Well, that first year we rented a house for the players. It was a big house, about a block away from the park. We had some coaches live

*The transportation has been updated, but this is how the team got around to different games shortly after we started up. The poverty in that country will break your heart, but the hope and kindness will fill it.*

there, too. That helped keep everything organized, and helped the coaches, too.

The way that park was set up, there were these huge trees behind the outfield walls in left and right field. After a while of training there, word was spreading around town about what we were doing.

We found out that scouts from other teams would get the information about when we were training, and then they'd climb up into those trees and watch us. They were spying on us. They'd watch for a few days, and if someone caught their eye, they'd try to sign them when they were walking the block from the stadium to the house.

We were doing the work identifying players and training them. Then, other teams were swooping in and trying to steal our guys.

We had to get that changed. So after that first year, we found a park in Salcedo. We were there on a 30-year lease. The Royals gave us $10,000 to make some improvements to the stadium, so under the stands we built some housing. We put bunk beds there under the stands, built a classroom so the players could learn English, built a kitchen and dining room to keep them fed. Silverio had an office there, too.

We weren't going to run the risk of our guys signing with someone else after a good practice anymore.

The academy paid off for us pretty quick. The first player we signed was a pitcher named Jose Nunez, who made it to the big leagues with Toronto. And the academy gave us Melido Perez, who helped make the Floyd Bannister trade. Hipolito Pichardo, who got 10 years in the big leagues with us, the Red Sox and the Astros. There were a lot of others to follow through the years.

We needed this extra pool of players.

If you saw a player down there, you had to act quickly.

Freddie Ferrera was a great scout down there for Montreal. He knew the Dodgers had an outfielder he really liked in one of those 30-day tryouts, and had heard from a contact of his that the Dodgers were about to release him. This player had a lot of talent. He had a big arm, could move pretty well and the ball took off his bat like a rocket.

So Freddie hears the Dodgers are about to release this kid, and he drives over to the Dodgers' complex on a moped. As soon as the player walked out of the complex, Freddie put him on the back of the moped and drove over to the Expos' complex.

That's how the Expos signed Vladimir Guerrero.

Vlad went on to make nine All-Star teams and win an MVP. He could hit just about anything. You couldn't throw it far enough out of the strike zone for Vlad not to hit it somewhere.

And he broke in with the Expos because a scout acted on a tip, and acted quickly.

• • •

Ruben Pujols is probably a name you've never heard. No, he's not related to Albert. He was this catcher in the Dominican, from a little town on the extreme west side of the country, right on the border of Haiti.

Silverio called me one day and he told me about this prospect, said he's a good catch-and-throw guy, needed to develop with his bat, but is worth a look. Now, you never turn down the opportunity to see catchers. Nobody has enough catchers. So we hop in the car and take a look.

We're there about a half hour or so, working him out in this field with a lot of open space behind the outfield fence — which happened to be the direction of the Haitian border. We're pretty impressed with the kid, especially for that age. He's got a good arm, especially. And even in batting practice,

*This is Hipolito Pichardo, who pitched 10 years in the big leagues for us, the Red Sox and Astros. He was one of the first big leaguers we signed out of that academy. Our international presence has since become one of the best in baseball. Salvador Perez has the chance to be the best of the bunch.*

*Photo Courtesy of Kansas City Royals*

83

he's hitting home runs over that fence and into the pasture. Cows are getting out of the way of these balls, it's a sight you don't forget.

And then came a sound I'll never forget.

Gunfire.

*Boom, Boom, Boom!*

You don't forget that sound. They were shooting at us! At first, you don't react right away because it's such a shock. We sort of look around at each other, like, *"Is this really happening?"*

And then we scatter. We run for cover, wait for the shots to stop, and jump in the car with Ruben and take off as fast as we can. It's the closest to death I've ever felt.

As it turns out, especially at the time, the relationship between Haitians and Dominicans wasn't very good. They would usually leave each other alone, but I guess the violence would escalate when there were outsiders around. You can tell by the cover of this book, I don't look Haitian or Dominican.

When we got back to the academy in Salcedo, we calmed down a little bit.

"Oh, that happens often," Ruben told us. "Especially when they see strangers."

But before the gunfire, we saw enough from Ruben to sign him. We put him in the Gulf Coast League at 18, but he never made it past Class A ball. He never could hit the breaking pitch. That's one of the things that's hard to predict sometimes.

So Ruben Pujols is one of thousands who had a lot of talent, but not quite what it takes to make it to the major leagues. You've probably never heard of him.

I'll never forget him.

• • •

The Japanese came into the Dominican, too.

They play some serious baseball in Japan. It's almost as much a part of their sports culture as it is in the Dominican. A few years ago, when Daisuke Matsuzaka made his big league debut for the Red Sox in Kansas City, there was nearly as much media there as would show up for a World Series game.

Japan has a different level of passion for baseball. And a different kind, too. It's very serious, more of an occupation than a recreation. When Matsuzaka threw an unplanned bullpen session on an off day in Kansas City, before that first start, the stadium was swarmed with Japanese media. They had to get every detail to report back home.

"The mound was nice," he told them in Japanese.

Anyway, when the Japanese came into the Dominican we knew the climate down there was changing. They built a beautiful, modern complex. The complex was built in a way that even on days when it rained, they had a roof over the pitchers and catchers. And they had security, everywhere. From the outside, you could see the guards positioned up top on the corners. It looked kind of like a prison. They had a big, red iron gate that was the only way in and out.

Once we got an invitation to see what they had from the inside. There was one player they had signed, and they were willing to sell him to a big league club.

At the time, getting in that complex was like going over the Wall of China or something. The talent in that player was obvious, too. He had this buggy-whip swing, was powerful and was playing shortstop. Could run pretty well, too. The first guy I thought of was Ernie Banks.

We tried like hell to sign the kid, and there was a time I thought we had him. We missed out on bad timing more than money.

We were that close to getting Alfonso Soriano.

• • •

The Dominican is a beautiful place, and the people there are usually so helpful and nice. You can have some of the best meals in the world there, too, but you have to know where to look. You hear stories about needing to be careful, but you don't really understand until you make a bad decision.

Before I ever went down there, I heard from some friends who spent a week in the hospital after eating some pork on a stick after a workout. They were driving down the road, and they just thought it looked so good. Big mistake.

I learned my lesson there firsthand, too.

I was there with Bob Hegman, our farm director at the time, and we're watching some of our own players, getting extra eyes and reports on our own guys. Well, toward the end of the game, this lady is walking around the park selling cookies.

I'm telling you, these cookies looked delicious. They were delicious, too. Some of the best cookies I've ever had in my life. Chocolate chip, soft, moist. Just terrific.

I didn't think much of it — most of the food advice you get there is about the tap water and pork — until the middle of the night. I woke up around 3 in the morning, and I was so sick I couldn't walk. Sickest I've ever been in my life. The room is spinning, I can't focus. I crawl on my knees to the toilet.

I can't sleep. I could hardly leave the bathroom. It was just miserable. At one point, I look at the clock and it's about 4 a.m. and I realize Silverio is coming by the hotel at 7 to pick us up for a game in Salcedo. I don't know how in the world I'm going to make that work.

About 5:30 in the morning, Hegman calls.

"Art," he says, and he sounds as bad as I feel. "I think I'm dying. I can't move."

I tell him I feel just as bad. You can't miss games down there, though. It's the only reason you're there, and there's a code of honor among scouts about showing up to the games no matter the conditions. I've known scouts who've gotten into car accidents but still made sure to be there for the first pitch.

Then about 6:30 in the morning, my phone rings again. It's Silverio.

"Sorry," he says. "We're rained out today. No game."

I've never been so relieved to not see baseball. I stayed in the room all day, and within about 24 hours, whatever was in those cookies passed. I made it to the ballpark the next day, with a lesson learned:

Boil your water, and only eat at the hotel you're staying if you can help it at all. Everything else is a risk.

But that's all part of the Dominican.

• • •

Silverio's brother worked for the government and had a connection to the President of the Dominican, so he invited him over for the opening of our academy there. He couldn't make it — I think Fidel Castro came over on a last-second, surprise visit — but the vice president was there.

You know how you see the President of the United States in those caravans, with the flags on the limos? It's the same thing in the Dominican, except they're big black Lincolns instead of limos.

There had to be six or seven or eight guys dressed up in suits. It was the vice president's security team. It was 100 degrees that day, so everybody's sweating but they don't budge. He came marching up the stairs, this big good-looking man, smiled a little, cut the ribbon on our complex, and we were officially open for business. We beat the Phillies 3-2 that day.

I love going to the Dominican. I absolutely love it. It really gives you that feeling of the old days of scouting, where you see a player at a game, and if you like him you can sign him there at the table. It's like it used to be here in the States, before the draft.

The younger scouts, I tell them that, and they look at me funny. The draft is the only way they know. And the draft has its wrinkles. It's a different challenge to pick out your judgments of a player, see how they align with another club's and see who turns out to be right. It's a constant motion of tweaking certain judgments, and learning which areas are underserved, why one kid did or did not make it to the big leagues. You're always adjusting.

But in Latin America, it's a little closer to the Wild West. I like it that way. I like the feeling that whatever game I'm watching, if I can see a kid with all the tools and ability and hunger to be a big league baseball player, I might just walk out of that stadium having signed the next Salvador Perez.

*The Royals were nice enough to dedicate the academy in the Dominican to me. This plaque hangs outside the facility. The Royals have really reinvested in the Dominican and the rest of Latin America in recent years, and you're seeing it pay off with guys like Salvador Perez and Yordano Ventura.*

• • •

Salvador is an important part of this, a good player to emphasize here. After Mr. Kauffman died, we had a board of directors that ran the Royals for a while and their charge all along was to minimize costs to make us more attractive to a buyer.

Well, one of the costs that was minimized was our time and presence in Latin America. We didn't abandon things down there, but we sure didn't have the focus and energy there that we had in the 1980s, when I was scouting director.

It takes resources and patience to really do it right in Latin America, and the situation just didn't allow for that.

Those ways started to change around 2006, when David Glass hired Dayton Moore. Glass was tired of the losing, and he wanted to build the Royals back from the ground up. When he interviewed Dayton, one of the things they spent the most time on was an international scouting program. Dayton and David agreed that this was one of the best ways for the Royals to get their farm system back to where it was in its heyday, and in a fairly quick matter, we went from one of the lightest international scouting programs to the best.

Rene Francisco deserves a lot of that credit. He and Dayton worked together in Atlanta, and Dayton trusts Rene to find players in the Dominican and other places. It's really paid off, too, if you follow our farm system. A lot of our best players have come from around the world.

Salvador is the brightest star for us in this regard. He made the All-Star team in 2013, and that was so great that he was able to be the catcher when Mariano Rivera pitched his last All-Star game. That's such a great picture they have of those two, the only ones on the field as the players from both sides wanted the focus to be on Mariano.

Speaking of Mariano, have you heard the story of how we almost signed him?

Probably not. I haven't told anybody until now.

• • •

We were *this* close. To this day, I still know in my heart that we should've had Rivera before the Yankees.

This goes back to the late '80s, and we had Herb Rayborn working for us. Herb was one of the best scouts in Latin America. Connections everywhere. He was supervising the Dominican, Venezuela, Panama, Nicaragua and Colombia.

Every time you'd talk to Herb, he'd tell you about some guy he had "hidden in the bush." That was his term. *Hidden in the bush.* And he wasn't just talking, Herb really did have players all over the place.

Well, one year, he tells me he has a couple in Panama. This is around September or October, but the kids aren't eligible to sign yet. They can't sign until after the first of the year.

"I've got them," Herb says. "Nobody knows about them."

Now it's time for contracts after the season is over, and we always had a pretty standard raise. It was nice, but nothing that was going to make you rich. Herb has a little hang-up with his. The Yankees liked the work he was doing for us, and they were offering Herb a $5,000 raise. Herb says he doesn't want to leave, but we all understand that a raise is a raise.

"I don't know if I can get that approved," Schuerholz says.

John tried, but it didn't happen. The money just wasn't there, so we lost Herb to the Yankees.

You know who those two guys in the bush were?

One was Rivera, who will breeze into the Hall of Fame on the first ballot. The other was Ramiro Mendoza, who was a pretty decent relief pitcher for many years with the Yankees.

I asked Mariano about that story, after he was with the Yankees and had become a star. He remembered it well.

"Herb was like a father to me," Mariano says.

I don't think anybody knows that story.

# Chapter
# 7

# The changing times

*I*'ve been fortunate to see Ted Williams in his prime, Willie Mays in his prime, George Brett in his prime, Albert Pujols in his prime, and Mike Trout at the beginning of what should be a brilliant career.

When I started scouting in 1953, we sent in reports with a two-cent postcard back to the Yankees. Now we can sit at a ballpark and enter all the information on our iPads, and cross-check that with other reports, both from other scouts and on other players. Instantly, I can see how hard Chris Dwyer is throwing his curveball for Northwest Arkansas even if I'm in Kansas City watching James Shields throw that good changeup.

We tend to think that technology has only made the big changes in recent years, but that's not necessarily true. Even things we know as so basic now, like cell phones, have changed baseball as fundamentally as they've changed our every day lives.

I remember being in Greenville, S.C., for the ACC baseball tournament in 1994 to see a young shortstop from Georgia Tech named Nomar Garciaparra for the first time. There's always a lot of talent in that tournament. Just that year, Paul Wilson was the great pitcher for Florida State who ended up going first overall to the Mets. Todd Walker was a second baseman for LSU, he ended up going eighth to the Twins. Heck, even on Garciaparra's team, Jason Varitek was the catcher.

But Nomar was a guy who really stood out. He had that quick, compact swing that you could be relatively sure would translate to the harder fastballs and late-breaking curveballs that he'd see in pro ball.

And he was so smooth in the field, great hands, quick feet and a strong arm. You knew he could stick at shortstop.

Anyway, he was so good I wanted to call back to the office right after the game. So I finish my notebook, close it up, pack my stuff and — I know how this sounds today — go find a pay phone.

And you know what I saw?

A scout already in the phone booth, doing the same thing I wanted to do, and two more guys waiting in line in front of me.

Today, of course, we just call up our bosses on the cell phone.

I know it doesn't sound like much, but it sure has changed the way we do our jobs — just as it's changed the way people live their lives.

I will say this, though: Nothing disturbs me more than getting a phone call during a game. I won't answer it, unless it's a true emergency. It bothers me seeing young scouts do that, too. You'll

*Photo Courtesy of Kansas City Royals*

*This is a reminder of one of the bad changes to baseball and scouting over the years. This is a picture of all seven full-time scouts (plus one part-time scout, and two executives) the Royals had after the 1976 season, when baseball's creation of the scouting bureau had almost everyone cutting staff. We had about 25 full-time scouts before the bureau opened up, and I still believe the cuts led to us having some of our weakest drafts before we beefed up the department again.*

be watching a game, with a top prospect, and the scout sometimes isn't even paying attention. They're not looking. Their head is down, looking at their phone.

It sounds simple, but that's one thing I tell young scouts: When you're at the game, watch the game. Whatever is on your phone can wait until the game is over.

There have been many changes in baseball over the years, of course. I can go all the way back to when World Series games were always played in the daytime. I've seen our great game changed by an influx of international talent, the split-finger fastball, weight training, bullpen specialization, more detailed and available scouting reports, bigger stadiums, more media attention, the amateur draft and so much more.

When I started, scouts were getting $.06 a mile, $6 a day for food and $6 a day for lodging. The average salary for a major league player was $13,000 (that's $110,000 in today's dollars) and the highest paid player was Ted Williams at $85,000 (today, that's like $720,000).

I remember asking Ted once, long after he retired, what he thought he'd be paid today.

"Half the franchise," he said.

There were only 16 teams back then. No free agency, no player agents, no radar guns, no video camera scouting, no batting helmets — and knock down pitches were allowed.

But by far the two ways it's changed the most are through technology and so much more money being paid to players.

• • •

In the last 10 or 15 years, there has also been a subtle but important change in the way we look at players, in the way we evaluate players.

Statistics have become such a bigger part. We always looked at on-base percentage and innings and strikeouts, but today there is just so much more information. You can use numbers and video to get a better idea of a player's defense, especially, the range he has in the outfield and what his arm is like.

The statistics are the natural evolution of scouting. We'll always use the 20-80 scale (a numerical grading system of a players' tools with 20 being a poor rating and 80 a top tier player), but this is a supplement to that. A guy can have enormous power, but you want to make sure it shows up in the games, not just batting practice. You don't want what we call a 5 o'clock hitter.

This information is harder to come by when you're scouting the amateur player, of course, though even with draft prospects — especially if they're college kids — you can sometimes find out how they do against the curveball, or what percentage of the time they throw first-pitch strikes.

But most of the time with amateurs, you still have to go by what you see. The numbers can be so skewed for college and especially high school kids. Some high school kids play games that end 25-0, and they might never see a pitch to hit because they're so talented, or if they do it's thrown by a guy who might as well be throwing batting practice.

You run into this a lot when a kid plays in an area where the talent is particularly uneven. There was a Kansas City kid some time ago, Damian Rolls. He was a spectacular talent, and he passed every eye test you could want — I remember he used to stand a bit upright at the plate, and wiggle his body and bat like Ken Griffey Jr. We saw a lot of him at Schlagle High School, but there were many games where he'd be walked every time he came to the plate and his team would win 14-1 or something. You're much better off seeing those kids in the summers, when they're playing better competition. No amount of statistical information is going to give you an idea on his talent. Damian ended up going with the 23rd pick in 1996 to the Dodgers.

The statistics and in-depth breakdowns are much more important for big league scouting, signings and trades than when you're looking at amateurs. That's because the competition is more even, obviously, but also because the information is more prevalent and relevant.

Our guys have these video programs where they can watch every single final pitch of a strike out. Or what they did against 2-1 curveballs, first-pitch fastballs or any pitch in a full count. If you're a pitcher, you can hit a few buttons and find out what you looked like against that night's cleanup hitter.

It can really help with defensive positioning. Rusty Kuntz is in charge of our outfielders, and Dale Sveum will help with our infielders. Both of those guys will use the breakdowns we get from our analytics guys to see where they should position, for instance, where Alcides Escobar should play when Joe Mauer comes to the plate. Or how deep Alex Gordon needs to be against Miguel Cabrera.

One of the reasons you see us and other teams — the Tampa Bay Rays are famous for this — use so many shifts is that we have a lot more information to tell us when it can be useful. It's a mantra in our game that you can never have too much information, so if we can steal an out or two in a game, that can be the difference between us losing and winning that night.

Having that information can help in other ways, too. In 2013, for instance, our manager, Ned Yost, was having trouble finding a lineup he really liked. We wanted Alcides Escobar to be our No. 2 hitter. If everyone is performing to their capability, he's probably the best guy for that spot because his hand-eye coordination is so good for hit-and-runs, he's a good bunter and he can run a bit. But Alcides was really struggling with the bat the previous year, so we needed to shake things up a bit.

Mike Groopman and John Williams, our analytics guys, ran some numbers and came up with what they thought was the best lineup. The most drastic change was moving Eric Hosmer from third to second, and Escobar from second to the bottom of the order. Salvador Perez moved up a bit, too, from sixth to third or fourth. Ned liked it. He made a minor change or two to keep us alternating left- and right-handed hitters in the middle and bottom of the order, but otherwise went with it.

Whether it was the change in order, the impact George Brett and Pedro Grifol were having as hitting coaches or just guys finding their swings on their own, we did start to score a little bit more after that.

· · ·

The trick, of course, is knowing what information to filter out and what information to give your guys.

Each player is different. Like in our clubhouse, Billy Butler wants all the information he can get. He has an amazing memory, it's almost photographic, so he can remember a lot of this stuff on his own. But he also wants to watch video. Some of the time, he just wants to see how his balance is at the plate, if he's dropping his hands or opening his hips too soon.

And sometimes it's specific to who we're facing that night. If we're going against Justin Verlander — I'm just using him as an example, though Billy has had some great success against Verlander — Billy will want to see how those at bats have gone in the past. Did he start him out with a fastball? A curveball? Does he go heavy on fastballs early, and bring the breaking stuff later in the game? Billy wants all of that information. He thinks it makes him better, and if nothing else, it makes him more confident, which can only help.

There are other guys who just want to know what the guy throws and then grab a bat and battle through. In our clubhouse now, Mike Moustakas is like this. In the past, George Brett was like this.

Despite the mantra, some guys feel like they *can* have too much information. They feel like they get to over-analyzing, they're thinking too much, and when the pitches are coming in at you in the blink of the eye, you want to be able to react, not think.

I've noticed that pitchers tend to like the information more than hitters. Pitchers want to have a plan of attack for each hitter, while hitters have to react to how the pitchers attack them. It can help to know how the pitcher has attacked you in the past, but sometimes that information won't help because the pitcher will change it up every time he sees you.

The information doesn't work for everybody. Each player needs to know what they're comfortable with, and what they don't need. That's important for the advanced scouts and coaches, too, to know what information is important to the player and what they should leave out.

Going back through the years with our club, managers Whitey Herzog and Dick Howser were both similar in this way. They would say some of the same things.

"Let's not over-complicate this," they'd say. "The game is hard enough."

• • •

One change in the game that I don't like is the emphasis on pitch counts. I firmly believe we've become prisoners to pitch counts, and that we use too much of a one-size-fits-all approach to how much work our pitchers can handle.

I've talked about this with pitching coaches. Some of them agree, some of them don't. Some agree but feel like their hands are tied, because there is so much more money invested in players now and organizations understandably want to protect those investments. This is part of what I mean when I say money has changed the game.

But today we protect them so much and we're at an all-time high in surgeries and amount of time pitchers spend on the disabled list. Teams end up spending millions and millions of dollars of salaries for pitchers on the disabled list. Some of that is unavoidable. There have always been injuries, and there always will be injuries. This is still a great challenge to the industry as a whole.

I know people say that repeatedly throwing a baseball 90 mph isn't natural, but I also know what Nolan Ryan says, that when we were kids we threw all the time, and in the old days pitchers threw a lot more between starts. It used to be their second day between starts was to throw live batting practice, and it seems like arms lasted longer then.

I don't know what, exactly, is the answer. There is no way to know for sure why a particular injury occurred. It could be misuse or overuse, but it could also be that particular pitcher had a weak ligament that was bound to tear. It could be genetics, not just whether he throws between starts.

Baseball should continue to explore for solutions to this problem.

• • •

You may not know or think much about another drastic change in baseball over the years. But the creation of the major league scouting bureau in 1974 shook our profession.

In the beginning, the clubs said this wouldn't cost any scouts jobs but we all knew better. The idea of it was to form a more centralized scouting center, to avoid five different clubs spending money to send five different scouts for essentially the same report on the same player.

In a perfect world, it would give basic reports on players and then if clubs wanted a closer look they would send their own guy to get more eyes on a prospect.

Of course it cost jobs. The Royals, we had a really good scouting staff. We had about 25 guys, which was one of the highest totals in baseball. But in 1975, we were down to seven.

The effects of this were everywhere in baseball. The reports from the scouting bureau would be distributed to the clubs, and then the clubs could use them as they saw fit. That meant more players to run down with fewer scouts, and it took time away from some of the better prospects you wanted to see.

You can imagine how this went over with the more established scouts. Some of them saw this as an act of aggression on the profession. I remember talking to George Brophy, who was the farm director for the Twins, asking him how he works with the reports from the scouting bureau.

"I'll tell you what we do with them," I remember George saying. "I tell our secretary, when those reports come in, file them in the wastebasket."

At first, the scouting bureau was merely an option for clubs. But by 1985 it was mandatory. Everyone was involved and everyone was paying for it. When it became mandatory, I'll never forget what Jack Schwarz, who was with the Giants, told everyone.

"I'm here with blood all over me," he said. "I fought this to the bitter end."

Fewer scouts meant bigger territories, so instead of getting more eyes on specific players, you were scrambling

*This is an old scouting report on Kirk Gibson, and believe it or not, this was state of the art at the time. It was done on a typewriter, and everything is what you see with the eye. That was all important, but time moves on and you need more.*

more to cover the same jobs you had before. When you saw a prospect, even a good one, a lot of times you could only see him once. The best reports always come when you've seen a guy over a period of time. A great player can have a bad day, and a bad player can have a great day. You don't want to get caught like that.

After a few years, the Royals admitted their mistake and by 1977 we started rebuilding the staff.

Once we were back to our accustomed levels, I changed my mind about the scouting bureau. They put me on the board of directors some time back, and I think they did this because they knew I wasn't a big supporter.

But I started to see it as an extra tool. It's just one more way to get information about prospects you otherwise might miss. Now, don't get me wrong. The information you get from the bureau is the same information everyone else has, so you're not getting an edge.

And nothing — *nothing* — will replace the veteran scouts you live with and die with to bring talent into the organization. Those are the guys you have to trust to see things the other scouts might miss. Those are the guys you have to believe are giving you an edge when you're on the road.

But if you use the reports in the right way, you can get a lot of good out of them. You follow up on the ones worth following up on, and hopefully your own scouts are getting information and observations that the bureau is missing.

The bureau reports are also good for medicals. You can get a preliminary report about a prospect's health, his arm strength if he's a pitcher, that kind of thing. They also give us video, which is very helpful. The quality of the video continues to improve and is a great asset in our draft meetings.

They've really come a long way under the direction of Don Pries, who is now retired, and director, Frank Marcos. They've also produced a lot of good scouts, like Lenny Merullo, Ralph Dillio, Brad Kolher and Jim Weldon. The bureau has produced many fine men who have been promoted to major league clubs in high positions.

It really has turned into a positive for the game.

• • •

There's no question that money has been a big change in the game, but not necessarily in the ways you think.

The best amateurs sign for millions, but the best amateurs have always signed for a lot of money. When Rick Reichardt signed with the Angels in 1964 for $200,000, the deal really pushed owners over the top in creating the draft.

Mickey Mantle made $100,000 that year.

Stephen Strasburg signed for $15.1 million in 2009, and that's a huge sum for an amateur player, obviously. But it was also a four-year contract, and even if the total of that four-year contract was just a signing bonus, it wouldn't have put Strasburg in the top 10 in baseball that year. Reichardt signed for twice as much as Mantle was making. It's all relative.

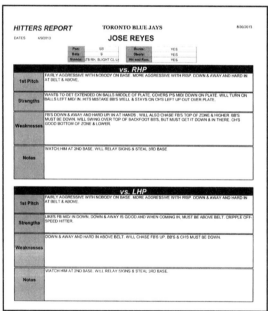

*This is a scouting report from 2013, when we played the Blue Jays. It's 23 pages, with everything from pickoff times to hot zones and what percentage of the time each pitcher throws each of his pitches and how often for strikes. I've included the page for Jose Reyes. Not that we warn our guys to be careful of him stealing pitches, and how right- and left-handed pitchers should attack him differently.*

So, there's always been a lot of money going to amateur players, but the biggest difference in the money now is that the negotiations for draft picks and amateur free agents are so much more involved.

Even into the 1980s and most of the 1990s, you didn't have much trouble signing your draft picks. Even for your top picks, you could usually get them done in a day or two.

But then agents really started getting involved, and I understand why. For some of those players, this will be the most money they ever make.

They have every right to get the best deal they can. But from a team's standpoint, it's especially nice when you see a player who you know wants to play pro ball and wants to get started as soon as they can.

That's one thing I always liked about Billy Butler. He knew he would make a lot of money with his signing bonus, but he also knew that the *really* big money was in the major leagues.

The best and quickest way to the major leagues is to get signed, so you don't lose that first summer of development in pro ball. Billy is talented and he's always been able to hit, but I believe the fact that he signed and got into pro ball so quickly helped him rise through the minor leagues so fast. He played his first big league game a few weeks after his 21st birthday.

• • •

When you've been around this great game as long as I have, one of the things you know for certain is that change is inevitable and most of the time should be welcomed with open arms.

I've seen scouts, executives, players and coaches fight change every step of the way, from the draft, to technology, to rising bonuses for amateurs.

I've always tried to get on board with the changes. You have to roll with the punches, and most of the time, the changes in place are good for the game and can even make your job easier or more effective.

That's what I thought the first time I saw Theo Epstein, who was still the GM with the Red Sox at the time, show up to an amateur showcase event with an iPad. I'd never seen one before, but when he told me he had every report for every draft prospect they were looking at in that thing, I knew this was the future and I should get ready.

One of the great things about baseball is the history, and how you can compare guys and eras through the decades. But if you want to make a living in baseball, you also have to be willing to adapt to change.

# Chapter

# 8

# You drafted the player, but can you sign him?

*N*one of it matters if you can't sign the kid.

That sounds obvious, but sometimes you can forget it. You can be on a kid since his sophomore year of high school; get to know his parents so well they cook your favorite meal; and get to know his friends and his girlfriend, his girlfriend's friends and his preacher. You can know his speed down to first and his arm strength in the hole and his favorite warm-up drill and his GPA and his favorite movie.

But none of it matters if you can't get the kid signed.

And I'll tell you this: Signing the kid is often a lot harder than you think.

• • •

Signing Johnny Damon was never going to be easy. He was a talented kid out of Dr. Phillips High School in Orlando, and probably the best high school prospect in the country going into his senior year — which is part of where the problems came from.

You see, his senior year didn't go so great. I mean, he was fine, still showed the good tools, but his numbers weren't where you'd want them for a prospect of his caliber as a senior in high school. Actually, his numbers weren't even as good as his sophomore and junior seasons.

There was a lot of noise around Johnny in high school. We'd go watch him play, and every time he came to the plate, the public address announcer would say, "Now batting, the best high school player in the country, Johnny Damon!"

So, numbers or not, Johnny expected to go in the first round. High in the first round, actually.

We took Michael Tucker with the 10th pick, hoping that Damon would still be there when our supplemental pick came up between the first and second round, 35th overall.

He was there, and as it turned out, he was the best player taken in that first round other than Jeter.

But we had a devil of a time getting that deal done.

• • •

Allard Baird was one of our top scouts at the time and was the first one into Johnny's house after the draft.

Johnny wanted that first-round money. He wanted what he would've had if he'd gone much higher in the draft, but of course that's not going to happen. The deal is stalling, so they call me in and we're at the house at noon. Allard and Brian Murphy are with me.

Johnny's brother, James, is there, and he's the one we're told was working as Johnny's advisor all along. James is the one holding the deal up, the one talking money. Johnny's mother didn't know much about baseball, but his father did. He was retired military, fought in Vietnam. He was there, but mostly just listened. Johnny's girlfriend was there, too, but she was in the other room reading a book, not saying anything.

The way these things often work is like a cycle. People sometimes think these negotiations are all about money, just going back and forth with different dollar figures, but that's not the way it works.

You talk about the opportunity of playing professional baseball, what you can offer the player in terms of support and facilities. You let him know he'll work with top coaches and compete against other talented players, and especially for a guy with Johnny's talent, the opportunity to move quickly through the minor leagues.

Every so often, you make a signing bonus offer, and you move forward from there. Well, with Johnny, every time we made an offer he would go into the bedroom with his brother. We thought they were just talking, two brothers, and that made sense. They were really close, and Johnny respected his brother.

What we didn't know was that every offer was going back to Scott

Boras, the powerful agent known for hard negotiating and pushing teams sometimes past the brink of reality. Scott has done very well for a lot of his clients, but there have also been guys who've pushed too hard and had to either sign a lesser offer later or missed out on the big leagues altogether.

Anyway, we're talking with Johnny and his family and we don't know about Boras until the girlfriend speaks up. This is four or five hours into the negotiations, and it's the first time she said anything. I think we started out offering around $200,000 and increased by $5,000 or $10,000 at a time.

"Johnny," she says, "Scott Boras told you you'd get a half-million if you go to Florida and come out after three years."

That's when we knew the negotiations were changing. This was a different deal than we thought we were getting into. You usually know who the player is being advised by, but Johnny and Scott kept this secret.

I looked at Allard.

"Uh-oh," I said. "We cannot leave this house. If we leave this house, we're not signing this kid."

So now we know they're talking to Boras, and the rules are changing a bit. Herk Robinson is our general manager at the time, and every once in a while I'm calling back to get a little bit more money, which I always got.

At about 6 o'clock — and remember, we got there at noon — Johnny's father looks at his son.

"Johnny, don't you think we should send out for some Kentucky Fried Chicken or something?"

That was another big moment for me. I looked at Allard.

"This is good," I said. They sent out for dinner. That means they're not going to throw us out. We've got a chance now."

So, now I feel good, but the brother is still being the tough guy. Johnny wanted to play baseball. He didn't want to go to college. He wanted to play, and we knew that. But the brother — through Boras — was holding us up. We're still going back and forth, hour after hour, pushing 10 o'clock at night. I've never been in anything like this. You're running out of things to say, running out of points to make.

After all this, it really is just about the money, and we're up to $230,000 now. Johnny never once made a counter-demand, which is a classic Boras move. He loves to do that. He thinks he can get a team to go above what the kid would sign for this way.

And that's about when the brother has to leave. He worked at Disney World, the night shift.

"Do what you want," James told Johnny, "but I'd advise you not to do it."

So James is out, but we're still talking. It is close to midnight, and I can tell we're really close. I call Herk and say that if we can get to $250,000 I think we're going to have a deal.

"Fine," Herk tells me. "Go to $250,000 and don't call me again."

When we made that offer, it was like a magic number.

"That'll be great," Johnny said.

I think he might've had that in the back of his mind the whole time. By the time we got the paperwork done it was 1 in the morning.

That made it a 13-hour negotiation, the longest I was ever involved in. And even then, it wasn't quite over.

As it turns out, Johnny didn't tell Boras he accepted the offer.

• • •

The longest face-to-face negotiation I ever had with a player was 13 hours in Johnny Damon's house. Finding out he was being secretly advised by Scott Boras was a setback, but once we sent out for fried chicken I knew we could get that done. I'm glad we did, too. Johnny turned out to be a hell of a big leaguer.

The next morning, Allard goes back over to Johnny's house. Johnny wanted to buy a Bronco, and he needed Allard to establish that Johnny had this money coming. My phone rings. It's Allard.

"Boras called Johnny," Allard said. "He told him not to honor the contract."

The contract's already done at that point. I tell Allard to tell Johnny I'm already headed back to Kansas City with it, but thankfully, the father speaks up and talks to Johnny. He told him their family is one that honors its word, and that he signed the contract for that amount of money and that he can't change his mind now.

So Johnny calls Boras back.

"Mr. Boras," he told him. "I'm happy with what the Royals have given me and if you want to represent me in the future, that's great. If not, that's OK too."

What can Boras do at that point? He couldn't void the contract.

So Boras continued to represent Johnny his entire career, through seven teams and 18 seasons and 2,769 hits and eight playoff appearances and two world championships — one with the Red Sox when they won their first title in 86 years, and the other with the Yankees in 2009.

Johnny and I became very close after that. When he was in Wichita, where our Double-A team was at the time, he called me on an off day and asked for a tour of Kauffman Stadium. As it happened, he played his last big league game in Kansas City. He was with the Indians at the time, and knew they were releasing him the next day. He sought me out and asked to take a picture together. I was there for his first big league game, and his last. I still have that picture.

Really, the only fallout from the signing was that Boras didn't speak to me for almost 10 years.

• • •

It never took me 13 hours to sign a player again, but once I got three players signed in one day.

This was back in 1983, and I'm sitting at the state high school tournament in Springfield, Ill., watching a young Joe Girardi. I loved him as an amateur, and wanted to draft him but his parents were strong for education and Joe was such a smart kid he had a scholarship to

Northwestern. There are so many forks in the road for so many players you end up seeing in the big leagues, and players you don't. You never know how things will work out, you can only hope for the best and that people make decisions for the right reasons.

Anyway, I get a call and it was Tom McDevitt, the coach at Eastern Illinois. He had a third baseman named Kevin Seitzer, who I tried to sign out of high school but his parents wanted him to go to college. That spring, Kevin got hurt. Not everyone knew he was hurt, but I could tell. He was an above average runner, a 4.2 guy from home to first but with the injury he was getting down at 4.7 or so. That's when all these teams were seeing him, so he was losing draft position. McDevitt calls and said Seitzer's healthy.

"We've got a game tonight, too," McDevitt said. "Right there in Springfield, where you are. Old Chamberlain Park."

I go down there to see him and Seitzer is back to his old 4.2, moving around the field just fine. I call back to Kansas City and say we've got to move this kid up. He's back to where I saw him before.

So the next day, in the middle of the Illinois state tournament, they tell me they got Gary Thurman out of Indianapolis in the first round. A little while later, another call. We got Seitzer in the 10th round. I felt really good about that one. And then a third call, this time that we got an outfielder named Jeff Schultz out of Evansville in Southern Indiana in the 22nd round.

## Royals sign Thurman to 'highest bonus'

By MARK SCHNEIDER

North Central's Gary Thurman signed a contract with Kansas City of the American League Wednesday afternoon for "the highest bonus the Royals have ever paid in the free agent field."

Thurman signed a one-year rookie free agent contract that is renewable each year for six years.

Art Stewart, Kansas City's Midwest scouting supervisor, said it is against club policy to disclose the amount of player contracts but added the 18-year-old high school senior signed for "the most a free agent has ever signed for with the Royals."

The all-state football and baseball player became the first high school athlete from Marion County ever to be chosen in the first round of the major league baseball free agent draft Monday. He was the 21st player selected.

It also marked the first time in five years Kansas City had not made a college player its No. 1 selection.

STEWART SAID the Kansas City organization was very pleased.

"Gary was made for Royals Stadium and there's no telling how great he can become," Stewart said. "We really feel his full potential is untapped. When he starts playing every day, I don't know how good he can be."

Stewart said Thurman will have

"the best of both worlds and that doesn't happen often to a young man his age."

"We feel Gary is comparable to Willie Wilson at this stage," Stewart said. "He has great speed with potential to steal bases. He could have a better arm and he might hit with more power."

The 5-10, 170-pound center fielder who bats and throws right-handed will leave next Wednesday for Sarasota, Fla., where he will begin playing in the Class A Gulf Coast Rookie League for the Sarasota Royals. The league runs from June 23 through August 30.

Kansas City then will give him a two-week vacation before he is to return to Sarasota for the Royals' instructional league during which he will be with the top 20-25 rookies in the organization.

Thurman said he will return to Indiana after the instructional league for a semester of school, although he said he hasn't decided which college he will attend.

"WHEN I heard that I had been drafted in the first round, I pretty much made up my mind that I was going to sign," Gary said. "I'm very pleased, and very excited with the way things have worked out.

"I'll be able to travel, play baseball and go to school. I'll go (to school) some place in the state so I can be around my family and friends."

Thurman said that he was both thrilled to be drafted in the first round and relieved he would no longer be hounded by scouts. "It was hard to concentrate on the North Central team with all the attention from all the scouts.

"There were telephone calls all the time. The phone would ring at midnight and 1 a.m. It was wearing me out. I'm glad it's all over."

Thurman helped lead North Central to a school record 24-2 slate and the No. 1 ranking in the state before the Panthers were upset by Chatard in Tuesday's sectional championship game.

Gary Thurman puts pen to big league contract. Mother, Cecilia, Kansas City scout Art Stewart look on

*This is a clipping from the day I signed three draft picks that made the big leagues in one day. I'll never forget that day. This is me with Gary Thurman, our first round pick in 1983, and his mother. As it happened, I was in the Midwest and within driving distance of him, Kevin Seitzer and Jeff Schultz. I got all three signed in about a 20-hour day. I slept pretty well after that.*

So I'm looking at the map, planning out my day. The best place to start was with the first guy we had, Thurman in Indianapolis. Back then, signing first round picks wasn't like today. You didn't have guys holding out and going back and forth over weeks or even months. We got Thurman signed in about three hours, for $60,000.

Next up is Schultz, in Evansville. I get there late in the afternoon and get him signed pretty easily by 7 that night. I'm going to call it a night but then I talk to Kevin and he wants to meet.

"Kevin, I'm all the way down in Evansville," I say. "That's a five-hour drive. There's no way I could even get there until after midnight."

"Come on up," he says. "I want to sign tonight. I want to play."

One thing you learn pretty fast: When a player wants to sign, you sign the player. I'll tell you the other side of this in a bit.

I get to Kevin's house around 1 in the morning. I remember it was a nice little place, across from a farm field. His mother puts on a pot of coffee and gives us some cookies. We sit around the table for an hour or two and get Kevin signed.

By then, I've been up for about 20 hours straight, in the car, going over deals. I shake Kevin's hand, thank his mother, find a Holiday Inn down the street and sleep until 1 in the afternoon.

• • •

Sometimes, you just have to be creative. Lou Maguolo, who was such a great scout for the Yankees, went to Kansas to sign a young outfielder named Norm Siebern.

Lou was this little guy, but he had a big personality, and always drove a big Lincoln. He got a new one every year. He gets to the house, and they're going back and forth with the money. Lou is up to $3,000, and he can go a little higher but not much. Norm is thinking about it, but he also might go to college.

Well, Norm's mother is nice as can be, and she's got some cookies and a cake and everything else out on the table. She's trying to make some coffee, too, but she's having trouble with this stove. This is going on in the background, you know, while Lou and Norm are talking about baseball and the contract and the Yankees and everything else.

But at some point, Norm's mother just kind of gives up on the coffee. She must've tried everything she could.

"This is terrible," she said. "I'm embarrassed."

But instead of being disappointed, Lou saw an opportunity.

"Mrs. Siebern," he said, "how about if we put a brand-new stove in the deal?"

Mrs. Siebern smiled, and looked at her son.

"Norman," she said, "you sign that contract right away."

And that's how the Yankees got an outfielder who played on two world championship teams, won the Gold Glove as a rookie, and played in three All-Star games.

• • •

Sometimes, it's even easier than that. Back in 1975, Rosey Gilhousen saw this boy in a small, NAIA school who had some nice statistics but he had very marginal stuff.

So, anyway, this boy meets Rosey and he asks — begs, really — if he can sign with the Royals if nobody drafts him. Rosey likes that attitude, and the kid did lead all of NAIA in victories, so, sure. But there won't be any money available.

The boy is fine with that, thanks Rosey for his time, and I think Rosey actually forgot all about that conversation until after the draft. His phone rings, and it's this kid. The kid explains who he is, reminds Rosey of his promise, and asks when he can sign.

Rosey says it's late, he's about to go to bed, so maybe in the morning. The kid asks if he can do it that night. He's dying to play pro ball. Rosey says sure, but you have to be over within an hour.

The kid makes it with a few minutes to spare, and I don't know if it's because he was impressed or felt sorry for the kid, but Rosey threw in a $500 bonus.

And that's how the Royals signed Dan Quisenberry, who made three All-Star teams, closed for four playoff teams including our World Series winner, and was inducted in the Royals Hall of Fame.

Quiz didn't fit any of the boxes you usually want to check for a prospect, but got by with trickery, precision, never making mistakes and guts.

• • •

We got Kevin Appier ninth overall, and that was a scouting success. Guy Hansen later became our big league pitching coach, but he used to be one of the best scouts in the country. He saw Bret Saberhagen as a shortstop and thought he'd be a better pitcher, then saw Jeff Conine as a pitcher and thought he'd be a better hitter.

Guy and I went to Antelope Junior College to see Appier pitch, and they're playing at East Los Angeles Valley Junior College. We pull in and the backstop comes up to the parking lot, so where you sit as a scout, you're on asphalt. It was 100-and-some degrees outside that day in California, and we're dying back there on that asphalt. Just dying. But on the field, an amazing thing — the hotter it got, the better Ape pitched.

"Guy," I said, "We can't miss this guy. We gotta keep seeing him."

It was more of the same every time we saw him pitch, so we had Appier as the best pitcher on our board. Most of the other teams had Mike Harkey, who went fourth overall, but there were five other pitchers who went ahead of Ape in the draft that year. We were thrilled when he was there ninth overall — but we still needed to get him signed.

This was early in the time agents really got involved with draft picks. Appier's guy was Dennis Gilbert, a really well-known agent who had Jose Canseco and Saberhagen and a bunch of guys.

Appier opens by asking for $125,000. Now, at the time, we'd never given a player even $100,000. We're not even close. We raise our opening offer to $90,000, they come down to $115,000 and we go back and forth and we get up to $100,00 and that's our limit. We can't go over that number.

After a few hours, Dennis comes down a bit more.

"A hundred and five thousand," he said, "and you can have your first-round pick signed in 15 minutes."

John Schuerholz is our general manager at the time. I call him.

"John, we can have him for $105,000 and he'll report in the morning."

"No way," John said. "We can't go that high."

I beg with John. Joe Burke was our club president then, and these things needed his approval. Please, I told John. Please just tell Joe how important it is we get this done.

I'm waiting almost an hour before I hear back from John.

"You've got $105,000," he said. "But Mr. Burke said this boy better be able to pitch."

• • •

So we're talking about the importance of getting guys signed, and earlier I told you that if a player wants to be signed you need to sign him as soon as possible. I can't think of a better example than Deion Sanders.

You know Deion as the great cornerback, the pro football Hall of Famer who's now on TV as an analyst. Well, back in 1985, he was a two-sport star out of North Fort Myers High in Florida.

We liked him a lot on the baseball field. He may've been the fastest player I've ever seen other than Bo, but we liked other things about him, too. He had some nice, line drive, gap power. He worked hard. He was flashy, and wanted to be noticed, but he could back it up. I'm telling you, if this guy would've signed out of high school and played only baseball, he'd have been a star in our game.

But, obviously he was a football star, too, and that made a lot of teams back off him in the draft. We think we can sign him, though, so we take him in the sixth round.

He tells us he'd like to play baseball for us, but he has this full ride scholarship to play both sports at Florida State. In those days, sixth round picks got about $25,000. So I tell Deion we can give him $40,000, pay for his education, and provide an incentive package.

"That'd be great," he told me.

That's it. We've got a verbal agreement with Deion Sanders to join the Royals. I feel really good about this, and call our scout in the area and get him on the road. The scout tells me he can be there about 9 o'clock, but he stops just short of Deion's house — and waits.

He didn't go in the house.

Even though we had a draft pick who agreed to a contract and wanted to sign.

Deion lived in a bad part of town, so I think the scout didn't want to go by there late at night. But the next morning, when he pulls up to Deion's house, there's a beautiful silver Corvette parked in front.

It's too late.

If we had been there the night before, we sign Deion Sanders and he's a Royal.

But Florida State got to him that night and acted quicker than we did.

It's only the second time I've ever fired a scout. You have to get in the house. I don't care if you have to take a cop with you. You have an agreement over the phone, and that means you have to get it on paper.

To top it all off, the next spring we're in Fort Myers for a Grapefruit League game and Deion comes by. Dick Howser was a Florida State guy, and he invited him. Deion's there in shorts and a t-shirt, watching batting practice, and this is as mad as I've ever seen John Schuerholz. He comes up with fire in his eyes.

"This kid doesn't belong here," he tells Howser. "Get him out here. He told the Royals he would sign, and then he didn't sign."

Even then, we all knew it wasn't necessarily Deion's fault. We had to get the deal done that night, not in the morning.

Deion Sanders could've been a Royal and, as it turns out, could've been in the same outfield as Bo Jackson.

Can you imagine?

# Chapter

# 9

# How a phenom named Rick Reichardt changed the game

*H*e was like Roy Hobbs, from the *The Natural*, only this boy was about three decades ahead of Hollywood and real flesh and blood in the part of Wisconsin they call the North Woods.

There are certain parts of your life, even after more than 60 years in this business, that you never forget. For me, one of those moments came on April 16, 1961 when I was in Stevens Point, Wisc.

I wasn't even looking for this real-life Natural, either. I was there to watch a pitcher in a small-college game. The first pitch is at noon, so it's still early afternoon when I'm packing up my things and getting ready to head for the next prospect. I hear the old man's voice from behind me.

"I hear you're with the Yankees," he says.

Yes, sir," I say.

"I've been a Yankee fan for years," he says. "You know, there's this big kid who can hit the ball a country mile at the high school here. They're playing at 3:30 today. It's only a mile down the street."

I thank the man. The old scout's motto about leaving no stone unturned means I have to go check it out. I'm curious. I hadn't heard anything about a high school kid in the area, but then, that's part of scouting. You're supposed to be the first eyes on tomorrow's great stars.

And that's how I got in on the ground floor with one of the great amateur talents of all-time, a young man by the name of Rick Reichardt.

Maybe you haven't heard that name before, but every scout in the game knows the story. It's not just about a great young talent, not just about a career eventually cut short by an unfortunate injury.

It's about a young three-sport star who fundamentally changed baseball and the way players come into our great game.

• • •

I get to the high school in time for infield and I didn't need a program to see who the old man was talking about. Rick Reichardt, clear as day, had to be the big guy — 6-foot-3, 200-and-some pounds — at third base. I'm the only scout there, which is hard to believe but made the whole experience more intense.

I always loved scouting those remote areas, because you could find that hidden diamond. There's some of these in the Dominican and other places in Latin America. You just get a different feeling when you can discover a kid on your own, instead of hearing about it from another scout or in the newspaper.

Reichardt's hands are OK, and you can tell he doesn't have the movements you want from a third baseman, but that arm. Oh, that arm. He's whipping the ball across the infield, and it's a clothesline. No arc to the throw, just laser after laser across the diamond. You see that right away, and you hear it, too, popping into the first baseman's mitt time and time again.

But it takes more than a good arm. So now we're at batting practice. You have to picture the scene. The leftfield fence is 370 feet or so away, and behind that is the school. It's two or three stories high, just beyond the fence.

Well, Reichardt digs into the batters box and he swings at the first pitch. He fouls it straight back, nothing big, but right away you see big league bat speed. For a scout, seeing something like that on the first swing of an unknown kid way up in Wisconsin, it takes your breath away. Now I'm sitting up on the bleachers a little bit more, wondering what comes next and, *boom!*

The balls are exploding off his bat, one after the other. They're going over the fence, and a couple of them, over the fence, out of the park and way up onto the roof of the damn school!

My first thought: *This is too good to be true.*

My second thought: *I should've got that old man's name, because he deserves a commission once this boy becomes a star.*

The game starts, and the first time up, Reichardt hits a bullet into the gap for a double. The next time up, he tops the ball, a dribbler down the third base line and you should've seen him fly down to first base. I had him at 4 seconds flat, from the right side, which would've made him one of the fastest guys in the big leagues.

I've been there an hour or so, and already this unknown kid has shown me the great arm, great speed and tremendous power from a big man.

I'm telling you, watching him then gave me the same feeling I'd have so many years later seeing Bo Jackson for the first time. He was the best amateur player I'd seen since Mickey Mantle.

*This is a Yankee*, I thought.

So after the game, I wait for him to come out of the dugout and introduce myself. He's telling me everything I want to hear from a prospect. He plays all the sports, but baseball is his favorite.

This is 1961, the great Yankee year where Mantle and Roger Maris are going back and forth chasing Babe Ruth's all-time single season home run record. I'm dropping their names and going through the great tradition and high standards of the Yankees. I tell him how interested the organization would be in a talent like his, and ask if he'd like to come up to New York to work out for us.

He was all for it.

"Just talk to my dad," he says.

• • •

Dr. Fritz Reichardt was the team doctor for the Packers. He was a wonderful man. He and his wife Bunny had nine children, and he'd give free physicals to kids in the area. He sewed clothes for his girls, built cradles for all of his kids, and helped his children and others in sports and through school. He was in the Navy during World War II, and at one point traveled through Brazil and the Dominican Republic giving free medical care to those in need.

Like I said, just a really impressive man. Which made signing his son even more enticing. The only thing better than signing a rare talent like Rick would be signing a rare talent like Rick who comes from a really solid family like that. You want to know a boy has been raised with good values and work ethic, and there would be no wondering with Rick.

So, I meet Dr. Reichardt and I'm going through my whole spiel about Rick's talents and what the Yankees can offer and how this can be a good relationship for both sides.

It turns out that Dr. Reichardt has always had a plan for his son. His first year of high school, Rick ran track and set all sorts of records. The second year, Rick played basketball and made all-state. His third year, he played football and made all-state in that sport, too.

And all the while he played baseball, because that was his favorite. But I'd never met a boy who had a high school experience like that, of putting special emphasis on a different sport each year with such a clear long-term plan in place.

"Dr. Reichardt, your son has major league ability," I say. "We'd love to bring you folks in, let you see New York, see Yankee Stadium, meet the players Rick would be playing with. His baseball future is unlimited."

"Art," he says, "I'm sorry to disappoint you but Rick is going to the University of Wisconsin."

Rick had a full-ride football scholarship there. It was his home state school, and where Dr. Reichardt went. I told Dr. Reichardt we could offer a very large bonus, and pay for school. He was very nice, and very firm.

"This is what we're going to do," he said. "He's not going to sign under any circumstance, for any amount of money."

You can't give up on a talent like that, though. Rick was playing on a city team that summer. They had games every Saturday and Sunday. I was there nearly every weekend. Dr. Reichardt was at a lot of the games, too.

It's July, and Donna is with me. She's pregnant with our daughter and getting to the point where she's really starting to show. It's the only time she didn't sit next to me at a game, because the sun was really starting to get hot. She needed some shade.

All the while, Reichardt is putting on a tremendous display. Home runs, stolen bases, everything you want to see. I don't know if Dr. Reichardt felt sorry for me or what, but he comes up and asks us over for a Fourth of July party they're having.

They have this big, beautiful home, and it was like a movie. The kids are all running around the yard, playing volleyball, basketball, there's music, everybody's having a good time.

At this point, I'm still the only one who knows about him but I know that's not going to last. Especially if he goes to college. Everyone is going to see this kid's talent. So as we're leaving that Fourth of July dinner, I try one more time to convince Dr. Reichardt.

"We're sticking with the plan," he said.

• • •

He played in a state tournament the summer between his sophomore and junior year at Milwaukee County Stadium, where the Brewers play, and that's where his profile really went national. There were so many scouts at that thing, and he's hitting balls clear out of the stadium.

So, now I'm not the only one who knows about him, but I still have an edge because I saw him first and have a relationship with the family.

"When I play pro baseball," he told me, "I really want to be a Yankee."

Reichardt becomes a two-sport star at Wisconsin. He's the best hitter in the Big 10, and he's also playing running back for the football team. Big league clubs are really starting to take notice.

By this time, Billy Martin was retired as a player and had moved on to scout for the Twins. He comes in to see Reichardt on a Friday night, and you see the great arm in infield practice and some of the power in BP, but in the game they walk him twice and hit him once.

"Crissakes," Billy snarled. "They sent me all the way out here for *this?*"

He took off that night, and the next day Wisconsin has a doubleheader. Reichardt goes 6-for-8 with three home runs, one of them a tape measure shot.

The scouts are all over his games by this point. Heck, Charlie Finley — he was the owner of the Kansas City A's then — came in himself. As it happened, Finley actually gave Reichardt the biggest bonus offer but nobody knew what was going on with the A's so they were never a really serious contender.

The Angels sent a big entourage. They brought their general manager, scouting director and even their owner. I told one of their guys it looked like everyone was there except for Trigger, the owner's horse.

After Reichardt's junior year, his father leaves it up to Rick about whether he'll finish college or enter pro baseball. Rick wants to play pro ball, so now it's time to get serious here with the negotiations.

By this time, Reichardt isn't quite the physical talent he was out of high school. Football took some of his speed, and a little bit of his arm. But he was still a rare prospect, and still had that great power, which is the most important thing. He was still a good comparison with Mantle. Mantle was faster, and a switch-hitter, but Reichardt's power was very close and his arm was better.

The family is in control of the whole process, and after some deliberation, they decide they're going to visit five interested franchises: Detroit, Boston, Philadelphia, the Yankees and Angels.

The ground rules are that Rick and his family will meet with everyone, not work out, and that whoever signs him will give him a bonus and pay for the expenses of the travel.

We all agree.

• • •

The Yankees put on the full-court press for Reichardt and his family. New York was hosting the World's Fair at the time, but Dan Topping, our owner then, had the fair closed for several hours.

That was just the beginning of it. "Hello, Dolly!" was playing on Broadway, with Carol Channing in the lead role, and you couldn't get a ticket for a $1,000. Naturally, we had tickets for the entire Reichardt family in about the third row, stage center. We also took them to the nicest restaurant in town, a great steakhouse.

The next day, we bring him in the Yankees' office and he's thrilled. The kid wants to be a Yankee.

Topping is doing the talking, and he's laying it on thick. He's going through the tradition of the Yankees, and that he can be a part of something great here. Up to that point, the most we'd ever offered an amateur player was $125,000. That was for Jake Gibbs, a catcher out of Mississippi who ended up being a backup guy for many years.

"We are prepared to give you more money than we've ever offered a player," Topping said. "We are offering you $150,000 to be with the greatest team in the history of baseball."

Right there, I thought we had him. The look on his face told me we had him. He wanted to be a Yankee.

But he had one more trip to take.

The Reichardts go out to California, and Autry gives them the big-time Hollywood treatment. They pick him up in a convertible limo and take him around town and have him meet the stars.

The Angels use every trick in the book, and they kicked the bonus up to $200,000. I'm not saying the Yankees would've done it, but I was so disappointed we didn't get a chance to match the offer.

At the time, I thought I lost the next great power guy for the New York Yankees. I was devastated. The only consolation was that I lost him to the Angels and Nick Kamzik, a dear friend and the best man at my wedding.

Reichardt's official bonus was $205,000.33. The family spent $5,000.33 touring the five clubs.

And baseball owners went ballistic.

Mickey Mantle hit .303 with 35 home runs and 111 RBIs in 1964, and he made $100,000 from the Yankees. Harmon Killebrew led the league with 49 home runs and he made $50,000. Brooks Robinson was the AL MVP, he was in his prime and made $35,000.

Hank Aaron, Carl Yastrzemski, Al Kaline, Bob Gibson, Ernie Banks, Juan Marichal, Sandy Koufax — all of these stars, eventual Hall of Famers, and none of them made anything close to what this college kid out of Wisconsin just signed for.

Baseball owners were apocalyptic. They felt like they were losing control of the game.

So that year, they didn't waste any time. They created a draft.

All because of Rick Reichardt and that otherworldly talent I first saw up in the North Woods when he was a high school senior.

• • •

We think of the draft as a part of baseball now, but it really required some adaptation in those early years. Nobody knew what to do with it.

The draft has always been an inexact science, but that first year, Johnny Bench went in the second round, Tom Seaver in the eighth, and

Nolan Ryan in the 10th. It was hard to know where to send your scouts, how to spend your time.

Before the draft, you'd pick five or six of the best players in your territory and see them as many times as you could. Five, six, seven, eight and, if you're lucky nine or 10 times. You really got to know the boys and their families.

With the draft, you couldn't do that. You didn't know who would be available to you, and in which round, so you had to build up reports on as many kids as possible.

Baseball lost its intimacy in scouting. It used to be a very personal thing, and you'd filter your world down to a handful of prospects. It limited your reach, but you knew a lot more about each player. You felt more certain in the guys you were watching.

A lot of scouts couldn't adjust. Some of them quit, if you can believe that.

The first year of the draft was chaos. Absolute chaos. Clubs didn't know how to prepare for it. The Yankees were no different.

Baseball's first draft was held at the Roosevelt Hotel in New York. They did it like they do the Rule 5 draft today, with this big conference room and all the clubs set up at these tables. When it was your turn, the scouting director went up to the microphone and announced the pick.

Well, once, when a selection was announced everyone turned their heads clear across the room to Jack Schwarz of the Giants. He's this old, rugged guy who wanted everything in the organization. As soon as the pick is announced, Jack is screaming.

"YOU DIRTY SON OF A BITCH! YOU TOOK OUR PLAYER!"

Jack is waving the card in his hands, with the same player that was just selected. A few other guys in the room had to hold him back from charging.

I'll tell you what. Holding the draft in New York like that only lasted a few years. They didn't want scenes like that happening.

So they went to a conference call. Now, guys still cussed other teams for stealing a player, but at least this way there would be no threat of violence.

• • •

The adjustment to the draft was hard for all of us. I was a younger guy, and my philosophy had always been to adapt to change, so I didn't have as much of a problem with it. If this is the way baseball was going, then this was what we had to adapt to.

I liked it more without the draft. And that's not me being an old scout, that's just because I felt like in the old days, the scouts who really worked were the ones who had the advantage. You had to hire bird dogs, you had to dig, you had to have your eyes and ears all over the place.

There was more of an emphasis on the detective work, along with the evaluation. That part of it always thrilled me. You could show up to a ballpark to watch one guy, and then be enthralled with someone completely different. Sort of like what happened with me and Reichardt that day in Stevens Point. Except, before the draft, you could sign the boy on the spot.

Those types of stories can still exist today with a guy who goes through undrafted or something like that, but the odds of that happening are so long it's unbelievable.

That's part of why I always loved going to Latin America so much. Finding the talent, and setting up the tryouts, and the ability to sign a great player on the spot took me back to what scouting was in the old days. There's a different thrill you get discovering and signing a player.

But I also understand that baseball needs to keep up competitive balance as much as possible. It wasn't fair to a lot of clubs when I was with the Yankees and we could just come in and offer a boy the most money.

I also know the rule benefits teams like the Royals, who can't spend with the Yankees and Dodgers and Angels and clubs like that. It's funny how baseball comes full circle in a lot of things. In recent years, before baseball instituted its slotting system, agents would team up with prospects and circumvent the draft.

The most famous case of this was Rick Porcello, who was the top high school pitcher in the 2007 draft. Baseball was really trying to keep amateur bonuses down, but Porcello had chosen Scott Boras as his advisor and Boras was floating the idea of a bonus of $8 million or more.

That scared a lot of clubs away, and Porcello dropped all the way down to the Tigers with the 27th pick. He signed a contract worth about

$7 million, which irritated a lot of the teams trying to follow baseball's guidelines because the Tigers had basically gotten the best prospect in the draft with the 27th pick.

Today, baseball has spending limits that attempt to do a better job evening the talent that teams can get through the draft. The ironic part of that is that the Royals had actually been spending more in the draft than many big market clubs. There are people in small-market organizations like ours who think the rules go against us, when they're meant to go for us.

For instance, we never could've signed Wil Myers in the third round in 2009 if we weren't willing to give him first-round money. And we never could've traded for James Shields if we didn't have Myers. Being able to "overspend" for Myers in 2009 helped our organization, but the same rules aimed at evening the field for small-money clubs like ours will take away those types of opportunities in the future.

That's OK. It just means we have to do a better job evaluating talent than other clubs, which has always been the key to scouting anyway.

# Chapter
# 10

# Mr. K

You know, I never thought I'd leave the Yankees. I loved the Yankees. For a boy growing up when I did, reading and hearing stories about Lou Gehrig and Babe Ruth, and then Joe DiMaggio and Whitey Ford — all the greats — there was nothing better than the Yankees.

There's a reason I named my semi-pro team the Chicago Yankees, long before I even thought about working for them.

And, really, I had no complaints about my time there. It was everything I dreamed it would be. I got to work with great scouts like Tom Greenwade and Paul Kritchell, and work for the greatest organization in baseball. Going to games and scouting, it meant something when you told someone you were with the Yankees. That gave us a leg up with a lot of players, which we used to our advantage. Kids wanted to be in the pinstripes, and the scouts knew it.

The Yankees weren't just a company where we worked. It was a real family, where your bosses cared about you as a person and you cared about all your colleagues as people because you were all in this great journey together.

In the 17 seasons I worked with the Yankees, the big league team played in 10 World Series, winning six. Those were largely the Mickey Mantle years — he debuted with the Yankees the same year I did — but those were also the teams of Casey Stengel, Yogi Berra, Phil Rizzuto, Hank Bauer, Whitey Ford and Roger Maris.

There was just nothing like it.

That all began to change in 1964, when Dan Topping and Del Webb sold the Yankees to CBS for $11.2 million. They put an Englishman named Michael Burke in charge and right from the start you just knew it wasn't going to work. Burke was a very successful businessman — he also ran Madison Square Garden, the NHL's Rangers and the NBA's Knicks — but he simply wasn't a baseball guy. He didn't know what an organization needed from the inside to be successful.

He changed everything. He changed how we reported to our bosses, the information they wanted, even our expense accounts. We used to be a family, where you're really looking out for your brothers and sisters. But after CBS took over, it became a corporation. You went from feeling like you had a real identity in the organization, to feeling like you were basically a number in a file. The creation of the first-year player draft in 1965 hurt the Yankees, too, obviously, because we could no longer outspend other teams for the amateur talent we really liked.

You could see it on the field. We were losing some of our really good players, and weren't able to replace them. It's not a coincidence that CBS's first full year in charge was the Yankees' first losing season since 1925. The Yankees went from playing in 15 World Series over 18 seasons to missing 11 in a row.

They really didn't get back to their real high standards until George Steinbrenner took over in the 1970s, but by then, I wasn't around.

In all my years with the Yankees before CBS took over, I never could've imagined a better opportunity.

And truthfully, even with CBS in charge I wouldn't have left for just any opportunity. It had to be a great one, a special one, something that would replicate and even exceed what was so fulfilling about working with the Yankees.

That opportunity presented itself in the late 1960s, when Lou Gorman and Cedric Tallis, two baseball lifers I respected and liked, told me what a man named Ewing Kauffman was building in Kansas City.

• • •

The Yankees wouldn't let me out of my contract so I officially joined the Royals immediately after their first season, in November of 1969.

We all met in January of the next year for a special meeting of the higher-level baseball operations people at Municipal Stadium, where the Royals played their first four seasons. Our first meeting — well, *my* first meeting with them — came in a blizzard. You could see the snow falling outside. It was all a lot of us could do just to get there.

I can say whatever I want now, but, honestly, back then I wasn't sure if I made the right decision. I mean, I had a good job with the Yankees and for everything I didn't like about CBS, it was still the *Yankees*, it was still an established franchise. It was all knew. There I was, giving all of that up for an expansion franchise? No expansion team had ever fast-tracked much success. It's hard to get a franchise going from scratch. I told you the problems that Donna had with my decision. Well, let's just say she wasn't the only one in baseball who thought I was making a mistake.

And if I was being 100 percent truthful, I wasn't certain they were wrong.

Not until I met Ewing Kauffman, anyway.

When he walked in that first meeting, I don't know how to put it other way than there was presence in the room, even among accomplished baseball men. He just carried himself with this dynamic air of confidence. He came in wearing that beautiful, designer, Royal blue suit and you had that feeling that you're meeting someone special. The best way I can describe it, for me, was like meeting the President of the United States.

He sort of glided into the room and introduced himself to those of us who hadn't yet met him. Then he takes his coat off, rolls up his sleeves and addresses the room with the perfect blend of confidence and humility.

"Thank you all, for coming," he says. "I want to talk with this group because I understand you are the nuts and bolts of what makes the baseball machine go. You are the people who will make us successful, or a failure."

The motivation was amazing. Sitting there, you just got a special feeling about him and the group he assembled. He was a terrific leader, and the way you knew that was because he made you want to work hard for him, and would give you whatever you needed to be successful.

"They tell me you people are among the best in baseball at what you do," Kauffman said. "You are the ones who will go out into the world and represent our organization. I want you to be proud of this organization, and I want you to do the kind of work that will make the rest of us proud."

Ewing Kauffman — nobody called him Mr. K until a few years later — hadn't been talking more than five minutes, and already I knew I made the right decision. Even as much of a die-hard Yankee as I was, I knew I was in the right place.

Outside those windows, it was snowing blankets on us in Kansas City. But inside that room, we were ready to run through walls for this man.

• • •

A lot of people don't know this about Mr. K, but he wasn't really knowledgeable about baseball. Not when he first bought the team, anyway. He was a wonderful man, of course, a businessman and entrepreneur who turned a start-up he ran out of his basement into a powerhouse in the pharmaceutical field that ended up creating more than 300 millionaires.

He was raised in Kansas City, graduating from Westport High School in 1934. He went on to serve in the Navy and when he returned started the business he called Marion Laboratories. His middle name was

*Photo Courtesy of Kansas City Royals*

*Mr. K always dressed to impress, didn't he? That's him on the right, in 1980, the year George Brett hit .390, with general manager Joe Burke and manager Jim Frey.*

*This is from my senior year at Schurz High School on Chicago's North side. That's me on the right, I was captain that year, and played shortstop. To the left is Gene May, our third baseman, who signed with Cleveland but never made the big leagues.*

*Can you pick out what's different about this picture? That's Mickey Mantle sliding into the base there. Take a good look. You see his uniform number? He wore the no. 6 for a short time as a rookie, before making no. 7 so legendary in Yankees history.*

*This is Mickey Mantle in his first year of pro ball, with what was then a Yankees affiliate in Joplin. Mantle is one of the game's great scouting stories, signed by Tom Greenwade before anyone else knew who he was.*

This is the semi-pro team I had with Jim Bouton, the one I took to all the prisons to keep Bouton hidden. I'll never forget the time we had a game interrupted because the sirens were going off for a missing prisoner. Turns out he was hiding with the laundry, and we finished the game. Later, I signed Bouton and he became my first big leaguer with the Yankees, and a 20-game winner, though most people remember him for his book, "Ball Four."

*Photo Courtesy of Kansas City Royals*

*This is Tom Poquette, the first big leaguer I signed for the Royals. I actually found him with the help of Lois Brandenberg, who I put on as the Royals only female associate scout. Poquette played the game so hard that the Royals had to put padding on the outfield walls after one particularly hard crash.*

*Photo Courtesy of Kansas City Royals*

*These are the rings we won for the 1980 American League pennant, and the 1985 world championship. Mr. K had promised George Brett he could design the ring. George wanted a KC in the middle made out of diamonds, and they had the mock-up and everything. But once they saw the actual ring, they agreed it didn't look quite right. So instead, they put 26 2-pt diamonds in a circle on each ring, representing each of the 26 teams in baseball at the time.*

*Photo Courtesy of Bob Snodgrass*

*One of my prized possessions, the ring they gave me when I was named baseball's Midwest Scout of the Year from the Scout of the Year Program in 2008. There is a movement for scouts to be permanently recognized at the Hall of Fame in Cooperstown, and the Scout of the Year Program has been at the front of that push.*

*Photo Courtesy of Kansas City Royals*

*This is Dick Howser, the great manager who led us to the 1985 World Series championship.*

*Photo Courtesy of Kansas City Royals*

*Winning that world championship in 1985 was the best feeling I'd ever had in baseball, and here I am with the trophy and three people who worked so hard to make it possible. That's Dean Taylor on the left, who was then assistant director for scouting and player development. He's since been the GM in Milwaukee, and is back with us as vice president for baseball operations. To Dean's left is Linda Smith, the great administrative assistant we've had for so many years. And to my left is Bonnie Morgan, who then was an administrative assistant in player development.*

*Photo Courtesy of Kansas City Royals*

*Players and even some other scouts joke that they can't read any of my notes, but over the years I've come up with a system that makes sense to me. This is the way you remember what happens in a game, and who you need to watch for and why. This is the fuel of what we do in a lot of ways.*

*This is one of the hardest hits you'll ever see on a baseball field, Bo Jackson taking out Rick Dempsey so hard that Dempsey flew back and broke his thumb. When Bo was running, it was like a locomotive hitting you.*

Photo Courtesy of Kansas City Royals

Photo Courtesy of Kansas City Royals

*Bo was such a phenom because he could do so many things. That's what stood out to baseball people. We talk about his power a lot, but that speed; he changed the rules. He'd beat out grounders to second base. He'd get picked off, but was so fast he'd beat the throw anyway.*

*Photo Courtesy of Kansas City Royals*

*This was taken on opening night in 1973, and yes, I said opening night. They didn't always play the first few games in the daytime. That's Jack McKeon, then our manager, with Mr. and Mrs. K.*

*Photo Courtesy of Kansas City Royals*

*Look at those thighs. Such great power. Bo Jackson hit home runs so hard and far that Buck O'Neil used to scream over from across the aisle, "Art, I lost it! I think it's in orbit!"*

The late Jose Lima was one of the great characters in our game. We signed him in 2003 out of an independent league, without even watching him pitch in person, because we were desperate for pitching. We'd heard his fastball was back to average, and took a chance on his breaking pitches and competitive spirit. He won his first eight decisions for us that year. Lima Time!

*Photo Courtesy of Kansas City Royals*

*This is me with my daughter Dawn, grandson David, wife Donna and Frank White when Frank was managing in our system with Wichita (Double A). I was there scouting some players, but the opportunity to see our old friend Frank meant we made it a family trip.*

*Tony LaRussa is one of the great minds in the history of the game. Getting to know him, both personally and as a baseball man, was a great thrill. We thought about the game differently, but always respected each other's viewpoints. He's one of those guys you're lucky to talk baseball with.*

*I've always liked scouting the minor leagues, and here I am looking at our Triple A team in Omaha. You just never know what you're going to see in the minor leagues, and which player out there you can help make a dream come true.*

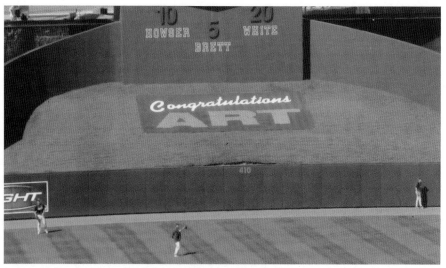

*Being the first scout inducted to the Royals Hall of Fame was one of the highlights of my career. Donna lived long enough to hear I was honored, but not long enough to see the ceremony. She was as much a part of it as me.*

*Buck O'Neil and I sat across the aisle from each other at Kauffman Stadium for so many years, we became like family. This is Buck and Donna before a game. They always enjoyed each other's company so much.*

Photo Courtesy of Kansas City Royals

138

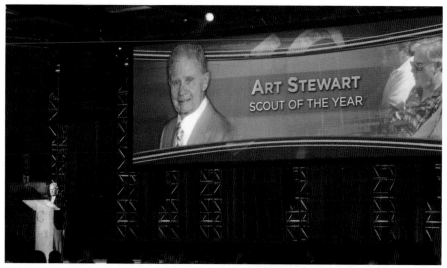

*This is from the Scout of the Year ceremony from 2008. I was thrilled to be recognized, of course, but the more important thing to me has always been that scouts in general are acknowledged for their hard work and part of the game.*

*Photo Courtesy of Kansas City Royals*

Mike Sweeney, one of the great gentlemen this game has ever known, signed this picture for me. We drafted him in the 10th round, and this is kind of funny, but it was on the tip of an associate scout who happened to be Mike's father. Mr. Sweeney got a bonus every time his son was promoted through the system.

*You won't find two guys more different than this. That's Bobby Brown on the left, a great intellectual who later became American League president and a cardiologist. And that's Yogi Berra on the right, famous for sayings like "Baseball is 90 percent mental; the other half is physical." That's one of the great things about our game, is the different people it attracts.*

*You think I'm joking, but sometimes we'd take a mule from the hotel to the ballpark at our academy in the Dominican Republic. Not the smoothest ride, but it got us there.*

*Here I am with three of my favorite people in baseball. From the left that's Buck O'Neil, the great Negro Leagues player, manager and baseball's first black scout. To his left is Bobby Mercer, who had the unenviable task of replacing Mickey Mantle in center field and later became a very good broadcaster. And to my right, of course, is Frank White, the eight-time Gold Glove winner.*

*Photo Courtesy of Kansas City Royals*

*One of the great honors of my professional life was when the Royals made me the first scout inducted into the team Hall of Fame. What a night, with the team lining up like this to recognize me.*

*Photo Courtesy of Kansas City Royals*

*This picture is of the two longest tenured members of the Royals' baseball operations. I started in November of 1969, and George joined the team in the June 1971 draft. George has continued to be an integral part of what the Royals do, regularly helping the guys in spring training, going on the road to work with minor leaguers during the season and even putting the uniform back on to be our hitting coach in 2013.*

*Photo Courtesy of Texas Rangers*

*Here's George waving his cap at the crowd there in Texas, which gave him a much-earned ovation for one of the great careers in baseball history.*

*This is George with Dawn and David in Las Vegas in 2008, when I got the Scout of the Year Award. After a while, you start to think of these people as your family. George and I were — and still are — part of the Royals family.*

*Billy Butler is one of the great young hitters in our game, and talking to him about his approach is always a thrill. You learn something every time you get an opportunity to talk hitting with Billy.*

Photo Courtesy of Kansas City Royals

143

Artwork by John Boyd Martin

*This is the portrait the Royals commissioned for my Hall of Fame induction. It was done by John Boyd Martin, the same guy who did most of the portraits you see of the team Hall of Famers. He uses an actual photograph in these things, which I think is part of why they turn out so realistic. I'm sitting behind home plate here, obviously, taking notes but the thing I really like is that Martin made sure I looked happy. I've never had a bad day at the ballpark.*

Marion, and he didn't want his first or last name on it — part of that was humility, I think, but he also didn't want people thinking he was the company's only employee.

Mr. K was fearless, creative and demanding. He was like that in business, and he was like that in baseball.

He bought the Royals because a friend convinced him it was the only shot Kansas City had to have a major league baseball team. Kansas City had and lost the A's, so if the city got a second chance it probably wouldn't get a third.

But once Mr. K bought the Royals, he wanted to make them as good as possible. That's just how Mr. K was. No matter what he was doing — becoming an Eagle Scout as a kid, driving Marion Labs, or the philanthropic foundation he started that helped so many kids in and around Kansas City — if Mr. K was involved, it was going to be first-class all the way.

So, he did this in so many little ways. One of them was in how he treated his employees. He had the best profit sharing in all of baseball. He paid his people well, too — a lot of scouts made $25,000 to $30,000, which was very good money back then — but the profit sharing put it over the top. It's how he was able to attract so many top scouts and executives from other organizations. With the profit sharing, there were scouts who retired from the Royals with $600,000 to $800,000 in their bank accounts.

Mr. K treated all of his employees well — he had chauffeurs, but he never called them that; they were his "associates" — and he had a special affection for scouts. Someone must have told him before he got started how important scouts were to bring in the best players to the organization.

So when Mr. K was figuring how to operate, he knew his scouts would be driving all over the country to see baseball players, and they'd be representing the organization — *his* organization — when they're doing it so why not have the best? Mr. K gave us company cars, and he wanted us to have Cadillacs, which was unheard of for scouts. Most organizations just paid your mileage, or if you got a company car it would be the bottom of the line.

But Mr. K wanted to give us Cadillacs, and he even had them ordered when he went to an owners meeting and word leaked about the cars. The other owners jumped all over him. They told him he couldn't do that, that he was turning everything upside-down.

Mr. K relented, but only to a point.

Instead of the Cadillacs, he gave us Pontiac Catalinas — which were built on a Cadillac chasse.

When Major League Baseball approved pensions for non-uniformed personnel in 1975, it was way behind the Royals. We already had pensions, so our controller told Mr. K he could take all of the money he was putting into pensions back.

Mr. K wouldn't hear it.

"Put it in their profit sharing," he said.

Once, Mr. K closed a meeting with some advice.

"I'm only going to tell you this one time," he said. "If you have any spare money, I advise you to put it in Marion Laboratories. It will help your family."

At the time, the stock was selling for about $7. Several of us bought some. I bought about a thousand shares. That stock went up to $80, and split. Then it went up to $80 again, and split again. The stock split not twice, not three times, not 10 times, but 13 times.

Our daughter got a great education with that money.

Working for Mr. K was a joy. He respected you, asked questions and saw his top responsibility as helping you do your job.

You had to produce, though.

Mr. K didn't stand for losing.

• • •

When the Royals started, at that time, expansion teams had never been all that successful in baseball. Not right away, at least.

Everything took time. A lot of that is the unavoidable nature of baseball — you have to draft players, nurture them through the minor leagues, and often live with them through the growing pains of transitioning to the big leagues — but Mr. K didn't like hearing any of that.

Like I said, when he took over the Royals he wasn't exceptionally knowledgeable about baseball, but because of the way he was, he used that to his advantage.

"We spend a lot of money on bonuses on these young players," he told us once. "But, gentlemen, how do we know they can see? Do we take them to the eye doctor?"

It's hard to believe today, with the skyrocketing bonuses paid to draft picks, but at that time, nobody tested the eyesight of prospects.

So Mr. K got Dr. Bill Harrison, one of the top vision specialists in the country, to develop an eye test with various slides to determine the quality of a prospect's vision. The most important slide measured depth perception, which is critical because without depth perception a player will never be able to see and hit a ball during night games. There are any number of reasons guys often can't transition from amateur baseball into the major leagues. Bigger stadiums, better pitchers and harder curveballs, you know the list.

But every once in a while you'd see a prospect who hit really well as a high school or college kid and couldn't hit in pro ball for a reason you usually didn't think about. Some guys don't have the kind of eyesight to pick up the ball during night games. You don't see that in high school or college because those games are almost always played during the day, but in pro ball, you're playing under the lights.

I remember there was a really good prospect out of Peoria, Ill., a catcher named Richard Bengston. He was a strong guy with everything you want out of an amateur prospect, and we were really high on him like everyone else — until we tested his eyes.

As it turned out, our tests showed he'd have a hard time picking up the ball at night. We took him off our draft board completely, but the Mets selected him 13th overall in 1972. Bengston spent three years at Class A ball, and hit .207 in 32 games of Double-A ball. That's as close as he ever got to the big leagues.

That was a theme with Mr. K. He kept hearing that baseball scouting was an inexact science, which it is, but he made a fortune in pharmaceuticals so the way his mind worked he wanted to make it as scientific as possible.

That's where the eye test came from. After about two years, Mr. K released the patent for other clubs and it really changed the way baseball prospects were scouted. Mr K also helped develop a test to measure bat speed. We were among the first organizations — if not *the* first — to use video and high-speed cameras for scouting and coaching.

Because he hadn't grown up in the baseball world, he was unaffected by baseball convention. He was thinking outside the box, because he didn't know what the box was.

It was the driving force behind us becoming the quickest expansion team to the playoffs in baseball history.

• • •

One of the other ways Mr. K made his experience in business pay off for us in baseball was specific to us scouts.

The fact that we were the organization's first line and communication to the big leaguers of tomorrow was very important to him. If we were the first impression that the amateur stars and their coaches who are so important would have about the Royals, then that first impression needed to be as positive as possible.

So toward the end of my first season with the Royals, in September of 1970, he brought in Gene Speery and Bob Pruitt, who worked with Marion Labs in sales education.

They wanted us to treat our jobs the same way their pharmaceutical salesmen treated theirs.

No detail was too small to be irrelevant. Baseball can be a very laid-back atmosphere, kind of folksy, but Mr. K wanted us to be as professional and alert as anyone would be in any corporation in America.

The way you sat in your seat was important, for instance. They wanted our backs at least six inches off the backs of the chairs, so you're sitting on the edge, showing interest in the meeting. Hand gestures were important. You had to be

*Ewing Kauffman wasn't much of a baseball man when he bought the Royals. Not everyone realizes that. He bought the team so Kansas City would have big league baseball again. But he turned his outsider persona into a strength, because he always thought outside the box. Here are the notes I took from the day he had his two top sales instructors from Marion Labs come in and give us some advice on how to "sell" the Royals as scouts.*

148

confident, but not arrogant. Informative, but still listening to what the prospect and his parents say.

They made it clear that management needed to be dedicated to helping us, but we needed to reciprocate for management. Mr. K believed in innovation, that the only way to accomplish what others aren't accomplishing is to do things others aren't doing.

You had to be able to think on your feet, to keep your cool when you're talking to prospects, and to always remember what you look like when you're in front of them. You had to not just be sincere, but *look* sincere.

They went over everything. Always call ahead to re-confirm an appointment. Ties and sport coats when you're meeting with prospects. Walk with pride, with purpose.

You had to be busy, too. One of the ways that Marion got out ahead of other pharmaceutical companies was by expecting so much out of those employees who were so well compensated. You were paid well, with great benefits, but that meant you had a responsibility to earn it.

At Marion, their profits were driven in large part because their employees generated more leads and profits on an average basis than other companies. Their goal was for each Marion salesman to generate the same number of calls and profit as two salesmen would for a rival company.

It was the same thing in baseball. We scouts were paid well for our work, and in exchange we were expected to generate more leads and baseball talent than our rivals. Everyone would be well compensated and recognized. If we scouted and signed a top player, we would be recognized by our bosses and, in exchange, we should recognize our associate scouts for their help.

A good example would be the Bo Jackson signing. Mr. Kauffman and John Schuerholz and others in the organization recognized me as the scouting director and our scouting department in general, but I always made sure that people knew Ken Gonzales did the real leg work.

It's only fair. And when things are rolling like that, success tends to follow.

• • •

You didn't get into Mr. Kauffman's office too often, but when you did, he made sure you felt comfortable. There was never a question about who was in charge, but he didn't want anything to get in the way of open communication.

If you looked behind his big desk, you would see this old baseball in a beautiful display case. A local businessman gave it to Kauffman as a token of appreciation for bringing major league baseball back to Kansas City — and it was something else.

The man was a great baseball fan, and as a kid he went to St. Louis for a series between the Browns and the Yankees and got Babe Ruth and Lou Gehrig to sign a ball. He saw that the Philadelphia A's were coming into town after that, so he stuck around and got that same ball signed by Jimmie Foxx, Mickey Cochrane, Lefty Grove and Al Simmons — all of them eventually made the Hall of Fame.

"That ball should be in a vault," I told Mr. Kauffman.

The year before he passed away, in 1992, he came in and stopped by my office. At first, he just wanted to introduce me to his new chauffeur — his *associate*. We ended up talking about a lot of things, old memories. It was very reflective, even more so now that I think back on it and the fact that he passed away the next year.

"By the way," he told me on his way out the door, "I know you've always admired that baseball I have in my office. I want you to have it."

My heart skipped a little bit.

"Mr. K," I said, "I can't take that baseball. That's more than just a ball, more than just a piece of memorabilia. I just can't do it."

Mr. K wasn't convinced.

"Art," he told me, "you're either going to take that ball or you'll be relieved of your duties."

We both laughed. I still have that ball, and will cherish it for the rest of my life.

• • •

Working for Mr. Kauffman was one of the great joys of all my years in baseball. He took such pride in owning that team, and watching it grow from a start-up behind all of our competitors into one of the best teams in the American League for most of the 1970s and 1980s.

Times were different in baseball back then, of course. We had a lot of advantages that are now disadvantages for the Royals. The economics of the game were such that we could compete with anyone in terms of payroll, even the Yankees. George Brett earned every penny he made from the Royals, of course, but it's important to remember that in those days a team in a market like ours could afford to keep George always among the highest paid players in baseball.

That doesn't exist anymore, and it's a major hurdle that teams like the Royals have to deal with.

But Mr. K's success wasn't *just* because the Royals were in position to spend as much as other teams. It was his vision that drove all of us, and set up the structure that helped the Royals become a perennial winner.

The most important things he did were simple when you read them as words, but much more difficult in practice, or else everybody would do them.

He hired the best people he possibly could, then made them generously compensated and appreciated, and, most importantly, demanded that they perform up to high standards.

And he was never content with the status quo. "That's how we've done it in the past" was never an acceptable reason for doing the same thing in the future. Mr. K was so smart, and always able to think a step or two ahead of his competitors. He invested long-term and generous contracts for cornerstone players like George and Frank White, because he saw value in keeping the players happy and giving fans some assurance that their favorite stars would be in Kansas City deep into the future.

But his greatest innovation, at least in my eyes, he unveiled to us in that first meeting in January of 1970.

He didn't tell any of us this at the time, but the real reason for that meeting wasn't to motivate us or compliment us or give us any warm baseball feelings in the dead of winter.

Toward the end of that meeting was when he was talking about the eye tests and measuring bat speed and all the other ways he wanted to speed up the trip from start-up to champion. He just refused to accept convention, that he needed to be patient.

One of the things that drove him crazy was that we only had such a limited way to acquire talent. We could draft, and we could trade — and the men he hired traded for Hal McRae, Amos Otis and others for virtually nothing — but that was basically it. Free agency wasn't nearly what it is now.

And Mr. K wanted more ways to infuse our organization with talent, to give us more to choose from and quicken our rise.

So after he had us so fired up, and his vision for the organization articulated so well, he got a smile on his face, stood up from the table, grabbed a rolled-up blueprint and spread it out in front of us.

He had just purchased 121 acres in Florida. We were holding spring training at Fort Myers in those days, but Mr. K had bigger plans. He had plans for that area that went way beyond just helping the big leaguers prepare for the season.

He was going to step outside baseball convention and create a talent pool all of his own.

"This," he said, pointing at the blueprint, "is where we are going to create the Baseball Academy."

We had heard bits and pieces about this so-called Academy, but none of us really knew what he was talking about.

From the way the rest of that meeting went, I had a feeling it would be special.

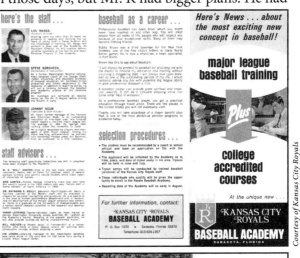

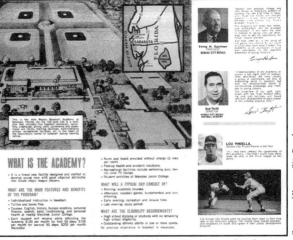

*Courtesy of Kansas City Royals*

*The other thing that was so good about Mr. K was that he gave us all the resources we ever needed to build a top franchise. This is an overview of the complex he built us in Sarasota, Florida. It was state of the art when we built it in 1970.*

# Chapter
# *11*

# The greatest year in Royals history

*I*'ve heard George Brett say that the best thing about the greatest accomplishment in Royals history is seeing how many people it affected, and how many people had the exact same joy as him.

We run into people all the time who want to talk about 1985. George was our best player, the most recognizable face, so he gets it more than any of the rest of us, I'm sure. And over the years, one of the things he notices is the detail of people's memories, and the pure excitement in their faces when they retell the stories.

At some point, George says he started to understand something: It doesn't matter if you were the All-Star third baseman or the 25th man or the scouting director or the bullpen coach or a ticket seller or the guy selling lemonade or a regular fan — we *all* had the same feeling.

An entire community of people remember exactly where they were, what they were feeling, and can rekindle that joy at a moment's notice.

And the more you talk to people in the community, the more you understood that we were all in it together. A team, a coaching staff, a scouting staff, a fan base — everyone.

I know it's the greatest feeling I've ever had in baseball, even better than any of the championships we won with the Yankees, because this one was built from the ground up. It took so many of us working hard and setting good examples and following great leaders to do what we did.

• • •

Sometimes people are surprised when I say the 1985 team wasn't the best in Royals history, but it's how I feel. I'm not alone, either. Some of the best players on that team — George Brett, Frank White, Hal McRae — say the 1977 team was better.

We had the best offense *and* the best pitching staff in the American League that year. Dennis Leonard won 20, and completed 21. That was the first year George really started hitting home runs, and Al Cowens drove in 112 for us that year. We won 102 games, breezed to a second-straight division title, and had the Yankees on the ropes in the American League Championship Series.

We just needed to win one of two at home, but we lost them both, including blowing the late lead in the decisive game. That loss stayed with all of us, for years. Right up until 1985.

That 1977 team was deeper, and more talented than any of other great teams. But it's not the one people remember, because it's not the one that came together and played with such guts and fun and fearlessness on the way to winning the first (and so far only) World Series in Royals history.

I always say that 1985 team was as close as any I've been around, and got closer to its maximum potential than any team I've been around. That group was such a joy. They loved each other, and their organization. That was the definition of what people talk about when they say baseball teams need all 25 guys pulling in the same direction.

That season changed so many of our lives, and changed the history of the Royals and sports in Kansas City.

• • •

It's easy to look back at the magic of that year and think it was all predestined, but that's hardly the case.

George Brett truly carried us that year. He had, perhaps, the best season of his Hall of Fame career: He hit .335 with 38 doubles, 30 home runs, 112 RBIs, led the league in slugging and walked more than twice as often as he struck out. He even won the Gold Glove.

Of course, some of that was because we didn't have much depth in the lineup. Steve Balboni hit 36 home runs that year (still our franchise record), Hal McRae had the last good season of his tremendous career, Frank White hit 22 home runs for us, and Willie Wilson was a terror on the base paths. But we finished next-to-last in offense that year, and at the All-Star break, nobody could've had any idea what was coming.

We were just two games over .500, in third place in our division, and 7-and-a-half games back of Reggie Jackson and the Angels. It wasn't the season we were hoping for, at least not yet, and that's when Ewing Kauffman did something I'd never seen an owner do before.

Mr. K really liked to stay out of the way. People remember him for waving from his suite during the seventh inning stretch, and always being so gracious when he was meeting Royals fans, but he was careful to stay out of the baseball team as much as he could. He'd meet with us scouts and executives, and wanted to be informed and involved in decisions, but the way he saw it, the clubhouse and the field belonged to the players and coaches.

That made what he did just before the All-Star break so memorable. He came down to the clubhouse after our last game before the break, which we won 9-5 in Cleveland — Willie had four hits and stole a base.

All the guys were sitting in front of their lockers when Mr. K addressed the room.

"Gentlemen, I know we're not where we want to be in the standings, but I want you to know we're all in this together," he said. "I believe in you. I want you to forget about the first half of the season. In your lockers you will find an envelope with a few hundred dollars. Take these days off, enjoy it, and let's go like hell and win the second half."

Well, back then, a couple hundred bucks was a lot of money. And with the way the season was going, you can imagine how excited that made the guys.

We came back after the All-Star break and won 11 of our first 14, cutting that deficit all the way down to two games in just two weeks.

You never know how things are related, but that's about when we *really* started believing.

• • •

Scouts look at the game differently, you know. I don't just mean the way we see bat speed on a hitter, or footwork with a middle infielder, or a repeatable delivery with a pitcher.

I'm talking about the actual teams out there. We see a collection of individuals who were scouted and developed and work through the struggles of the minor leagues to play on our sport's biggest stage.

When we see big leaguers, it's almost like we're looking at a photo album. We remember how that player was first seen, who signed him and how he ended up with that team.

That 1985 team was just like that. Five of the eight starting position players in that World Series for us were either drafted or signed by us as amateurs. That included George Brett in the second round, but also Frank White out of the Royals Academy. Also, our starting pitcher in four of the seven games, plus our closer, were drafted or signed as amateurs.

There was a lot that went into making that team, of course, and we wouldn't have been there if not for the trades and free agent signings that brought us guys like Charlie Liebrandt, Hal McRae and Buddy Black (for a player to be named later). But as a scout it makes you feel so good when you see a team built mostly from the draft make it all the way to World Series, especially when it's *your* team.

With that in mind, one of my fondest memories of that 1985 team is how we got Willie Wilson, the great outfielder and base stealer for so many years.

It all came from Al Diez, a guy who wanted to scout for us so bad that he moved his family out East for a part-time job. That's all we had open at the time, so he took a chance, and really worked hard to become a great scout.

In 1973, I remember Al talking about this kid in New Jersey. He had a big, strong body. And he was fast. So fast.

Everybody knew about Willie, but nobody knew quite what to make of him. A lot of clubs were scared off because Willie had a football scholarship at Maryland, and was telling everyone he wanted to play football. Some other teams were turned off because Willie had bad body language playing catcher on his high school team — yes, *catcher* — which wasn't showing off his talent.

But Al didn't stop. He kept after Willie, got to know the family. He started to realize that Willie's body language was bad because he hated playing catcher, but agreed to do it because nobody else would. You'd rather not see the bad body language, but at this point, at least there's a logical explanation for it. It's not that he didn't want to play baseball (which is what some clubs thought). It's that he wanted to be in the outfield, which would've allowed him to shine more.

Al also found out the family had some financial problems. So Al started pushing the bonus money, pointing out what the family could do with a big check. Now, it's critical that Al had their trust before he started doing this, otherwise he comes off as a car salesman. But because he knew them, and understood where they were coming from, the family saw it for what it was — a genuine conversation — and an option they hadn't thought much about.

"OK, I'll play baseball," Willie eventually said. "But the money has to be right."

Nobody else had this information, because nobody else had this relationship. So all these other teams are passing on Willie, either because they perceived he had a bad attitude about baseball or because they thought he wanted to play football.

But we kept at him, and agreed that if he was available when we were picking 18$^{th}$ that we'd take him. We planned on giving him $75,000, at least, and ended up at $90,000.

Willie was so happy when we signed that contract. He paid off the money that his family owed, and then became such a key player for so many of our great teams, including our World Series champion — he was our leadoff hitter, our centerfielder, stole 43 bases and led the league with 21 triples that year.

All because we had that relationship with the family, and had information that others didn't.

• • •

A lot of clubs thought we took Mark Gubicza far too early in the 1981 draft. Where we saw a big, strong (6-foot-6 with a sturdy frame) right-handed pitcher with guts, a lot of clubs saw a herky-jerky, violent delivery that made his arm an injury time bomb.

We might have done that too, honestly. You usually don't like to spend high draft picks on guys who've put mileage on their arms with those really violent deliveries, but we had Tom Ferrick scouting for us then. Tom pitched nine years in the big leagues, and was a really good scout, particularly on pitchers.

He watched Goobie a lot, and what he saw was something else, entirely. He didn't think the delivery was too violent, and what violence there was in the delivery could be smoothed out with some technical tweaks.

But other teams thought we were crazy for drafting him in the second round. Goobie was from Philadelphia, but the Phillies passed on him to take another right-handed pitcher, a guy named Johnny Abrego who ended up getting a cup of coffee in the big leagues.

It wasn't just the Phillies who passed on him.

"You've got a guy who's going to blow out," we heard those words over and over.

Well, Goobie did "blow out," I guess, but not until he'd pitched 13 years for us, helped us win that 1985 World Series, and did enough to earn induction to the team Hall of Fame.

• • •

The heart of that team was George, obviously, but other than that, the real strength was our pitching.

And the pitcher people probably remember the most is Bret Saberhagen, the skinny kid from Grover Cleveland High School in Reseda, Calif., who we got in the 19th round of the 1982 draft.

It was an interesting story, because if we felt strongly that he'd become what he became we wouldn't have waited until the 19th round to draft him — and the other teams in baseball would've selected him long before the 19th.

But this is another good scouting story, because it was Guy Hansen who saw a lot of Sabes in high school and really sold the scouting department on his potential.

Sabes didn't look like much. He was about 6-feet tall, maybe 160 pounds, with what some scouts saw as a max-effort delivery. He was a good player in high school — even threw a no-hitter in the city championship game as a senior at Dodgers Stadium — but there were a lot of concerns about him. Not just the size, but he kept coming up with a sore arm. He didn't pitch much.

Who wants to draft a runt high school pitcher whose arm can't handle amateur ball?

But Hansen saw some potential, thought there were some things in the delivery that could be corrected to both increase the quality of his pitches *and* limit his injury risk. So we took a chance in the 19th round, and he really shot through the system, making our opening day roster in 1984 after just one full season in the minors.

He never had that overpowering stuff you like to see from an ace, but he had such a good feel for pitching, for keeping hitters off balance, and that pinpoint control. In 1985, he only walked 38 guys over 32 starts and 235 1/3 innings. He won 20 games for us that year, won the Cy Young Award and was the World Series MVP. He only gave up one run in two complete games against the Cardinals in the World Series.

Those are the kinds of things that often have to happen for a World Series winner: You find a great player, or two, hidden under rocks.

Nobody personified that better than Sabes.

• • •

The playoffs that year were such a thrill ride for all of us. I still say that George Brett's Game 3 of the ALCS was the greatest individual performance I've ever seen — 4-for-4, four runs, three RBIs, a double, two home runs and probably the best defensive play he ever made.

Looking back, we probably don't even make the World Series without that performance, and the history of the Royals and all of us involved with the club is much different.

That series against Toronto was so strange. We were down 3-1, and came storming back to win it in seven. Well, late in the seventh game, we probably only need six or seven outs to win it and the game is stopped for some birds in the outfield.

I'm sitting with Avron Fogleman and John Schuerholz, and Fogleman's freaking out, "John, you gotta do something!"

Well, what's John going to do? But then, a little later In the same game, a guy goes streaking across the field and then some drunk falls out of the stands.

I'm telling you, we really thought the jinx was on. We're sitting fairly close down to the field, up by five, but you never assume anything in baseball — especially not with the World Series on the line. But people all around us are getting up, leaving the stadium, headed out to the parking lots.

"Good luck in the World Series!" they're telling us, like the game is already over, and we're thinking, what in the heck are all these people doing? This is Game 7!

*Kansas City hasn't had a celebration like this since 1985. This is Sabes in the championship parade. He was the best pitcher in baseball that year, just three years after we drafted him in the 19th round. If we knew he'd be this good, we wouldn't have waited that long to take him, but we did feel good after the strong scouting reports we had on him from Guy Hansen.*

Later, we realized it was the opening night for the Maple Leafs at the Toronto Garden. All of these people that were leaving would rather watch the first game of the NHL season than the seventh game of the ALCS.

. . .

After it was all over, we beat the Cardinals 11-0 in Game 7 and the way that game played out there was no drama in the outcome. The whole thing felt like a countdown to a huge party, building and building and building.

I remember so much about that night. The iconic picture of George and Sabes hugging after Darryl Motley caught the last out. And, of course, the champagne celebration in the clubhouse, sharing hugs and laughs and memories with people you work so hard for — the sport's ultimate joy.

But I'll tell you something else I remember. It's Ewing Kauffman, walking off the stage after the live TV interview they do with the trophy presentation. He's in his best blue sport coat, pure joy on his face. This is a man who only bought the team so that his hometown would have major league baseball again, but then once he bought it, he figured he might as well work as hard as possible to make it a model franchise.

Mr. K never failed at anything in his life, so owning a baseball team wasn't going to be any different. And after all of our successes in 1977 or 1980 or any of the other seasons, there would have been a little hole in all of our records without that night in 1985.

I was thinking about all of that as Mr. K walked by. He put his hand on my shoulder and pulled me in for a big hug.

"Art," he said, "this is one of the greatest days of my life."

# Chapter
# *12*
# Inside the draft room

The NFL calls it the war room, and, at times, we should call it the war room, too.

Rosey Gilhousen had disagreements with someone most every year. Al Kubski was a national cross checker for us, almost turned our draft room into a boxing match. They're going back and forth about a player. I can't remember who it was, but Rosey really likes the prospect, Al thinks we're wasting our time and all of a sudden the argument goes from baseball to somewhere else entirely.

"Rosey," Al tells him, "you're a prick!"

Rosey is this short, heavyset guy, and his face is red as a tomato. Neither one of these guys are the type to back down. Rosey must've said something back, because Al starts to lunge across the table like he's going to throw punches. It took two or three of us to hold him back.

"That's it!" Rosey screams. "I'm done!"

He packs all his reports into his big leather bag and storms out of the room. Slams the door. We have to chase him down in the hallway, grab him and play on his emotions to get him back in that room.

I can't tell you what year this was, where they nearly came to blows.

Because this type of thing happened more than once, at least it did in the old days.

You have to understand that the draft is the most important day of the year for every scout in baseball, and aside from the two teams that make the World Series, it's the most important day for their organizations, too.

This is the scout's Super Bowl. This is the final exam they spend 365 days preparing for. This is the one test of a full year's work, 12 months of their lives spent driving 50,000 miles around the country eating bad food on the go, sacrificing sleep because after the night game in St. Louis they need to make it to a day game in Memphis the next day. They become detectives, weathermen, psychologists and coaches for this day. They build relationships with prospects and their families, both out of love for the sport and an effort to find any edge over the next guy.

All of that work is either validated or wasted on draft day.

I always told our scouts, "you are the first line of productivity." The better you scout, the better the organization. All of the functions of a major league baseball organization go back to scouting: winning games, ticket sales, marketing, public relations and attendance. It all goes back to scouting, and the quality of players you bring in the organization that, of course, means getting the most talent for the money you spend.

Whatever you think of our big trade for James Shields, we probably can't afford a pitcher like that on the free agent market. There are only two ways for us to get an ace like that: We have to draft and develop him, or we have to trade for him with guys we've drafted and developed.

Both ways go directly to scouting. They say the Royals are in the best shape as an organization as we've been in nearly two decades. I agree with that, and it's because we're putting the most emphasis on scouting as we've done in nearly two decades.

All of that goes back to scouting, and draft day.

Which is why I've never slept the night before a draft. Never.

• • •

One of the most important parts of being a scouting director on draft day is being able to "scout the scout." As much as we're all objective, and try to look at each player the same, we all have our favorites and our quirks.

Over the years, I know other scouts have come to know me as more optimistic. I always try to see the *can* in a player, not the *cannot*. So I know that when I give an opinion on a player, the scouting director and other scouts might take that into account.

Just like when there's a scout who sees an injury around every corner, or typically undersells a player. The scouting director and other scouts take that into account, too.

The goal, of course, is to be even-handed with every evaluation. But as long as each specific scout is consistent with his approach and reports, it works out fine. It's sort of like what we say about the umpires: you can have a high strike zone, or a wide strike zone, we just want you to be consistent.

That's one of the reasons it's so important to spend time with scouts in each territory. Especially for the cross-checkers, and *especially* for the scouting director. That's why you travel with these guys, driving through the hills of Kentucky or the freeways of California. You get to know the men very well this way, and their families, and they get to know you. You do that long enough, and it becomes a family.

This was pretty easy and enjoyable for me when I was scouting director, because I was blessed to have Dean Taylor, an excellent assistant scouting director whose baseball expertise was exceptional. He was so good that I bragged to John Schuerholz about him too much and I lost him. He became John's assistant GM and has gone on to a great career in baseball as a GM and now the Royals vice president of baseball operations/assistant GM. It was truly a hard-working, veteran staff. Guys like Rosey, Kenny Gonzales, Brian Murphy, Al Kubski, Al Diez and Tom Ferrick. Those guys were so great to work with. I got to know them, and they got to know me. There's no substitute for looking eyeball to eyeball with a scout. You scout the scout, like we say, and you get to know which scouts should move the room on a gut feeling and which ones might still be a little green.

That time we spend together during the scouting season, on the road, really paid off on draft day.

It's like if you run a marathon, you have to have good shoes. If you have good shoes that you trust and know and are comfortable with, then you were in much better shape on the day of the race.

Having good scouts and knowing them well is only part of it, like having good shoes is a critical part of training for a marathon — but only part of it.

You still have to do the training.

• • •

Today, they bring you in one at a time to talk about your players. It's like you're sitting on a jury box.

When I was scouting director, I'd bring in guys in the same area at the same time. Like, we'd have our west coast scouts together, then bring in the Midwest scouts, then the southeast, and so on. The reason I did it like that, a lot of times guys in the same region would end up seeing some of the same players. They might have been there to scout the shortstop on one team, but they'd also get a look at the catcher on the other team. The more views you have of prospects from scouts you trust, the better off you are.

We'd bring the scouts in, and have all the names on a big blackboard. You'd separate the players into categories by how much you thought of them — excellent, good, average and fringe. Then we rank them in preferential order. We always took the best player available.

It worked for us, but times have changed. The reason we do it the other way now, getting the scouts' views more independently and removed from each other, is that so much of the scouting now — especially the best prospects — is done in showcase events of players from all over the country.

That means that if you have a scout on the West Coast, say, in LA … well, not only has he seen the better prospects from around the West Coast (say, the Bay Area) but he's probably seen the best players from Texas, Chicago, Florida and Michigan, too.

We divvy up the prospects differently now, too. We look at them by position. And not just position, but experience. So you look at all the pitchers together, but then you rank the high school pitchers together and the college pitchers together.

But however you do it, this is the most important day of the year for a lot of reasons. What you see in the draft and in the organization are the players we draft, but for us scouts, that's just the beginning.

Your scouting director (and, by extension, your general manager, team president and owner) are judging you on every report you give — whether we sign the player or not.

I used to have a sheet that I'd keep on every scout in our organization, and each player in their territory. A form of this is still used today. Basically, you're creating an old-fashioned scale. You track every player in every territory, with what that player signed for, what round they were drafted in, and you update it every year with what level that prospect made.

I kept a folder on each scout. You weigh the money spent against the progress of the player, and at the end of the year, the production better outweigh the money spent.

• • •

On draft day, everyone is excited. You have a full scouting department that have the energy of kids on Christmas morning, but the seriousness and focus of law students taking the bar exam.

There is a fine line you have to walk as a scout when you're talking to your boss about a player. The really good ones won't oversell a bad player, and they won't undersell a good one. They're not afraid to go against the conventional view on a guy, and they won't stretch the player's ability in an effort to get the bosses on their side.

Because a good scout knows that no matter the outcome of the draft, his judgments on every player will stick with him, good or bad. That's why those history sheets are important, to remember how everyone does over time.

There are thousands of players to go through but each decision is important enough that in the right situation you might spend two or three hours debating two players — which one goes in the fourth spot among high school catchers, for instance, and which one goes fifth.

The hours you put in are immense, but if you have the right group the time flies by because you're doing what you love and you're all working together. It's nothing to have an 18- or 20-hour day during draft time and be frustrated that you have to sleep for a few hours before starting it all again the next day.

Keeping everything straight when the bullets are flying is why it's so important you have smart people who know the terrain around you. And not just scouts. Linda Smith has been the manager of scouting operations in the scouting department for so long. I can't even think about what it would be like without her. She saves us all a lot of headaches, confusion and time, working all night before the draft. She had everything in perfect order when the draft commenced the next day.

Part of what takes so long is there are so many aspects to each prospect. Especially these days, the most important thing you have to do is weigh your value on the player to the player's value of himself. If we think a player is worth a $1 million bonus but he has an "advisor" who won't let him sign for less than $2 million, then it's not a good fit. But if your value matches up with the player's perception — or, in those very rare circumstances, even *exceeds* the player's perception — then you have a good situation.

That's where the term "signability" came from in scouting circles. You have to have that signability right in your report, or else all the other information doesn't matter. We've been pretty good with this. Scott Boras was advising Mike Moustakas, and there were some reports that he wanted a really big number to sign, but we felt confident he wanted to play pro baseball. It went right down to the last minute — literally — and Moose got $4 million, which is a lot of money but considerably less than some of the rumors before the draft.

If a guy's price doesn't match yours, then you can't draft him. I can't say we've ever completely taken a guy off the board because he was advised by any particular agent, but there are times where if the talent is equal you go with the guy who has a more reasonable expectation of a signing bonus.

You go through a similar process with the medical reports on players. Guys who have significant risk — or, just as importantly, significant *perception* of risk — go in another category. But if you have good information, and independent thinkers, you can sometimes find value here.

For instance, in the 2013 draft, Indiana State lefthander Sean Manaea might've been a top-5 pick but battled a hip injury early in the season. That scared some teams off, which meant he was still available for our supplemental pick after the first round. Our information was that Manaea's injury wouldn't be a problem going forward. Time will tell, but as it turned out, we got what we feel like are two first-round talents with only one first-round pick.

Navigating the medical concerns is so important, we keep a trainer in the draft room to help throughout the whole process.

It's actually good to have differing opinions on the same player from different scouts. That's why a real good general manager and scouting director will be careful who they hire. They want to bring in men who will work together and respect each other, but also unafraid to challenge each other — and secure enough with themselves not to take offense at being challenged.

You want to keep an engaged, spirited, productive environment where everyone feels free to give their opinion and is expected to respect the other opinions in the room. That's the only way you can get to a point that, no matter who "wins" a specific debate on a player, everyone in the room lets it go when the decision is made.

• • •

One other part of running a good draft that you might not think about is scouting the other teams. You have to scout your competition in the draft.

Over the years, I've developed a knack for getting information. I guess it's a combination of being around for a while, knowing a lot of people, having a lot of conversations out in the field and a good feel about what certain scouts and franchises are thinking.

George Brett still talks about this when we see each other. He's sat in on some draft meetings with us, and loves to hear the part where I tell everyone who will and won't be available when we pick. When we get to the draft, Peter Gammons, the longtime ESPN reporter, always finds me.

"You got the list, Art?" he says.

Terry Ryan, who led the Twins' resurgence in the late '90s and early '00s as general manager, likes to joke with me.

"Hey Art, who are we taking this year?"

Through the years, we've probably been 80 percent accurate on the top 15 or 20 players taken.

Well, one year, I sure wish I'd have known *all* of the picks ahead of us.

This was 1992, and we were picking 10<sup>th</sup>. We knew who each team ahead of us was taking — with one exception. The Yankees were picking sixth, one of the few times they've picked in front of us, and I couldn't get any crumbs on who they were taking. Their scouts just kept saying, "We don't know yet." And the scouts on other teams who are usually tuned in didn't have a feel for it either.

I was especially on edge about this draft, because the top player on our board was a shortstop out of Kalamazoo named Derek Jeter. We had a scout named Ray Jackson who became close with Derek and his family. We felt good about the whole situation, but, well, you know how that turned out for Jeter and the Yankees.

From our side, we still managed a pretty good draft. The star of that draft was Johnny Damon. You know all about Johnny, and I told you the backstory earlier. But we also got Michael Tucker, who had a nice career and was the player we sent to Atlanta for Jermaine Dye. We took Jim Pittsley with a compensation pick, and he got to the big leagues quick. Jon Lieber was our second-rounder, and he had a very good career.

All together, we drafted nine guys who made it to the big leagues, including one borderline Hall of Famer (Damon), one All-Star (Lieber), and one regular big leaguer (Tucker).

That's a pretty good draft.

But if we got Jeter, it would've been the greatest draft we ever had.

• • •

In 1968, just four years into the draft era, the Yankees are picking fourth. We usually didn't pick that high in the draft because we had such good teams, but we had a bad year the prior season and to be honest, as a scout, you look forward to drafting high. It's a chance to really pick the best players in the country, instead of the best among those who are still left at the end of the first round.

We're down to two. There's a catcher from Kent State in Ohio, a four-year guy with good instincts behind the plate and a bat that we thought had potential. And there's a big first baseman I had from Notre Dame High in Niles, Ill., which is a suburb of Chicago.

The high school kid is Greg Luzinski. They called him "The Bull," and he could hit the ball so hard and far it looked like a meteorite in the sky.

As scouts, we're going back and forth, back and forth, and finally we settle on Luzinski. Power hitters are just so important in our game, and it's hard to pass up that kind of raw, natural power.

You always want to take yourself out of the process, as a scout. The process has to be about the players, not your own biases. But I was so excited about this pick. It's a good problem to have, but with the Yankees, you don't get a lot of opportunities to take the best player available.

So I'm getting excited about Luzinski's power in Yankee Stadium when Ralph Houk, our old manager (who grew up in Lawrence, Kan.), walked into the room. You have to remember that the Yankees were in a bad spot then. We finished 10th in the league in 1966, and ninth in 1967. We were below .500 and already out of the race in 1968 when the draft came along, and Ralph, understandably, was interested in one thing.

"Gentlemen, I have one question," he said, and he didn't mention names because he didn't have to. We all knew who it was down to. "If we take the college kid out of Ohio, or the high school kid from Chicago, who gets to the big leagues and helps the New York Yankees the quickest?"

Well, naturally, everyone in the room knew the answer. It was the college catcher.

We lost Luzinksi.

You know who we that college catcher was?

Thurmon Munson.

He debuted for us the very next season, and the year after that, hit .302 and won the American League MVP. We won 93 games that year.

That was the first of two MVPs for Munson, and by the time his career was over, he helped us win two World Series. What a player.

Luzinski turned into a heck of a player. He hit 307 home runs, made four All-Star teams, and in 1975 led the National League in RBIs.

But we were all thankful Houk came in that room.

• • •

We had another situation like that with the Royals. This is 1995, and we're picking 19th. That was the draft where Darin Erstad went first, and that a lot of people may remember had Kerry Wood, the great high schooler out of Texas who starred for the Cubs before suffering some arm problems and transitioning into a very good closer.

We were split between two high school outfielders from Puerto Rico, one you've heard about and one you probably you haven't: Carlos Beltran and Juan LeBron.

This is that inexact part of scouting, because obviously Beltran is building a Hall of Fame case while LeBron never made it past Double-A ball. But back then, we all had both players as first-round picks. As to who was better, we had a very divided camp. Allard Baird, Guy Hansen, Brian Murphy and Chuck McMichael all pushed for Beltran.

The Beltran backers came on all points of the spectrum. Hansen liked Carlos' bat speed, but thought he was a bit of a gamble as a first-rounder. Allard really liked Carlos's athleticism, and thought he'd develop some power. McMichael actually had Carlos as the best player in the draft. In his report, he wrote "best available, complete package."

LeBron's biggest ally was Johnny Ramos, the great scout we had working that area. He loved both players but leaned toward LeBron. Johnny was our authority in Puerto Rico, and for good reason. He had an in with Roberto Alomar, but we didn't give him enough money. So when Ramos compared LeBron to a young Juan Gonzalez and Amos Otis, it really swung some minds.

We ended up taking LeBron, and we all felt great about it. Unfortunately, it just didn't work out.

But you should've seen our celebration when Beltran was still available for us in the second round. We felt like we drafted two first-round talents.

. . .

Another thing about how inexact baseball scouting is that it really changes the way drafts are judged. In the NBA, you have to hit on your first-round pick. In the NFL, you better get a few starters out of a seven-round draft.

But in our sport, if you can get one very good player and another starter out of 50-some rounds, that's a great draft.

The result is that you can always second-guess yourself. For any team, in any year, you can go back through an old draft and change a franchise's future by shifting around picks.

Just as an example, let's go back five years to the 2009 draft. You can't make complete judgments on baseball players five years after a draft, but that's a pretty good number.

The Cardinals are one of the best-run organizations in baseball. They won the World Series in 2011, and have been in the playoffs each of the last three seasons. And they had an excellent draft in 2009. Their first-round pick was Shelby Miller, who won 15 games with a 3.06 ERA in his first full season in 2013; Joe Kelly, who's won 15 games with a 3.08 ERA in two seasons, and Matt Carpenter, the second baseman who led the National League in runs, hits and doubles in 2013.

Pretty good, right? Every team in baseball would be *thrilled* to have a draft like that.

But instead of Miller, what if they took Mike Trout in the first round? He's probably the best player in baseball right now.

And in the second round, instead of Robert Stock, a catcher who finished last season in Class A ball, what if they took Patrick Corbin — he won 14 games, pitched 208 innings and made the All-Star team for the Diamondbacks in 2013.

Brandon Belt could've been theirs in the fifth round. Belt had 56 extra-base hits for the Giants in 2013. In the seventh round, they

*Here I am with Dennis Leonard at the draft in 2009, which was televised on ESPN2. I'm one of the few who's been scouting since before the first draft in 1965, all the way through today when they're on TV. We've come a long way, from the time they moved the draft to a teleconference because there were almost some fights between scouts over who we were drafting.*

could've had Paul Goldschmidt, who led the league in homers, RBIs and slugging percentage in 2013. The Cardinals don't need a catcher with Yadier Molina, but they could've had Yan Gomes. The Blue Jays took him in the 10th round, with the very next pick after the Cardinals took a pitcher who's still in Class A ball.

And on and on and on.

Like I said, you can play this game with any team in baseball, in any season. I only picked the Cardinals as an example because that's such a strong organization, with so much success. And they *did* have a great draft in 2009, but what if they had Trout and Corbin and Goldschmidt?

I'll give you an example with us: our 1986 draft might be the best in franchise history, and one of the better drafts in recent baseball history. We found eight big leaguers the year after winning the World Series, which you hardly ever see. I told you the Bo Jackson story, but we also got Tom Gordon in the sixth round. All he did was pitch 21 years in the big leagues, with three All-Star selections.

The top of that draft was loaded — Matt Williams went third, Kevin Brown fourth and Gary Sheffield sixth. So we didn't have a chance at any of those guys, not picking 24th, but instead of picking Tony Clements (a high school shortstop from Chino who never made the big leagues), what if we took Kevin Tapani, who won 56 games in his first four seasons?

In the second round, we took a high school outfielder who stalled in the minors, but we could have had Dean Palmer, who hit 26, 33, and 38 home runs in his first three full seasons (and who later hit 34 homers for us after we signed him as a free agent in 1998).

In the rest of the draft, we could've had Pat Hentgen (fifth round to the Blue Jays, 1996 Cy Young winner), or Rod Beck (13th round to the A's, three-time All-Star), or any other number of long-time big leaguers.

And that doesn't include stars like Steve Finley and John Olerud, who were drafted but didn't sign.

Even in the years you have a great draft, you could've had an all-time draft.

• • •

Major League Baseball put the first round of the draft on TV in

2007, and we nearly didn't make it. Mike Swanson, our vice president of communications, is driving on the highway toward the hotel. Frank White and Dina Wathan, John's daughter who works for us in media relations, were also in the car.

When the big truck in front of us lost a wheel.

Thank goodness Swannee was driving. We're going about 60 mph with traffic and this wheel is coming right for our windshield. Swannee makes this quick turn, no hesitation, and that wheel bounced by us by inches.

We almost missed that draft.

We'd have been in the ditch, at best.

That was the year we got Moustakas in the first round. Someone would've had to call that pick in.

• • •

We had one of those classic debates back in 2002, in some ways, the same kind of debate baseball fans have every night with friends at the ballpark or on text messages or at the bar:

Do you want the slugger?

Or do you want the ace pitcher?

Do you want Prince Fielder?

Or do you want Zack Greinke?

It doesn't always happen like this, but this was one time where everything we said in that draft room about both of these guys turned out to be true.

We were picking sixth that year, and there were clubs who had pitchers who ended up going lower in the draft higher on their boards than Greinke, but we really liked him. He was a smooth athlete — I know a couple clubs who said they'd take him in the first round as an infielder. Most of the time when you're debating college pitchers against high school pitchers, what you're really doing is debating a more polished guy with someone who might have a higher ceiling.

Well, with Zack, he had that higher ceiling being a high school kid but we also saw that polish. He had great balance on the mound, a real presence and a feel for pitching that you just don't see in guys very often. He could run that good fastball into the mid-90s, with movement, but he also knew how to trick guys with offspeed stuff. It was really something to watch him pitch.

With Prince, there were no mysteries. No unknowns. He was this big, powerful piece of machinery who could hit the ball out further than you could see. He had the good genes, of course. Everybody knew about his father, Cecil, who we actually drafted in 1982. Cecil had that natural power, too, that country strength. He ended up hitting 51 home runs for the Tigers in 1990, and 44 more the next year. Both totals led the American League. Prince had all that potential, and he was a much better athlete than his dad — plus he hit from the left side.

This is the pitch chart I kept on Zack Greinke's major league debut. We drafted him after a long debate between him and Prince Fielder, and I'm not ashamed to tell you I was one of the guys pushing for Prince. As it turned out, we couldn't have gone wrong. Prince hit 50 home runs in a season, and Zack won a Cy Young.

In that draft room, when we talked about Zack, we talked about a guy who could win a Cy Young Award someday.

And when we talked about Prince, we talked about a guy who could hit 50 home runs in the big leagues someday.

Like I said, it doesn't usually happen like this. Scouting means you're wrong about a guy more often than you're right.

But in this case, we were right about both. Zack won the Cy Young for us in 2009, and Prince hit 50 home runs for Milwaukee in 2007.

But before all that happened, we had to choose between the two. I can say this now: I argued for Prince over Zack in that draft room.

And I'll tell you why.

• • •

In the lead-up to the draft, the club wanted as many eyes as possible on all the top prospects — with a special emphasis on Zack and Prince.

They sent me to Sebring, Fla., where they were having this big event for Florida high school all-stars. And they wanted Frank White to go with me. They thought it would be a sign of goodwill since Frank and Cecil knew each other so well.

Good idea, too. We get there and Frank gives Cecil this big old hug. They're smiling and laughing and telling old stories. Meanwhile, Prince is having that real good batting practice that you want to see from a high draft pick and when it's over, Cecil asks if we want to meet his son.

Of course we do. The two biggest knocks against Prince in the draft were that he didn't play a premium position (you'd rather your real high draft picks be centerfielders, shortstops, catchers or starting pitchers) and that he had a bad body. In the scouting jargon, they often call it a soft body — more jiggle than muscle.

So we're there in Florida, and Frank meets Prince. They shake hands, and Frank sort of puts his left hand on Prince's shoulder and grabs it, you know, like you do sometimes when you're trying to show friendship or affection. We're all standing there talking for a bit, and Prince is as nice as he can be. He's a sharp guy, comfortable and really likes to talk ball, which is always a good sign.

Anyway, after we walk away, Frank looks at me.

"I don't know who says this kid has a soft body," Frank says. "When I grabbed his shoulder, it felt like a hunk of granite."

That was one thing people missed about Prince, actually. He does look a little pudgy, and that's his natural body type. You can see where he gets it when you see his dad.

But you know what? At those All-Star games, they always have workouts. They have the prospects go through drills that the scouts want to see and time and one of the main ones is the 60-yard dash.

Nobody's interested in Prince for his speed, but he ran the 60 in 6.9 seconds. That's fast enough that it would've qualified him for the old Royals Academy.

Of course, you know how that draft turned out. I was pushing for Prince, because I've always thought that if you're trying to start a ballclub, you take the hitter over the pitcher because he plays every day. Maybe that's old-time thinking, but it's what I've always thought.

Now, don't get me wrong. I loved Zack as a prospect and I was thrilled when we took him. As it turned out, we couldn't have gone wrong.

Zack was our pitcher of the year as a 20-year-old in 2004. Everyone knows how he went away from baseball for a bit in 2006, and then when he came back he really started to fulfill all that potential. He won 13 games and threw 202 1/3 innings with a 3.47 ERA in 2008, and then in 2009 had one of the greatest seasons for a starting pitcher this century: 16-8 with a 2.16 ERA over 229 1/3 innings, 242 strikeouts and just 51 walks. He won the Cy Young Award, almost unanimously. That was even more impressive considering we were a big disappointment as a big league team that year, losing 97 games in a season we hoped to be much better.

And Prince, of course, quickly turned into one of the great power hitters in the big leagues. He hit those 50 home runs in 2007, and drove in 141 runs in 2009.

If it was just up to me, we'd have drafted Prince. But like I said before, once the decision is made all of the scouts have to get behind it so that's what I did. I'm thrilled we drafted Zack, and that I got to see him up close and get to know him.

As it turned out, the decision between Greinke and Fielder was like a diamond or piece of platinum.

• • •

I've been part of every draft that baseball has ever had, and the biggest difference from the old days to now is the information that's available and discussed.

We used to have the names on an old blackboard; now they're printed off on magnetized panels, color-coded and organized around all four walls of the room. Video screens show the strengths and weaknesses of the players we're discussing, and trainers have gone from sitting by a phone to sitting by us in the room.

In the old days, sophistication was defined by the scouts who *typed* their reports, instead of writing them out with a pen.

Now you have these numbers guys pulling up every stat you can think of on demand, and instead of arguing about who has the better swing or more fluid pitching motion, you can pull it up on the video screen and see for yourselves.

We've come a long way.

But I'll tell you this: even back in those days, we still figured out a way to get players who could play.

# Chapter
# 13

# Prisons and a wife-swapper: a scouting story

*Y*ou get a lot of mail when you're a scout. More mail than you feel like you have time to read, actually, and a lot of it is from amateur baseball players around your area who want to be seen.

Most of the mail will be sent to your ball club, so every once in a while you'll get a big package of mail forwarded to you. Some guys, to be honest, ignore most of those letters. They feel like they already know about the players in their area, and that if a kid has to resort to cold-calling big league clubs for a chance then he's probably not much of a prospect.

I might've thought that, too, but when I was just starting Tom Greenwade told me to always follow up on those letters. At least make a phone call, find out the kid's schedule, his goals, his strengths. Part of scouting is finding kids who love the game and want to play. By definition, these letters are being written by kids who fit that description. So I always kept that in mind.

Another bit of advice that stuck with me through the years: Never leave a ballpark early. That came to me from Paul Kritchell, the legendary scout who signed Lou Gehrig, Whitey Ford, Phil Rizzuto and so many others. It sounds so simple, but you'd be surprised how many scouts don't follow it. You'd be surprised what you can find if you follow it.

Or, at least, I was.

These two bits of advice helped me sign two very successful pitchers for the Yankees, two men who would go on to shake up the baseball establishment in their own and very different ways.

• • •

The letter came to me from a boy in Illinois playing for a summer team in Genoa, which is a small country town not too far from Rockford.

Fritz Peterson was a left-handed pitcher who had just completed his freshman season at Northern Illinois, but didn't want to go to school anymore. He was going to drop out, with the idea of signing a pro contract. The letter was very enthusiastic. He wrote about how he was a Yankee fan and that playing for them would be a dream come true. He even sent me his schedule for the summer.

So I follow up on the letter, talk to Peterson for a little bit, and find out when he's going to pitch. You should've seen this ballpark. I'd never seen anything like it. Many years later, when *Field of Dreams* came out, it reminded me of seeing Peterson for the first time. They had a cornfield for the outfield wall. When you show Joe Jackson walking out of the cornfield, that's exactly what the park looked like in Genoa.

Anyway, I pull up and I see Fritz warming up in the bullpen. No radar guns in those days, of course, but any scout can eyeball it and get a good feel for what the prospect has. What I see is an average fastball, but a really good curveball and a nice, loose arm. This is pretty good for a follow-up on a letter.

Then the game starts, and it gets better. Much better. He pitches a three-hit shutout, striking out 17. That's enough for me to know I need to see more of this kid, and that my bosses need to know about him.

I talk to him after the game, and he really wants to be a Yankee, but he says the Kansas City A's have seen him and arranged for him to fly out there for a workout.

"Fritz," I said. "Just promise me one thing. No matter what they offer you, please, before you do anything, would you give me a call?"

He agreed, and he calls me a few days later. The workout in Kansas City went well, like I knew it would. They offered him $10,000. Fritz told them he'd think on it, which gave us time to work him out ourselves.

As it happened, the Yankees were playing in Chicago that weekend so we got Fritz to drive up to Comiskey Park. He gets there early, before the players are even hitting. Fritz goes down to one of the bullpens, and he starts throwing, and it's just as good as what I saw that day in Genoa — maybe better.

At one point, someone taps me on my shoulder. I turn around and it's Whitey Ford.

"Art," he says, "don't let this kid out of the park."

Then comes manager Ralph Houk and pitching coach Jim Turner and they're all just as impressed. A few minutes later, it's Al Lopez, who was managing the White Sox at the time.

"Who's the kid?" he asks.

"Ah, just some kid from one of the neighborhoods here," I said, trying to downplay it so the White Sox wouldn't get interested.

I called the offices back in New York and told them how impressed everyone was. I believe strongly in the old theory that if you've got a guy, you can't ever let him get away. So we took him into the visitors' clubhouse.

We gave him a $12,000 bonus and signed the contract on a trunk in the visitors' clubhouse at Comiskey Park, without the White Sox, the A's or anyone else knowing a thing.

Fritz Peterson developed into everything we hoped. He had that pinpoint control, hardly ever walking anyone, playing the angles of old Yankee Stadium as well as anybody before or since and changing speeds enough that he became one of the better pitchers in the American League. He made an All-Star team and won 20 games in 1970, and holds the permanent distinction of the lowest ERA of any starting pitcher in the old stadium's history.

And he did it for the Yankees, because of Greenwade's tip about always following up on those letter writers.

But Fritz Peterson would shake up baseball in a very different way.

• • •

Kritchell's tip about never leaving the ballpark early helped me and the Yankees in the spring of 1957 find a young man who would become an All-Star.

This starts with a really good prospect out of Bloom Township High School in the Chicago area. As it happens, the boy is a pitcher and his name is Jerry Colangelo. Today, the world knows Jerry as one of the great moguls in American sports. He went on to own the Arizona Diamondbacks in Major League Baseball, the Suns in the NBA, and helped bring the NHL to Phoenix. He also runs USA Basketball.

But back then, he was one of the better pitching prospects in the Midwest. And that's why seven or eight scouts showed up on that day in 1957.

We're all looking forward to seeing what he has, but when the lineup comes out, Colangelo isn't pitching. I still don't know why he didn't pitch that day, but it turned out to be a major break for me.

"That third baseman from Kankakee is playing five miles from here," one of the scouts announced.

That's all it took. They all hit the road. I wanted to go, too, to be honest but I remembered what Kritchell said about never leaving the park until the game's over.

So I stick around, even though I don't have a positive report or tip on anyone in the game. But that's about when I hear that *smack, smack, smack* from the pitcher Bloom has going, instead of Colangelo.

That gets my interest, so I get closer to the bullpen and I see a really strong fastball, pretty good curveball and the kind of natural athleticism you want to see in a prospect. The boy's name is Jim Bouton, who I first heard about from an old gentleman named W.K. Fred, and he pitches a magnificent game. I was stunned. It's the kind of thing you hardly ever run into, even in those days. This kid was really talented, but nobody knew about him because Colangelo was the big guy on that team. Bouton was overshadowed.

Bouton was already set to go to college, but I got him to pitch for me with the Chicago Yankees that summer. I didn't know this at the time, but he's since told me that he was scared out of his mind the first time he pitched for us. We had a guy named Jim Hansen on the team, and Jim was a very strong pitcher. He ended up getting $50,000 from the Cubs, and he was pitching the first game of the doubleheader. Bouton said he watched Hansen, so strong and in command, and wondered if he belonged.

I'll tell you this, too: There were scouts from the Pirates, White Sox and Cubs to see Hansen in that first game. They didn't know about Kritchell's rule, I guess, but in the second game Bouton was even better than Hansen.

"Holy smokes," I thought. "I've got to hide this kid."

So I worked the schedule in a way that I would only pitch Bouton where I knew scouts wouldn't see him. We had enough games in small, out-of-the-way towns that we made it work.

Prisons, too.

• • •

We played games in a lot of prisons in those days. We played at the Illinois Stateville Prison and the old Joliet prison. Those were always fun. I know Bouton really started to enjoy pitching at prisons. It wasn't as scary as you might think, but it was unlike anything else I did in baseball. You get in there, and you're expecting this really raucous crowd screaming at you and threatening you, but it's not like that.

As it turns out, the prisoners in the stands don't necessarily root for the prisoners on the field. If anything, they root against the other prisoners because there's some jealousy there that they're not the ones playing.

But most of them root for themselves, and I'll tell you what I mean: The prisoners bet cigarettes on the games, so they were rooting for their bets. You could feel the buzz in the stands throughout the game. They were constantly changing the odds, too. Bouton would break off a real good curveball, and they'd change the odds in our favor.

When Bouton would close out an inning with a strikeout, or we'd score a big run, there were at least as many prisoners cheering for us as when their own team did anything.

We only had something *really* out of the ordinary once, when the sirens start blaring. The prisoners in the stands sort of freeze. We don't know what the heck is going on. Then we hear that there's a lockdown, because a prisoner escaped. They take us into a room to wait everything out, until they know it's safe. After about 45 minutes, they found the guy hiding in a laundry basket.

*They didn't always look at Bouton as a pariah. Back in 1963, the first big leaguer I ever signed for the Yankees was one of the hottest stories in baseball. He was in his first full season with the Yankees, and well on his way to 21 wins. This is him posing for a picture with Johnny Sain, the great old pitcher with the Boston Braves ("Spahn and Sain, and pray for rain") with his grip on the curve that served him so well.*

And then we finished the game.

Of course, I knew I couldn't hide Bouton forever. Eventually, talent always finds the light of day, and that's what happened when Bouton pitched us to the city finals at the end of that summer.

Then he goes to college at Western Michigan, and he's pitching more, and pitching brilliantly, so there's no hiding him at that point. The word is out. But by then, I at least had a head start on the others, and obviously had a relationship with Jim and his family.

Jim pitched again for us the next summer, after his freshman year, and we go all the way to a national tournament in Battle Creek, Mich., and the place is crawling with scouts. That's when his family decided he would sign a pro contract.

The Detroit Tigers were on him hard, the Philadelphia Phillies liked him a lot, and four or five other teams. My relationship with the family was strong, but not strong enough that he would sign a lesser offer. The advantage I had was trust, and that they gave me the last appointment. Actually, we did the appointment over Thanksgiving dinner at their house.

We got it done for a package that included a $15,000 bonus and incentives that brought the total up to $25,000, and did it for the Yankees because of a few good breaks and Kritchell's tip about never leaving the ballpark early.

Here's Jimmy getting the champagne treatment from Joe Pepitone after he won his 20th game in 1963, 2-0. We won 104 games that year, but got swept by the Dodgers in the World Series. Bouton was great in his World Series game, going seven innings and giving up just one run. But we lost that day to Don Drysdale, who threw a complete game shutout.

Bouton won 21 games and made the All-Star team in his second season, when he was just 24 years old. He was great again the next year, winning 18 games, but soon after that he had arm problems and he was never that dominant starting pitcher again.

He ended up pitching parts of 10 seasons in the big leagues, but that's not what most people remember him for — just like pitching isn't what most people remember Peterson for.

• • •

The book came to my house with a Houston return address, and sometimes I wonder if I should be thankful I was no longer with the Yankees.

Jim Bouton — the quiet kid from Illinois who I found as a high school kid, hid in the prison games, signed with the Yankees and watched win 21 games in just his second big league season — had turned the baseball world on its nose with a memoir of his 1969 season with the Seattle Pilots and Houston Astros called, *Ball Four*.

The book was a collaboration with a sportswriter Bouton became close with in New York, and it's no overstatement to say it changed the way people saw baseball and the men who played it at the highest levels.

Before that book, there was something of an unwritten code that what happened in the clubhouse should always stay in the clubhouse. Baseball writers — even the great ones —would look the other way when they heard about players being out drunk, or running around with women in the bars, things like that. All the dirty jokes, drug use, basically everything that you wouldn't talk about in polite company or at the dinner table, the sportswriters wouldn't write about it.

But Bouton changed all of that, and he didn't hold anything back. He even talked about his own drug use, and the insecurities and uncertainty he felt going through a big league season. That was another eye-opener. Big leaguers had usually been seen as these powerful, fearless stars who didn't have any problems with confidence or self-esteem. Bouton told everything, right down to the cliques and disagreements that mark every baseball team.

One of the biggest revelations of the book was Mickey Mantle's drinking. The stories are now so well known that maybe it's hard to imagine a time when they were stunning, but nobody outside baseball really knew about it before Bouton's book.

He was always a smart guy, and I guess unaffected by convention, so Bouton stepped outside the baseball norm and brought the world into the clubhouse. But he was always so quiet, so nice, you never would've had any idea that all of this would come from him.

The baseball world freaked out. The commissioner came out and said it was bad for the game. He actually tried to get Bouton to say the whole book was made up, but Bouton refused and some of the guys he played with never forgave him.

There are stories about Pete Rose and other stars screaming at Bouton in games after the book came out. He became a pariah, of sorts, in the baseball world. Many felt that Bouton betrayed their trust.

I'll always love Jim. I was never mad at him, and we've always stayed in touch. But some of my best friends in baseball always looked at me as the guy who signed the guy who shook up the sport.

At the time, they couldn't imagine anything bigger or more personal. Then another guy I signed did something even more outrageous.

• • •

Today, you see the media circus created when Michael Sam, the former University of Missouri football player, announces he's gay before the NFL draft.

Well, what if two high-level professional athletes traded wives?

That's exactly what happened in the early 1970s.

I still don't know exactly how it got started. I was with the Royals by the time everything went down. I've heard a lot of stories, including that it really got going at a party when Mike Kekich took Fritz Peterson's wife home from a party, and Peterson drove Kekich's wife home from the same party. At the time, Kekich and Peterson were both in the Yankees rotation, about the same age. It made sense that they would be friends. They had a lot in common. But you couldn't imagine anything like this.

I'd never heard of anyone just trading families.

But that's how it happened. Kekich and Peterson were close friends, and they announced their "deal" in separate news conferences during spring training before the 1973 season. They traded wives, children, even dogs. You think the Royals made a big trade in getting James Shields, this was like the blockbuster trade to end all blockbusters.

The media circus that followed that was unlike most anything I'd ever seen. It's easy to look back on this now as the natural progression of things, as times changing, but back then it was pretty radical.

That was really the first time that papers and news networks had talked about the personal lives of professional athletes. It wasn't that athletes didn't do crazy things, or stray from their marriages from time to time. It's just that it wasn't broadcasted, or written about in the papers. Just like with Bouton's book, the commissioner went public to say he disapproved.

In some ways, the wife-swapping became a symbol to some people about how the Yankees had changed.

Kekich and Peterson's wife didn't last, but to this day, Peterson and Kekich's ex-wife are still together.

Kekich actually changed his name, and you don't hear from him much. But Peterson has always been around, and was even a chaplain for Major League Baseball for a time.

Ben Affleck and Matt Damon announced they wanted to make a movie about it called "The Trade," and even got Peterson to sign on as a consultant.

We'll see.

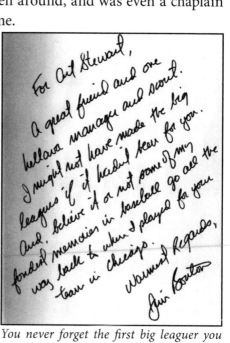

. . .

By the time all this stuff happened, I was with the Royals, so my involvement with two of baseball's biggest scandals in the early 1970s was mostly on the fringe.

I'd hear about it from my friends, of course, most of it good-natured but also from some who didn't like that two guys (whether I signed them or not) were shaking the baseball establishment like this.

After the wife-swapping thing came out, I got a call from Roy Hamey, my old general

*You never forget the first big leaguer you sign, and for a lot of big leaguers, they don't forget the scout who gave them a chance. I think the bond I had with Jimmy was heightened not just because I helped him and he was my first big leaguer, but because he played for me those years with the Chicago Yankees. This is the inscription from Jimmy on the copy of "Ball Four" that he sent me. A lot of people remember that book for rocking baseball with the secrets Jim told.*

manager with the Yankees who by then was retired. I answered the phone and heard Hamey's bulldog voice.

"What's going on with this, Art?" he said. "These guys you're signing, they keep creating these controversies that are upsetting the commissioner's office."

I stopped him.

"But Roy," I said. "They were both 20-game winners for the New York Yankees, weren't they?"

And it was never brought up again.

• • •

Of course, to most of the baseball world and general public, Bouton will always be the guy who wrote the book that exposed so much about what goes on behind the scenes in big league baseball. And Peterson will always be the guy who wife-swapped.

I'll remember those things, too, but when you're a scout you see the world a little differently. To me, Bouton and Peterson each represent scouting successes — talented players off the beaten path who we found, identified, signed and helped become successful big league pitchers.

I'll also remember them as the embodiments of two sound pieces of scouting advice, which you could alter by personalizing them.

I didn't leave the ballpark early on that spring day in 1957, which meant the other scouts left me alone to see an overlooked, hard-throwing pitcher who I ended up hiding in prison games and eventually watched win 21 games for the New York Yankees.

And:

I always followed up on letter writers, because by definition they are showing they love baseball and want to play, and I once watched a letter writer dominate a game at a ballpark with a cornfield for an outfield fence, eventually signed him under the White Sox's nose at Comiskey Park, and then became a 20-game winner with the Yankees.

Of course, it helps that they each come with great stories you can tell at parties.

# 14

# The greatest age in baseball's greatest franchise

*T*he most distinctive part of the Yankees' mystique is the pinstripes. You can talk about Babe Ruth and Mickey Mantle and Joe DiMaggio and Derek Jeter, but when you talk about everything the Yankees have stood for over the years, chances are at some point you're going to mention the pinstripes on the home uniforms.

The Yankees aren't the only team to put pinstripes on uniforms. The Cubs, probably most notably, have worn pinstripes for years and years. The Mets have done it. The Twins, the Phillies, a lot of teams.

But the Yankees made pinstripes famous. Those crisp, white home uniforms — never with names on the back — are the connection between the Yankees' first World Series champion in 1923 under Miller Huggins all the way to the last one in 2009 with Joe Girardi, Alex Rodriguez and C.C. Sabathia.

And you know why those pinstripes have endured?

I learned it in one of my first years with the Yankees, when George Weiss, the great Hall of Fame general manager, addressed a meeting of club scouts and executives.

"Gentlemen," I remember him saying, "we will always wear pinstripes, because pinstripes make a player look bigger."

That was the thinking behind it. If the other team thinks we're bigger than we actually are, maybe that plays in their minds a little bit.

I don't know if that works. It hasn't done the Cubs much good over the years. But it became synonymous with the Yankees' success, to the point that when people ask about my time with the Yankees, sometimes they phrase it like this:

"What was it like working all those years with the pinstripes?"

Well, I'll tell you what it was like.

• • •

There were so many strong personalities, and I don't just mean the stars people think of with the Yankees — guys like Mickey, DiMaggio, Yogi and Casey.

Hank Bauer was the toughest man who's ever played this game. He played rightfield for us for about 11 years, and later became a successful manager — he won the 1966 World Series with the Orioles. This is a guy raised as the youngest of nine children in East St. Louis, the son of an Austrian immigrant who lost a leg working the mills.

Hank joined the Marines after Pearl Harbor, and got malaria in Guadalcanal. He wasn't going to stop, though, and stayed in combat for nearly three years, earning two Purple Hearts. They say that his unit was ambushed by the Japanese, and only six of 60-some Marines survived. Hank was one of them even though he took some shrapnel. Just surviving what he went through with the Marines would be one thing, but then Hank returned to baseball and made three All-Star teams, and helped the Yankees win seven world championships.

*This is a picture that Yogi Berra signed for me. Yogi was the heart of some of the Yankees' best teams, both his personality and talent behind the plate.*

You didn't want to mess with Hank, either. He played baseball the same way he fought for his country. I remember once in Chicago, at old Comiskey Park, a relief pitcher we'd just brought up blew a two-run lead. After the game, the guys are filing into the visitors' clubhouse, and if you ever went into the visitors' clubhouse there you knew it was pretty cramped, with trunks lined up down the middle separating the small room.

"Hey, no big deal," the relief pitcher said. "We're still up in the standings."

Well, that set Hank off something fierce. Hank goes lunging across those trunks like a madman, and gets to this kid, pushes him up against the wall and grabs him by the throat.

"You dirty son of a bitch!" he's screaming. "We play every inning of every game to win, and if you're going to be part of this club you better start now or I'm going to kill you, you bastard!"

It took Yogi Berra, Mickey Mantle and Gene Woodling to get Bauer off this guy. That kind of thing wouldn't be tolerated the same way today, of course, but I'll say this, that pitcher learned what the Yankees were all about.

Those guys were like warriors. Every game was a war to them. That's how they approached it. They *had* to win. They had a lot of talent, many Hall of Famers, but that mentality is a big part of what made those teams so special.

• • •

Of course, not *everyone* was wired like Hank. Mickey Mantle was famous for not only what he did on the field, but what he did off it, too. Everyone with the Yankees knew he liked to have fun after the games, and they'd try to guide him in certain ways, but really what could they complain about when he was playing the way he was playing?

One night, again in Chicago, we're staying at the old Del Prado Hotel. They used to have a restaurant-bar-lounge type place in there called the Bamboo Hut. They had this bamboo hanging from the ceiling in a way that you could sort of hide out if you found the right spot. Well, this was in the days when Casey Stengel was managing us and he loved to hide out in there to see who was missing the 12:30 a.m. curfew.

One night I'm sitting in there with Mel Allen and Casey, and when that happens the time tends to fly by. On this night, it gets to be 2 or 3 in the morning and here comes Mickey into the hotel. Casey sees him. We all see him. But Mickey can't see us, so he just goes up to his room.

The next day, before batting practice, Casey calls Mickey into his office.

"What time did you get in last night?"

"Oh, Skip, I just beat the curfew by 15 minutes."

"Well, Mick, you must have a twin brother I saw coming in at 3 in the morning then."

Mickey looked like a boy caught with his hand in the cookie jar.

"Yeah, I guess I was a little late."

"That's going to be a fine, Mick. See me after the game."

So the game starts, and Mickey is hitting the ball all over the field. He hits this towering home run in the third, got another hit in the fifth, drove in three runs and basically won the game for us.

So afterward, Mickey comes into Casey's office.

"How much do I owe, Skip?"

Casey looks at him and sort of grumbles.

"Don't worry about it, today. We'll talk about it later."

Mickey never paid that fine. What could Casey do?

• • •

There were a lot of advantages to scouting for the Yankees in those days. Most of the time I worked for them was before the first-year player draft started in 1965, which was good for us in two very important ways.

First, a lot of the players we're scouting grew up Yankees fans, so the idea of joining the Yankees was very appealing to them. Second, the team made a lot of money, and understood the importance of investing in the best amateur players to keep the machine running.

Of course, that didn't always mean we got our guy.

Back in 1961 or so, I saw one of the best young pitching prospects of my life. His name was Denny McLain, from Mt. Carmel High School on the south side of Chicago. He had such a great arm, that fastball came in like an aspirin tablet.

Interesting thing about young Denny. It was almost always fastballs with him, sometimes changeups, but never curveballs or other breaking pitches. I got to know his father fairly well, so I asked his dad about it one day.

"I've never seen Denny throw a breaking ball," I said.

"And you never will," Mr. McLain said.

"How's that?" I shot back.

"All you'll see is a fastball and changeup," he said. "I want him to build up the strongest and most powerful arm in baseball, and I don't think a young player growing up can do that throwing breaking pitches."

And that was it. Mr. McLain was a strong presence in his son's life, so what he said went. That was important to remember later, before Denny's senior year of high school, when Mr. McLain tragically passed away. Denny's uncle took over the negotiations. He was close with the father, and swore to represent the family the way Mr. McLain wanted, which meant signing for the biggest bonus.

Denny had a very strong senior year, like you'd expect. There were no radar guns in those days, of course, but just eye balling it his fastball was probably 95 to 98 miles per hour. Toward the end of his senior year, he came upon a rough stretch, where he actually had a bit of a dead arm. Some clubs backed off, but I talked to his doctor who assured me there was nothing structurally wrong with his arm.

But because of the concerns there, it ended up only being about five teams that were heavy on Denny when it came time to negotiate a pro contract. I got the next to the last appointment with the family, and Denny was very excited. He wanted to be a Yankee, and told me as much.

Well, there was a rule back then, where if you signed a kid for more than $8,000 you had to keep him on the major league club for two years. The Yankees hated this rule, because with the teams we had in those days, we were always trying to win pennants. We didn't like the idea of keeping such a young player on the big league roster, taking up a spot that would've gone to a veteran who could help us win games — not to mention the possibility of disrupting the young player's development.

But there are exceptions to every rule, so I called Roy Hamey, our general manager at the time, and told him the situation: The kid wants to play for us, but he's so talented that he's going to get offers for more than the $8,000. If we can just match what other teams are offering, we'll get him. And I think he's worth it.

"We shouldn't do this," Roy said. "But I'll give you $12,000."

Denny thought $12,000 was good enough, but he also promised the White Sox he'd meet one more time with them. The next night, the phone rings around 7 in the evening. Donna tells me who it is.

"Denny," I say into the phone, "are you ready to be a Yankee?"

"I only have a minute or two, Mr. Stewart," he says. "But the White Sox have offered $15,000. I really want to be a Yankee, but we promised my dad we'd take the best offer."

"Dennis, where are you?"

"I'm at Comiskey Park. I told them I had to take a leak, and I'm calling you from a phone booth."

"Give me the number. Stay right there. I'll call you back."

I hang up, and call Roy.

"Roy, we have Denny McLain for $15,000," I say. "I just need $3,000 more."

"Art," he says, "we're $4,000 over the limit already. Another $3,000 to carry a young player for two years with no guarantees, on *this* team? I can't do it. I can't give it to you."

We were both so disappointed. I call Denny back.

"I'm sorry," I tell him.

"Me, too," he says.

Well, you know what happened with Denny. He signed with the White Sox, but they ended up letting him go a year later because of the rule about carrying a guy on the big league club. The White Sox had to choose between Denny and Bruce Howard (who, coincidentally, is the father of David Howard, the former utility player for the Royals). They chose Bruce, and the Tigers picked up Denny.

Denny took a few years to get going, but once he did, he was the best pitcher in baseball. He made his first All-Star team at 22, and by 24 won the Cy Young *and* MVP award. His 1968 season — baseball lowered the mound after this year to make the game more fair for the hitters — is one of the greatest statistical seasons a pitcher has ever had.

He went 31-6 (nobody has won 30 games in the big leagues since) with a 1.96 ERA in 336 innings. He completed 28 of his 41 starts, struck out 280, walked just 63, and allowed the fewest baserunners per inning of anyone in the American League.

His career was later derailed by some problems with drugs and the law, but for a time there he was the best in baseball.

The fact that we didn't get Denny bothered Roy and I the rest of our lives.

As a scout, you usually think about guys you lost more than the guys you get.

• • •

I still think I could've signed Lou Brock for the Yankees, if not for a scout who later became famous as one of baseball's greatest ambassadors.

This is back in the late 1950s, and the scout's name was Buck O'Neil. Even if some were slow to recognize it, those of us in the game knew that Buck was one of the top scouts in the country. He had such a great eye, and that gentle demeanor belied a tough, tough competitive streak.

They held the Pan Am Games at Wrigley Field, and Brock was playing centerfield for the American team. The Pan Am Games were a very big deal then. Everybody played.

Brock was outstanding, doing everything you want to see in a centerfield prospect. The Yankees gave me $35,000 to sign him, which I thought would be enough, or at least very close to it. Brock set up appointments for the day after the tournament, at a hotel on the south side of Chicago.

*Ralph Houk was the toughest man to ever play this great game. He was a major in the Army during World War II, and won a Purple Heart and Silver Star, and other awards. He also won a lot of games with the Yankees with a no-compromising, every-game-is-a-battle attitude.*

About a dozen teams had appointments, going one hour each, starting at 8 in the morning. Tom Greenwade, our legendary scout, was with me and our appointment was one of the last of the day, at 5 in the evening. We get over there a little early, and we see the guys who had the 4 o'clock appointment walk out of the room. They tell us there's nobody in there.

"You guys waiting for that young ballplayer?" said a gentleman who worked at the hotel. "He left early this morning with someone."

Well, what happened was that Buck had such a good relationship with Brock that he convinced him to bypass all the appointments and sign with him.

That's good scouting right there. Buck got a future Hall of Famer to so completely trust him that he didn't even listen to any of these other offers.

Buck and I remained friends for more than 50 years.

• • •

Like I said, scouting for the Yankees had its advantages, but that doesn't mean we didn't work hard. Doesn't mean we weren't creative, or aggressive, and let me tell you how we signed Mike Jurewicz.

Jurewicz was a premium pitcher with Pius High School in Milwaukee in 1962. He pitched his last game in the state high school tournament, and struck out something like 19 batters in a one-hit shutout. All the clubs were on him, and the ones the Jurewicz family liked the best had appointments the next day.

*Mike Jurewicz is one of my favorites signings of all-time. I sneaked into the house to sort of spy on the Orioles scout who was in ahead of me. I knew the Orioles' offer, and got him switched and signed with the Yankees. He's still the youngest pitcher to start a game for the Yankees, and could've been one of the greats if his arm held up.*

Mine was the last appointment — you might sense this as a theme; I always angled for the final appointment because I thought it was good to leave the last impression — which was scheduled for midnight.

Right before me, the 11 o'clock appointment,

was Phil Gallivan, the old Orioles scout. Gallivan was a pitcher for the White Sox for a brief time, and then became one heck of a scout. Aggressive, too. If he saw a kid at a tournament he liked, Gallivan would fly him right out of the tournament to Baltimore and get him signed.

Sometimes, just as a joke between us scouts, we'd see a plane flying over a game that says, "There goes Gallivan with a shortstop!"

So, anyway, with Jurewicz I get to the house a little before midnight, so I can be through the door as soon as Gallivan leaves. But it's getting past midnight. It's 12:05, then 12:10, now it's 12:15 and Gallivan isn't out. So I go down to the corner drug store, for a phone booth, and call the house.

Mr. Jurewicz answers and says his wife and Gallivan are still talking. Give us 15 or 20 more minutes, he says. Well, that's no good for me. They're really striking up a good relationship if they're still going like this.

So I get edgy, nervous, and when I get back to my spot in front of their house I don't want to just wait. I walk around the back of the house, and there's a door there, into the basement. I turn the knob, push the door, and it's wide open. I'm sneaking into the house. I probably could've been arrested, but at this point, I really want to sign this kid.

The way the house is set up, there are some stairs going up from the basement to the kitchen, where they're having their conversation. But about halfway up the stars, there's a vent, and I can hear what they're saying clear as day.

"Twelve thousand," I hear Gallivan say. "We'll start you in instructional league, but you have a chance to get up to the big leagues really fast."

I can tell they're leaving, so I race like hell out of the house and stand in front of my car. Gallivan comes marching out of the house, and he's just so confident. He even has a date set up for the next day, he's going to take the family out to a nice breakfast at the Pfister Hotel, which was a really plush place there in Milwaukee.

"Good luck, Art," Gallivan says to me. "But you're wasting your time."

Well, he didn't know I'd snuck in the house and knew he'd offered $12,000 — and he certainly didn't know I had $15,000 from the Yankees.

So we get into the house, and we're talking for about 15, 20 minutes when Mrs. Jurewicz goes upstairs to sleep with the expectation that her boy will be an Oriole.

Except I knew he wanted to be a Yankee, and by knowing what the Orioles offered the sales pitch was pretty easy. It didn't take long once I got in front of Mike. He dreamed of being a Yankee, so we talked about what that would be like deep into the night until it's about 3 in the morning.

"Dad," Mike says, "I want to sign with the Yankees."

"You know your mother really likes the Orioles," Mr. Jurewicz says. "She'll want to talk about it."

He goes upstairs to wake up his wife, and I assume he told her what was happening, but she was half asleep and maybe didn't remember because the next morning she's mad as hell. She's not the only one. Gallivan comes to the house the next morning to take them to breakfast, not knowing that Mike was now a Yankee. He was stunned at first, then angrier than the mom.

That's OK. Instead of the breakfast, I offered to take the Jurewiczes out to dinner at the Pfister. She's not too friendly at first, but we put on what we call the Yankee Spread at the hotel. No expenses are sparred for something like this, and by the time the evening was over, she was my best pal.

Mike Jurewicz ended up pitching at Yankee Stadium younger than any pitcher in Yankee history. I truly believe he'd have been one of the great pitchers in baseball, but his arm gave out after that first season. It was an elbow tear, the same thing they fix with Tommy John surgery now, but of course back then there was no such thing.

That elbow injury robbed him of a bigger place in baseball history. But the fact that the Jurewiczes didn't lock their back door means I'll never forget him.

# Chapter
# 15

# How the Royals Academy innovated scouting

*E*wing Kauffman always wanted an edge. That's what made him so successful in business, and eventually, that's what made him so successful in baseball. Nothing was good enough, at least not until Mr. K was convinced nothing was better.

He was so good at this. You'd tell him how something was, and he'd ask a dozen questions about why it couldn't be better. More times than not, those questions would unlock something you'd never thought of before, something that *could* make it better.

And then, Mr. K would sit back, give you all the resources you needed to make it happen, and never ask for any of the credit.

This is basically how he got the idea for the Baseball Academy. He didn't like that the pools of talent available to him were basically limited to the expansion draft and first-player draft. He thought there should be more ways to get players into the system, and figured that baseball was missing some talented high school and college kids — either because those players hadn't had the proper instruction, or maybe hadn't played enough baseball.

The idea was fairly simple. If you had all the great basketball players in the country who were too short to be top college or professional players, you'd have a lot of excellent athletes with the kinds of tools that might translate to the baseball field with top coaching. If you had hundreds and hundreds of "sales leads" like that, maybe you can find the next Mickey Mantle or Tom Seaver in there somewhere.

Kauffman basically wanted to create a pipeline of athletically gifted kids that would be exclusive to the Royals.

I have to be honest here, before we go in depth about the Royals Academy. Even with the respect and admiration I had for that man from the very first time I met him, I was skeptical about this.

Tryout camps?

We never did tryout camps with the Yankees, and I don't know of too many other teams around baseball that bothered. What was the point? A scout's job is to know where the good players are. Tryout camps, we thought, were a waste of time. A lot of to-do just so you can watch a bunch of kids who aren't good enough.

I heard that a lot from other scouts I knew around baseball, too.

"You're wasting your time."

"You're spinning your wheels."

*Photo Courtesy of Kansas City Royals*

*Helping start the Royals Academy was one of the defining experiences of my career. I didn't think it was worth it going in, but I loved working so closely with the prospects and watching them develop.*

And I didn't argue with them too much. In my heart, I didn't know if this would work.

But I also knew it's what my boss wanted, so I was going to give it my full effort. I'm glad I did, because it was one of the most enjoyable experiences of all my years in baseball — and a grassroots scouting effort that helped establish the foundation of our great teams in the 1970s and 1980s.

*This is the brochure we sent to around 7,000 high schools across the country announcing the Royals Baseball Academy. This had never been done before, so we had to make sure the publicity campaign announced it to the world. The turnout we got from this switched me from a tryout doubter, to a tryout believer.*

After that, those friends of mine giving me grief were instead jealous that we'd found all this talent.

• • •

The first thing we had to do was get the word out. Nobody had ever tried something like this, so we needed to make players and coaches aware. We needed to explain to them what this was.

We hired a public relations man named Sam Ketchum, and he put together what had to be one of the biggest PR campaigns in baseball history. He put together a questionnaire and brochure to send to nearly 8,000 high schools around the country.

We wanted to hear from anyone, but specifically athletic directors and coaches who might know of an athletic kid who hasn't had much time in baseball. We set up tryout camps all over the country, and Sam would go in a few days ahead of time to publicize. He'd put up flyers in store windows and light posts. He was really good at his job, getting us in the papers and on radio and TV. We were even in *Sports Illustrated*, so the problem was never going to be lack of awareness.

We made a lot of big promises to these kids, which was important. We told them — and by extension their parents and coaches — that we would use "the most modern, scientific methods" to identify talent, and then we would take care of them first-class all the way.

Boys selected from our tryout camps would be flown to the campus in Sarasota, where they'd live in a hotel-type dorm, eat tasty and nutritious meals, and have their first two years of college education paid for.

The way we had it set up, you'd go to class in the morning — English, speech, and finance classes, especially — and then the afternoons were devoted to baseball. If we took you into the Academy, it was all free for you. We even paid for your health insurance, and all medical care, and you got a salary. It cost the Royals about $1,000 to keep one student in the Academy for a month.

It was a beautiful complex, too. They had five baseball fields, each exactly the size of Royals Stadium. Eight pitching machines, and enough bullpen space for 18 pitchers to warm up at once. The locker rooms were big enough for 254 players.

Wasn't just baseball, either. They had an Olympic-sized pool, tennis courts, squash courts. Even two big lakes, that Mr. K stocked with fish on his own father's suggestion. Funny thing about those lakes, this being Florida, eventually alligators found the lake. One morning, Syd Thrift, who ran the Academy, woke up and found a big alligator sitting on his porch.

Once we got going, we had a great run of guest instructors, none better than the greatest hitter who ever lived, Ted Williams. We also had Wes Santee, the track star from Kansas, teaching the guys proper running technique. Mickey Vernon, who led the league in hitting one year, came down to work with them.

Tommy Henrich, who started in the Yankee outfield with Joe DiMaggio, helped out. And Charley Lau, the great hitting coach, would come down after the big league season and go through hitting technique with his video camera. Buzz Keller was our manager down there, and he was perfect for that team. Just a really good instructor, a lively guy.

So, hey, other than the alligators, this is a pretty good deal for the player, right?

But first you had to make it.

• • •

The first camp I ran was on June 6, 1970. They gave me Illinois, so we did the camp in Peoria, the day after the high school state baseball tournament finished.

I was still holding my skepticism about this whole deal, but that started to dissolve almost immediately. You see, we had the camp at Meinen Field, which is what they called Bradley University's home stadium at the time. There was a running track outside the field that led to the gate, which we had locked until registration started at 9 a.m.

We got there at 7, and there were already 100 kids in line.

And you know what else? The first kid in that line — the very first kid to fill out an information card for the Royals Academy — was a big, strong 16-year-old catcher named Danny Goodwin.

Now, that name might not mean much to you but Danny Goodwin has the distinction of being the only player in baseball history to be drafted No. 1 overall out of high school, *and* No. 1 overall out of college.

The White Sox took him first overall in 1971, and then the Angels took him first overall in 1975. I'm not sure why he didn't sign out of high school. His father was a very smart man, a chemist. Maybe the family wanted him to go to college. Whatever the case, Goodwin ended up playing parts of seven years in the big leagues, though he never became the great player a lot of us predicted.

But either way, his presence there — and first in line! — made it obvious to me that we were attracting some top players to these camps. Obviously, Goodwin was much too good of a prospect to need our tryout camp, but if holding these things across the country gave us an early (and exclusive) look on some players we'd be discussing in our draft rooms, then they were worth the time.

The way I saw it, a bit of baseball history was made there in what we were building.

• • •

After the turnout of that first camp, I knew the second camp would be a success, which was held in Chicago, the place I knew better than anywhere else in the world.

I put the camp at McKinley Park, which was at Western Avenue and Pershing Street. The location was important, because north of that park the city was mostly white and south of the park the city was mostly black. Having it at McKinley gave us the best chance at drawing from both sides of the city. We wanted it to be as inclusive as possible.

The park was also outlined by two bus lines, which made it accessible. If you can picture this, the fields there were sunk down a bit from the area around them. You could look up and see both bus lines unloading, and all morning, you're just seeing bus after bus unload dozens and dozens of kids with their bags and gloves and bats. It really was something, being down there and seeing all these talented kids coming at us in droves. At one point, Ketchum was so happy with the turnout he screamed out, "It looks like Normandy!"

By the time we started the camp, we had 408 kids in there. Combined with another camp we did the next day, we saw more than 600 kids we never would've seen otherwise in just two days.

You can imagine the logistics of getting that many prospects a fair look, but we were well prepared. We split them up and put them onto three fields — one for pitchers and catchers, one for infielders, and one for outfielders.

I had Dick Drott, who pitched for the Cubs and Astros, working with the pitchers and catchers. Al Smith, an All-Star outfielder and starter on the White Sox's American League championship team, worked with the outfielders. Then I got some associate scouts who had time in pro ball, and we worked with the infielders.

Any time you invite the public to come to a tryout for professional baseball, you're going to get some people who don't belong. I remember one guy came in with a big water tank on his back, ready for the whole day, but we had to turn him away because he was almost 30 years old.

The requirements were pretty simple. You had to be 22 years old or younger, and really, what we were looking for was athleticism. We wanted athletes with the tools to be big league baseball players, and then we'd turn them over to coaches who would bring out that ability.

The rule — and this was a strict rule — said that you had to show an average or above average arm, and you had to run the 60-yard dash in 6.9 seconds or better, which meant you were at least an average major league runner.

We didn't sign anybody out of that first camp, but we got a lot of names and phone numbers of kids we'd follow over the next year and eventually it turned into quite an asset for us.

The first prospect we signed out of a tryout camp was Orestes Minoso, who everyone called "Minnie" after his father. He was so smooth in the outfield, and made it to Omaha but couldn't hit the good breaking balls once he got that high in the system.

The first big leaguer we got out of a tryout camp was Tom Bruno, who got called up in 1976 to join our first division championship team. He was taken by Toronto in the expansion draft that winter, which means the organization got a good return on its investment.

Another guy we got the second year was Sheldon Mallory, who got some big league time with the A's. Mallory could run like hell, he broke some stolen base records in the minor leagues. We traded him for Pete LaCock, who played on three playoff teams in four years with us.

What I'm getting at here is it wasn't just Frank White, Ron Washington and 12 other big leaguers we found in the Academy. It was an infusion of talent that helped the organization build depth, and the big league team in many ways.

Like the case of Winston Cole.

• • •

Winston Cole was a big first baseman we signed out of a camp in the second year. We thought he had some potential, but he didn't make it two years with us before he helped us in a bigger way.

The big league team was trying to trade for Nelson Briles and the deal just wasn't going anywhere. The Pirates wanted a major league prospect. We didn't want to give up any of the guys they were asking for, and they didn't want to take any of the guys we were offering.

But at some point, Danny Murtaugh, the manager who led the Pirates to two World Series championships, walked in the room and told them he saw our Gulf Coast League team and really liked the first baseman.

We agreed, and we got Nelson Briles, who pitched two years in our rotation, winning 16 games the first year, and then we traded him for an outfielder who helped our big league team, too.

"The deal wouldn't have been made if Winston Cole hadn't been included," said Joe Brown, the Pirates' GM at the time.

I'll tell you, those Academy kids tended to look better when they were together. It really was a talented group, and if you watched them over a period of time, they sort of fed off each other. They were all competing against each other for promotions, of course, but there was also a camaraderie there — they were learning the game together, progressing together, building good relationships together.

And, boy, could they play.

That first class gathered in Sarasota on Aug. 10, 1970. They played 241 games together before graduating in December of 1971, and they won 162 of them — a .672 win percentage. That included the Gulf Coast League championship. They also went to Latin America for a 10-day tour, and went 10-4.

Word was getting out, and quick. These kids we signed off the street for nothing could play.

But there remained some skepticism.

• • •

Early in the process of the Academy, I came home from a trip and had a message to return a call from Lou Gorman, one of my bosses at the time.

"I know you just got home and your wife probably hasn't even washed your clothes yet," Gorman said. "But there's 10 days left in the Gulf Coast League, and we need a report on this first Academy class."

As it turns out, Mr. K was getting all kinds of different views on the Academy kids. Some people were telling him we had as many as 12 big league prospects, and some of the other owners were telling him the word was no prospects — just a big waste of time.

Mr. K wanted to know the deal.

So I go down to the Gulf Coast League, and I'm there a week, maybe a little bit more. It's the first time I've seen all these kids together, and I'm there to write a report on every player.

The guys I remember most vividly to this day are Minoso in centerfield, Frank White at short and our little jumping jack catcher — Ron Washington.

Frank was so smooth out there in the field. He was a big league defender even back then, at 19 or 20 years old. He just had that natural grace about him, with terrific instincts and baseball intelligence.

And with Ron Washington, you saw those leadership traits right from the beginning. He was too small to be a catcher, and we figured he'd have to change positions, but he was such a natural leader. Between hitters, he's yelling over at Frank, "Shade this guy up the middle!" You'd watch, and the guy would hit a grounder up the middle. Mr. K would be so proud if he could see Ron now, a big league manager who's been to the World Series.

Anyway, the games are going pretty well, and I'm about halfway through with the trip when Gorman calls.

"That Frank White kid is really playing well at shortstop," I said.

"Be careful how you write him up," Gorman said. "We think he may be older than he says, and that's why he's looking better."

Well, coincidentally, the next day I'm talking to Joe Tanner, who was working with our base runners and he tells me he has to go help Frank buy a car.

Because of the conversation with Lou the night before, that piqued my interest.

"Frank's not old enough to buy it on his own," Tanner told me. "He needs me to help him sign for it."

So then I knew his age was correct. I'm not sure where people got the idea that he was older, other than he was a big kid, and obviously developed physically. After that, I wrote him up as a big league prospect.

That scouting report is in the Royals Hall of Fame. You can see there that Frank became a much better player than I projected him. There was never any question about Frank's athletic ability or desire, just an uncertainty about whether he could hit enough.

*Here's a picture from Frank White's 2,000th hit that he signed for me. Frank is a dear friend and the best player we found in the Academy. A lot of people around baseball thought Frank was older than he was saying, but once we found out his age was real it just reinforced that we had a solid big leaguer on our hands. As it turned out, he was better than any of us predicted.*

I had no way of knowing then that Frank would play 18 years for us, make five All-Star teams, win eight Gold Gloves and bat cleanup for our World Series championship team in 1985. I certainly had no idea that I'd be there speaking at the unveiling of his statue in front of our stadium so many years later.

Frank went on to broadcast our games for many years, and has always been active in the community. You never know the different paths in life that will be presented, but the Royals and Kansas City are much better off for the Academy providing a way for Frank to display his talents.

*Photo Courtesy of Kansas City Royals*

• • •

My best day scouting our Academy began just before the first pitch of a game against the Pirates' Gulf Coast team. A big blue Cadillac pulled up to the field, and when you saw that you knew the owner was in town.

Mr. K had his wife, Muriel, with him. They pulled out two beautiful, upholstered Royals chairs and asked me to sit next to them. Mr. K had a smile on his face that entire day, smoking his pipe, watching his kids, asking a million questions about each kid and how we signed him.

I'm not sure he's ever rooted harder for the Royals, other than a big league playoff game.

By then, I had done many tryout camps, of course. I was prideful about what we were doing with the Academy — beating the system in a way, finding kids that every other franchise was ignoring.

And I knew that Mr. K had been hearing conflicting reports about how our kids stacked up, so I wanted him to know the real deal. I happened to know the bonuses of most of the kids on the Pirates' team, so I'm pointing these things out to him.

"That shortstop got $35,000 to sign," I'd say. "The leftfielder got $20,000."

He's the owner, so these things are important to him. All of our guys, we signed for practically nothing. The owner should know what he's getting for his money, compared to what other teams are getting for their money.

We beat the Pirates pretty soundly that day, and after the game, you could hear their coaches yelling.

"You guys signed for all this money, and a team full of guys who got nothing just embarrassed you!"

You can't overstate how good that was for me to hear, having been part of getting the Academy off the ground, right in front of our owner.

Mr. K liked hearing it, too.

When he left, he packed those chairs back into the Cadillac and turned to me. Winked.

"Pretty good day, Art," he said.

He took as much pride in those Academy kids as he did our guys with the big league team, and the kids loved him just as much.

"When Mr. K comes to talk to us," Minoso told me once, "it's like electricity flies through the room. He's honest, and it wears off on you. You want to run through a wall after he speaks."

• • •

A few years after that, I came home one day and Donna pointed out a gold-embossed envelope in the mail from the Royals.

Everyone who worked for the Royals knew that if you got that gold-embossed envelope, it's only from one person, and that's the owner of the club.

So I opened that envelope, and it's a handwritten note from Mr. K.

*Dear Art,*

*I appreciate all you've done to make our Baseball Academy successful. As a token of my appreciation, I'm enclosing this stock certificate for 300 shares of King Radio. My people tell me this stock will increase significantly, and perhaps you can use it toward your daughter's education.*

*Sincerely,*

*Ewing Kauffman*

*p.s. I would appreciate if you would keep this confidential.*

Well, just like the stock I bought of Marion Labs, Mr. K was absolutely right about King Radio. It was a company started by an engineering student at Kansas State, and they made parts for gauges and things like that in airplanes.

The story of the Royals Academy says so much of what I think of Mr. K. He was willing to think outside the box, and try something new that baseball hadn't considered and initially mocked.

He then put his best people in charge of it, helping them brainstorm ideas to make it as successful as possible, and then rewarded us all when it became productive.

There's no question the Academy was productive. Frank White, an Academy product, and George Brett are the only two players with their numbers retired. U.L. Washington hitchhiked to a tryout camp and made it all the way to the big leagues. A lot of Royals fans will remember him for the toothpick he kept in his mouth when he played, and for hitting .364 in the American League Championship Series when we finally beat the Yankees in 1980.

He was our regular shortstop from 1979 to 1983, meaning that for some of the best teams in franchise history, our double-play combination was two kids we signed out of the Academy.

Other teams used high draft picks and lots of money to fill their middle infield, but we were able to find a good shortstop and a terrific second baseman for next to nothing. That freed us up to use our resources in other places, too, which just made the rest of the roster and organization stronger.

• • •

Unfortunately, the Academy closed in 1974. It lasted only five years, but changed the Royals and even baseball.

Today, if you look at the academies that every team has in the Dominican and Venezuela and throughout Latin America, they're all using the template created by the Royals Academy in Sarasota. It helped

*Mr. K would be so proud to know that Ron Washington, who got his chance in pro baseball through the Academy, is now one of the most successful managers in baseball. Wash was actually a catcher when we signed him, but he had good feet and quickness so we moved him to shortstop. Even then, you could see all the leadership qualities that would make him a good manager.*

revolutionize baseball in that way. Our own academy in the Dominican was driven by Luis Silverio, who was part of the Sarasota academy, and told to copy as much as he could.

Mr. K made the decision to close the Academy as a cost-cutting move. The Academy was running about $500,000 per year to operate, and without an immediate payoff — there was no way to *know* who would become good big leaguers for us, if anyone — it was an easy line on the ledgers to eliminate.

Many years later, Mr. K came into my office with a bit of a serious tone. His health wasn't great, we all knew that, and there were times he was more reflective than others.

"Art," he said, "I just want you to know that one of the biggest mistakes I ever made was letting them talk me into closing the Baseball Academy."

I hated seeing the Academy go, too, but it was still hard to hear that from Mr. K. There's no way to know what the Academy would've given us if we'd have kept it open. There were some baseball people who recognized its usefulness, but thought it had run its course.

I don't know. They could be right. But I think we'd have kept finding good prospects that fell through the cracks of the system.

Either way, helping run the Academy from the ground up was one of the great professional joys of my life.

# 16

# Siphoning gas, breaking and entering, and how baseball has gotten me out of speeding tickets

*T*his scouting life isn't for everyone.

You're on the road constantly, and especially when you're looking at the amateur players it's a lot of small towns and long drives on the highway. You get to know where the rest stops are between Eau Claire, Wisc., and Rockford, Ill. You start to feel like a truck driver at times, knowing exactly when the signal from the rock station in Carbondale fades into the country station in Peoria.

It's a hamburger and hot dog menu most of the time. You spend as much time in your car as you do watching players, and even when you get to the game the chances of you actually signing the player you went to see are small — and the chances of that player making an impact in the big leagues are even smaller.

You'll have your heart broken by a player far more often than you'll be proven right. How many other jobs can you fail around 90 percent of the time and have it considered a success?

This whole thing is so unpredictable, and your job is to predict it. You have to look at a boy who's 17 years old and bet a lot of your owner's money on what he will look like at 22 and 25.

You have to decide whether he'll learn to hit the kinds of exploding fastballs he's only seen on TV, and then whether he can adjust off that fastball to hit a good slider. You have to decide whether he has it in his gut to work, to believe through the failure, and to stay strong when he's away from home and his girlfriend, and he's making peanuts on the busses in the minor leagues.

You have to decide how this young man will adjust from sleepy crowds in small towns in the Carolina League to sellout crowds at Comerica Park in Detroit when Justin Verlander is throwing 99 mph in the ninth inning. You have to decide whether he can handle the attention of professional baseball, and not just the media, but the way friends and family might ask for favors and all the temptations of being a ballplayer on the road. The next talented player to be sidetracked by too many women on the road won't be the first, and he won't be the last.

Nobody can know any of these things for sure, of course. That's why the failure rate is so high. All you can do is gather your information, see the player as often as possible, and believe what you see, trust what your brain tells you and listen to what your heart says.

And when you see a boy you really like, and you're able to convince your bosses to sign or draft him, and then you get the chance to get to know him better and watch him develop through the minor leagues and all the way to the big leagues … when it happens like that, it makes every miss on every other player worth it.

Really, there is just no feeling like that for a scout. Signing an overlooked player and watching him turn into a big league star — like Bret Saberhagen in the 19th round out of Reseda, Calif., or Salvador Perez for $50,000 out of Venezuela — is the same feeling a player has hitting the game-winning home run or striking out the last batter with the bases loaded in a one-run game.

That's why we do this. That's why we put so much into this.

And if you can understand that feeling, and value it, then this scouting life is for you.

• • •

This is back when the Royals were still training in Baseball City. I'm the scouting director then, and Allard Baird, who later became our general manager, wants to go see a young high school phenom named Alex Rodriguez in Miami. Rodriguez was playing a night game, and it's quite a drive from Baseball City to Miami, so we're trying to make up some time.

Now, if you've ever driven through Florida you know about the section of I-75 they call Alligator Alley. If you don't, well, it's exactly what it sounds like. There are gators all over that part of the state, in the waterways by the road. Sometimes, you have to slow down and stop right there on the highway because there's a gator going across.

The other thing about Alligator Alley is there are no gas stations for about an 80-, 90-mile stretch there across the state. Or at least there weren't at the time. So the last stop before we hit that stretch, there's this Cuban place that Allard always liked to stop at for coffee. We grab some coffee and we're on the road, about halfway across the state, and a light comes on.

"Oh my gosh, Art," he says. "I forgot to fill the tank up. We're on empty."

Of all the places to run out of gas, Alligator Alley would not be your first choice. So now we're starting to get panicked, because there's no way we have enough gas to make it the rest of the way across. A mile goes by, two miles, five miles, and there's just nothing. The gauge is below empty now, we don't know how much further we can go, and we see a little driveway off the road.

We pull in, because this is our only hope. It's a sugar cane farm. Surely this man has some gas cans for his tractor and things. We pull up in front of the house and knock on the door. An older gentleman answers, and he apologizes, but he doesn't have any gas in the barn.

"I don't know what we're going to do," Allard tells me.

Then the farmer speaks up.

"Hold right here," he says. "I might be able to do something."

I'll never forget what happened next the rest of my days. He pulls his tractor up next to our car, puts one end of the hose into the gas tank on the tractor — and the other end in his mouth.

He's going to siphon gas from his tractor to our car.

I've never seen anything like it, before or since. This man is sucking gasoline out of one tank, and putting it in another tank — and doing it for strangers.

It looked like he'd done it before, because after a minute or two he's finished. He takes the hose out of his mouth and smiles at us.

"I think you have enough gas to get to the next stop," he says.

And we made it to Miami in time to see the game.

This wouldn't be the last time Alex Rodriguez was the centerpiece to a story about scouting.

• • •

Muzzy Jackson had just joined the Royals as an assistant in player development. He's a great guy, and would later become Allard's top assistant. But at the time, he was trying as many different spots of baseball operations as he could, trying to find what suited him best.

He knew that Brian Murphy and I always left the spring training complex after workouts to see amateur talent in the area, had heard some of the hype around Alex Rodriguez and found out Rodriguez's team was playing in Hernando that night. That's maybe a 60- or 70-mile drive from our complex, so Muzzy asks if he can tag along.

"I want to get some knowledge on scouting," he says.

Sure, let's do it. It's me, Muzzy and Murphy, another longtime scout who has been so productive for us. Murph is driving, and he's really blazing down Interstate 4 and soon enough we see the red lights flashing behind us.

He pulls over to the side of the road. It's the same conversation you probably have with the cop whenever you get pulled over, and it feels like Murph is about to get a ticket. The cop is a younger guy, probably in his 30s, so I try to talk a little bit.

"We're baseball scouts for the Royals," I say. "Just headed to Hernando to see one of the best high school players in the state."

I can tell that got the guy's interest.

We start talking about the Royals, and Bo Jackson, and George Brett, and I see the cop is starting to weaken a little bit. So I get an idea, and I'm trying to be undercover about it but I think we all know what's going on.

"Are you a baseball fan?" I say. "Spring training's going on, and if you want to see some games, give us your name and we'll make sure you have nice seats."

The cop kind of nods, and he turns to Murph.

"You'll get to the game on time," he says. "Just slow down."

• • •

We get to the game — on time; the cop was right — and Rodriguez is out there taking BP and the ball is shooting off his bat. It's line drive power to all fields, solid all across the diamond. In the warm ups, nobody's killing themselves out there, but you can tell the arm is there. You can tell he's loose, good feet, very impressive.

Then the game starts, and it's something else. His first time up he lines a double off the right center wall. Then later, he bunts — bunts! — and beats it down to first base. Already, we've seen that he can run, we've seen the line drive off the wall, the great bat speed, a lot of tools.

I mean, this was a game that my Aunt Nellie could've scouted.

Alex is out in the field, and he's making all the plays. Goes into the hole to gun a guy out, comes in on a ball and makes the bare-handed catch and throw, dives on one up the middle. He even got the play in the hole where the shortstop has jump up in the air — the play that Derek Jeter has since made famous — and gets the guy at first.

The game's tied, so we go into extras and Rodriguez hits a bomb right out of the stadium. Dead centerfield. Wins the game.

There's a bunch of scouts there — Rodriguez ended up being No. 1 on our board, and everyone else's, too — and we're sort of shaking our heads at each other. We all know we've seen something special. We pack up our stuff, head out to the parking lot, and Muzzy climbs in the back seat.

"Jeez," he says. "This scouting stuff is easy."

His first trip ended up being one of the greatest amateur talents in recent baseball history, putting on one of the great displays of ability you'd ever see.

I've been in the game more than 60 years, and I've only seen two prospects who even come close. When Paul Molitor was a shortstop in college for Minnesota, he basically swept Texas by himself in a three-game weekend series. He did everything then. Even stole home to win one game. And Barry Larkin made some spectacular plays in the field as a shortstop at Michigan when I saw him, and went 8-for-10 in a doubleheader sweep of Ohio State. Those are the only displays I can think of that even come close.

Muzzy saw it on his first trip.

• • •

So we're headed out from watching Rodriguez, going back to Baseball City, and we're about halfway there. We're around Clermont,

Fla., and Murph must be speeding again because we get pulled over. *Again.*

The guy comes up, and it's the same conversation. This guy's older than the one who pulled us over on the way up, but, what the heck, I think, I'll start the baseball thing again.

"Hi, officer, we're just some scouts on our way back from seeing Alex Rodriguez, one of the best prospects in the country."

This stops him. It's always a good sign when they stop.

"Where was the game?"

"Hernando," I say. "Right near the Ted Williams Museum."

That got him going.

"Williams was a hell of a player," he says.

"Yeah," I say. "I was lucky enough to see him in person."

That was it. That's when we had him. We start talking a little more about baseball, and about the Royals, and he lets us go.

In one day, we got out of two speeding tickets and saw one of the great amateur prospects of all-time.

· · ·

I don't know if I should say this in a book, but the great game has gotten me out of more than a few speeding tickets. The key to it is conversation. I always use baseball, because it's sort of a universal language.

I'm not saying it always works. I've paid a few speeding tickets. But I've gotten out of more than I've paid, and it's all because of baseball.

In some ways, it goes back to what Ewing Kauffman told all of us scouts. You have to be a good salesman. You have to be able to talk, and be ready for any situation, never flustered, and think on your feet.

So, yeah. I guess I sell baseball a little bit there.

I can't promise it'll work for you, of course. But it does for me.

· · ·

You hear a lot about baseball's unwritten rules. You know, like, don't steal a base when you're up seven runs, don't show up a hitter after a strikeout, and don't bunt to break up a no-hitter.

Well, in scouting, we have our own unwritten rules about how to conduct yourself. They mostly involve respecting your fellow scout and staying out of each other's way, and the "punishment" for breaking the rules can be creative.

This doesn't happen as much anymore, but if you were a young scout and a veteran scout didn't like something you did, you might go out to the parking lot after the game and find a flat tire or two on your car.

Once, I got to a high school game in Chicago and this old veteran scout named Tony Kauffman was there. It was early enough that nothing was really happening at the park, and Tony told me the game got moved to the South Side. At 99th and Pulaski Road. So I jump in my car and head out there, but there's no game. He put me on a wild goose chase.

Tony won that day, but later, when there was a pitcher at Simeon High School who we were all trying to see, I called over to see when the boy was scheduled to pitch. Leroy Franklin was the coach. He told me Tuesday. I knew Kauffman was going to be there.

"Any chance you could switch him to Monday?" I asked. "I have an extra dozen baseballs in the back of my car."

Well, in those days, a dozen new baseballs was really something.

"You got it!" Leroy shouted back.

So I went and saw the boy pitch. Kauffman got there the next day and wasted his time.

• • •

One of the best parts of this job is that you never know what you're going to see. They say that every time you go to the ballpark, you'll see something you've never seen in your life.

When you're really lucky, that means Bo Jackson striking out on a ball in the dirt, breaking his bat over his leg, and then, realizing the ball got past the catcher, beating the throw down to first. Or maybe it's Nolan Ryan blowing away the side with nine fastballs, all 96 mph or harder. Or maybe it's Willy Mo Pena hitting the concession stand beyond the leftfield wall at Kauffman Stadium some years back.

Other times, of course, it's something as trivial as a ball getting stuck in the advertisement board behind home plate *twice* — that actually happened in the summer of 2013 — or even an act of Mother Nature.

In 2010, I went to see a prospect named Michael Choice. He became an outfielder with the A's, but back then he was with the University of

Texas-Arlington. They were playing in Corpus Christi, and this isn't a story about Michael as much as it is a story about what happened.

It's the longest game delay I've ever experienced, other than rain.

The stadium at Corpus Christi is right down on the Gulf of Mexico. It's a beautiful setting, with the water and the breeze and seagulls and all of that. Well, this particular game, right about the sixth inning, those seagulls must've wanted to see a ballgame because they flew right in and sat down in rightfield.

Must've been a thousand of them, at least. It looked like a Hitchcock movie. You could hardly see the green grass, it just looked like a sea of white out there. The umpire had to stop the game, and for 20 minutes or so the groundskeepers and players from both sides are trying like hell to clear the field.

Think about sitting in the stands, watching this. It was the damndest thing. Groundskeepers are running at these birds, players are running out there with their bats — not to hurt the birds, but just to scare them, so we can play again. Eventually, they did get some scare in the birds, but all that happened was the seagulls took off from rightfield and flew over to leftfield.

So now it's another 20 minutes or so of this, then a half hour, 40 minutes. All together, it must've taken an hour and a half to get those darned birds off the field.

A seagull delay.

Never seen something like that before.

Of course, sometimes the thing you experience at the ballpark isn't as harmless as a pack of birds.

• • •

This was back in the days of segregation. Times are, thankfully, so much more inclusive now. You hear a lot about baseball helping race relations in those times, and for the most part, that's true.

When I went to black neighborhoods as a white scout, usually you're treated well. Just by going in there, you're showing admiration for the talent you're seeing. People respect that. When it's sports, it's always about who can play, not what color they are.

But it wasn't always smooth.

Once, we're on the south side of Chicago, at 39th and Shields. We're there to see a kid by the name of Murray. Good talent, we were all excited to see him.

Well, at that particular complex, there was a railroad that went by the park. The railroad was set up on a bit of a hill, and all of sudden from the top of that railroad track, you hear, *BOOM! BOOM! BOOM!*

We look up there, and it's this huge guy in overalls, with a big shotgun in his right hand. He screams out to the field:

"THERE WILL BE NO BASEBALL TODAY IN THIS PARK WITH WHITEYS IN IT!"

That was all we needed to hear. The umpire puts his hands up to stop the game and says, "Gentlemen, that's it, we'll continue this game tomorrow."

We're hustling out of the stadium, and I hear one of the other scouts, a guy from the White Sox, say, "They'll never get me in this park again!"

I went back the next day. There was no trouble. Just a little scare. And a small one, in the name of progress.

• • •

The most scared I've ever been at a ballgame had nothing to do with a gun. The earth was shaking.

Everybody remembers the Bay Area Earthquake that disrupted the World Series in 1989. I was in the middle of it. Right next to Joe DiMaggio, as it happened.

Before the game, the warm ups are going on the field, and I excuse myself from Joe and the other guys sitting in the box closer to the field because I want to check on some friends who had tickets out in leftfield, in the upper deck of Candlestick Park.

I go up the escalators, all the way to the top. I walk out onto the concourse and I thought I was having a heart attack. That's what it feels like at first. Everything is moving. You look at the lights and foul poles, it's all swaying, back and forth, for what feels like forever. I run back into the concourse and out there in the parking lot, the cars are bouncing up and down like little toys. It's the most unbelievable thing I've ever seen.

Later on, they told us the shake lasted about 15 or 20 seconds. Once the ground settles back down, you hear and see and feel the panic around you and that's when it really starts to set in. I got back down to the field, and you see some of the players taking their children from their wives for safety.

Some people from the commissioner's office come over to our box and say, "Follow us." They have some busses to take us back to the hotel. We get on the busses, but the streets were jammed, there's chaos everywhere. We got within a few blocks of the hotel, and then walked the rest. You're making your way down these streets, and you hear barking dogs that you think might me trapped, people screaming, it was just heartbreaking. Nobody knew if another shock was coming, or when. Scarier than hell.

I'm with John Schuerholz, who's still our GM at the time, and he's as serious as can be. He makes it his mission to get us out of there that night. Dean Taylor, who's back with us now but then was one of John's top assistants, calls the airlines but the airport is closed.

So he rents a car instead. At least that way we can drive out there. But when we go to pick up the car the next morning, it turns out all the cars are behind this gate that won't open because the power's down.

Our only hope is a taxi. You can imagine how hard those were to get. Finally, we see this big station wagon cab come by. The only flight we could get was out of Sacramento. The cab driver is Russian, with a really thick accent, so he motions with his fingers like, *this will be expensive.*

"It doesn't matter," John says. "We need to get out of here."

Driving out of there, you see the fire hydrants going off and all the damage to the buildings. It's a sight I'll never forget.

It's quite a drive from San Francisco to Sacramento, and by the time we get to the airport, John, who has the best English vocabulary of anyone I know, has picked up a few words in Russian.

When we get to the airport, we all chip in, it's all the cash we had between us and the best money we ever spent — we were never so happy to be on a plane in our lives.

• • •

Of course, danger comes in different ways. Sometimes, it's subtle, hissing, out of your conscious until you can't get it out.

In the summer of 1977, I was in rural Kansas to see Bob Horner, who would be the first overall pick in the following year's draft. Horner won the Rookie of the Year, and is perhaps best known for hitting four home runs in a game in 1986.

Anyway, back then, he was playing summer ball for the Liberal Blue Jays and they had a weekend series I was trying to catch. Well, about 60 miles out, my tire blows. So I get out, and I'm messing with the jack and the bolts and all of that and in between I start to hear this sort of hissing sound. I don't know what it is, look around, don't see what it would be so I go about my business.

A few minutes into it, a state trooper pulls up.

"Young fella," he says. "You know where you're at?"

"I'm just changing my tire, officer."

"You're in the heart of rattlesnake country," he says.

That's when I look over my shoulder, down into this dip off the side of the road. It's maybe 15 feet down, and there are so many damn rattlesnakes crawling over each other you can't even count.

"Let me help you," the officer says.

You never saw a tire changed so quickly in your life. We were like a pit crew.

• • •

Some prospects you never forget. Everyone remembers Kirk Gibson for his "I-don't-believe-what-I-just-saw" home run off Dennis Eckersley in the 1988 World Series, and the MVP he deservedly won that year. But I also remember him for the breathtaking prospect he was out of Michigan State in the 1970s.

I'm telling you, this guy could do it all. He was a guy who really made your heart beat. The old stadium at the University of Michigan had major league dimensions, and behind the wall in right-center there was a hockey arena. He used to hit them on top of the hockey arena in batting practice regularly. At Northwestern, they had this three-story building behind the rightfield wall, McGraw Hall, and he's the only guy I know of who hit them on top of that building.

Northwestern, by the way, is the *coldest* ballpark in the country. Once you watch a game there, especially early in the spring, you don't forget it. Your teeth are chattering from that wind coming off Lake Michigan.

Everyone was on Gibson. He was that kind of athlete. He was coming out in 1978, and we were coming off our 102-win season in 1977 — the best team the Royals have ever had, in my opinion — and picking 25$^{th}$. Normally, we wouldn't even have thought talent like Gibson could fall that far, but he was also an All-American flanker for Michigan State so we thought some teams would scare.

When Gibson started saying that if they drafted him, they had to let him play his last year of college football, most teams were turned off. We actually liked hearing that because it gave us a better chance.

So we got to know Kirk a little bit, and I'll never forget what he told me over dinner one night: "There's no way I'll play for the damn Yankees."

My first thought: *Gee, I'm glad I don't work for them right now.*

My second thought: *He'd fit in perfectly with us.*

Gibson ended up being drafted 12$^{th}$ that year, by the Tigers. Bill Lajoie, who later became general manager when the Tigers won the Series in 1984, was one of the scouts on Gibson. He went to every Michigan State home game that season, and said it was one of the most agonizing experiences of his scouting career. Gibson played football just like he did baseball — hard, fearless and unapologetic.

Every time Gibson went over the middle, or caught a pass and lowered his shoulders into a linebacker, LaJoie's heart is jumping into his throat, scared to death he's about to lose his first-round pick to a football injury.

But in this business, there's no such thing as a risk-free prospect. The trick is finding the ones worth the risk.

• • •

You really do want to check out every possible tip. Back in 1993, one of my associate scouts in Michigan, Roy Mitchell, told me about a good-looking outfielder who was in prison.

Prison.

My experience with baseball in prisons was taking Jim Bouton there to pitch in the old days so the competition couldn't see him, but I'd never actually scouted a guy in prison. But Roy said this prospect was really exceptional, so I make a call to the Jackson State Prison.

I'm doing my homework on the kid before getting up there, because you have to be careful about who you bring into an organization. It turned out that the kid really came up in a hard way. His dad wasn't around much, and he grew up in a rough part of Detroit. He made some bad decisions, got addicted to drugs and alcohol, and eventually was put away for armed robbery.

The kid really began to play baseball in prison. He never played much before that. But he had a lot of athletic ability, and a real natural way around the field, so with Roy's tip and urging I made the trip up there.

The week I called, they had a game on Saturday that I'm going to go watch. I'm basically out the door on my way to see him when the phone rings.

Billy Martin was managing the Tigers at the time, and he got a similar tip to the one I got from Roy. Martin got a one-day parole, worked the kid out at Tigers Stadium, and signed him on the spot. I never did make it into that prison.

That prospect was Ron LaFlore. Later, CBS made a movie out of his story.

*Hard to believe we all used to dress like this, huh? Suit jackets for sure, and for some clubs you had to wear ties, too. This was a group of us at Milwaukee County Stadium watching a semi-pro tournament in 1961. Nowadays, just like a lot of places around, it's a little more casual. A lot of guys wear polos, some even jeans.*

LaFlore played nine years in the big leagues, and even made the All-Star team in 1976. He continued to have problems with the law every now and again after his career was over.

• • •

Scouts are some of the biggest characters you'll meet in baseball. I guess it takes a certain kind of man to be on the road, day after day, week after week, watching games filled mostly with players who will never make it to the majors. And it especially takes a certain kind of man to enjoy it, to crave it, to want to do nothing else.

One of the guys I'll never forget is Ellis Clary, a rugged, small baseball lifer who played for the old Washington Senators and St. Louis Browns. He  was a Georgia man, a strong Bulldogs fan who lived one heck of a baseball life. They used to say Ellis could make a dog laugh. He'd tell us stories about some of those Browns teams, and if you ever congratulated him on winning the 1944 American League pennant he'd point out that 18 players on that team were deemed unfit for the military during World War II.

"What a terrible job it was for Luke Sewell to manage that bunch of hyenas," he once famously said. "They drank anything that would pour. If you went out with them, you wore a football helmet."

Later on, he was a scout with the Twins, and really good one. We're sitting there watching a game once, and Luis Aparicio makes this great diving play up the middle. He really was something with the glove. I look over at Clary, and he's got the earphone in, listening to the game on the radio. I yell over, hey Ellis, what did they say on the radio about that play?

"The Bulldogs got the ball on Notre Dame's 2-yard-line!" he yells back.

Once, he had a heart attack during a game in Alabama. They rush him off to the hospital, and Spud Chandler, who was another long-time scout and one of Ellis' closest friends, tells the story about going to the hospital. Clary motions Spud closer to the bed, and whispers.

"I want you to do something for me," Clary says.

"Anything," Spud says.

"I want you to go down and get the mileage off that ambulance so I can turn it in on my expense report."

• • •

Back in 2002, we were picking sixth in the draft and most of the in-house discussion was between Zack Greinke and Prince Fielder, but I want to tell you about something that happened when we went looking at some other guys.

Most of the clubs had Adam Loewen as the top amateur pitcher in the draft that year. As it turned out, Loewen only pitched 35 games in the big leagues for the Orioles, but back then, everyone was on him. He was a big lefty from British Columbia, went 6-foot-6, and just a terrific athlete. He actually swung the bat really well, but we liked him better as a pitcher.

This is in the spring of 2002, so not too long after 9-11. We were in that stage where we knew we liked Greinke or Fielder, but we still wanted to keep our eyes open in case something happened.

Well, on this day I was in Salt Lake City watching a first baseman and Deric Ladnier, our scouting director at the time, calls to see if I can get up to Vancouver to see Loewen pitch. So I call the airline and they ask for my passport number. Now, I've always had a passport, usually to see guys in Latin America, but you never needed a passport to get to Canada. That changed after 9-11, of course, but I left my passport at home. I didn't know I was going to end up in Canada on this trip.

They won't sell me the plane ticket, but Deric really wants some eyes on Loewen, so instead of Vancouver I buy a ticket to Seattle. My plan is to see if I can get across the border in a car, even without a passport.

So I fly out, stay the night in Seattle, and then the day of the game I wake up early and head north. I get to the border patrol, and the guy asks for my passport. This is where I need the charm of our great game to come through for me.

"I don't have my passport, sir," I say. "I'm just going to see a baseball game. I'm coming back today."

"I'm sorry, there's nothing I can do for you," he says. "We have strict rules."

Then he pauses. I can see his eyes light up.

"You're seeing a baseball game, huh?"

"Yes sir," I say. "I'm with the Royals. I'm trying to see this really good pitcher, Adam Loewen."

Those were the magic words.

"Adam Loewen? He's one of the best pitchers in the history of our country!"

And that's how I got through border patrol. The guy even gave me directions!

You know, at the time, I was so happy to get through and see Loewen I didn't actually stop to think about how I was going to get back to the United States. But like I say, I was back the same day, through the same checkpoint, and actually saw the same guy on the way back through.

He wanted to know how it went. Loewen pitched really well, I told him. And with that, he waved me back into the United States.

# Chapter
# 17

# So, you want to be a scout?

*T*om Greenwade is one of the great scouts in baseball history. He's the one who found Mickey Mantle for the Yankees, and the story of how he did that is an instructional manual on how to do this job.

He first heard about this raw talent from Oklahoma in a conversation with Barney Barnett, Mantle's manager of a Ban Johnson league team. Everyone knew Barney, all the scouts. So Greenwade checked him out, and if you can believe this, back then he was known as "little Mickey Mantle." He was only 16, so he wasn't yet *The Mick*. He was a little guy, and played shortstop. Greenwade didn't think much of the kid, so he moved on.

The next year, another contact of Greenwade's, an umpire in that same league, convinced him to take another look. By this time, Mantle had put on some weight, all of it muscle, and now his speed was showing up on the field in a big way. He'd gone from a boy to a really intriguing prospect in less than 12 months.

Greenwade got to know the family a bit, and found out he was the only scout interested. Those contacts he developed in a Ban Johnson league in Oklahoma were paying off for him. It took seeing Mantle play a handful of times before Greenwade even knew Mantle was a switch-hitter, because his team was always facing right-handed pitching. But the first time Greenwade saw him bat righty, Mantle was shooting rockets all over the field.

Greenwade didn't waste any time. He got Mickey and Mickey's father in his car right after that game, and had the contract written up in 15 minutes.

You hear a lot about the Yankee dynasty in the 1950s and 1960s, and it's true we had a lot of advantages. But people often overlook that one of the biggest advantages we had was a strong scouting staff with guys like Greenwade.

I was lucky enough to meet Greenwade when I was young, and since we both worked for the Yankees, he was particularly helpful to me. I tried to remember everything he said, but one of his bits of advice sticks out far above the rest.

"When you're at the ballpark," he said, "keep your mouth shut and your ears and eyes open."

There are so many tips from so many scouts, different levels and different situations. But if there's just one piece of advice to remember about this business, that might be the best one.

Keep your mouth shut, and your ears and eyes open.

Actually, that's pretty good advice for a lot of walks of life. Not just scouting.

• • •

It's harder than it looks, even for baseball lifers. I told you what George Brett, one of the all-time greats, said about not knowing how we do it. John McNamara spent 14 years playing professional baseball, and 19 more as a big league manager. He was the skipper of the 1986 Red Sox, the team that might've won the World Series if not for that ball going through Bill Buckner's legs.

Anyway, after he was fired as a manager, he became a scout and he comes to Kansas City. This is a guy who's been around the game his whole life, and on the field as a player and manager and coach for so many years. He's seen and lived the game from the inside.

"Art," he says, "it's a different game sitting on this side of the screen. I thought it was tough on the field, but this is really tough."

Johnny turned into a pretty good scout. But there is an adjustment. It's not like watching a game from the dugout, and it's definitely not like watching it on TV.

The importance of a good scout is often overlooked, but hardly ever by people inside an organization. Casey Stengel managed the Yankees to five straight championships. He's the only person to ever do that, but the Yankees still depended first on the opinions of scouts when putting together those rosters.

George Weiss was the general manager then, and sometimes he'd give Casey the final decision on the 25$^{th}$ man, something like that. But for the most part, those rosters were built on the input and hard work of scouts.

• • •

The lifeblood of any scouting department, and by extension any organization's baseball operations system, is the territorial scout.

Sometimes we call him the area scout, but either way, he is the eyes and ears on the ground in nooks and crannies of the baseball world that the national cross-checkers and higher executives just don't have time to see.

The territorial scout is the one who knows his area better than anyone, the one with contacts in the legion leagues, high schools, junior colleges, and four-year schools. He's the one who knows the coaches, the assistant coaches, the umpires, the one who gets the first heads-up when an unknown amateur player becomes a prospect.

It's so important for a scout to be the first, or at least among the first, to make contact with a prospect and his family. The quicker you get to know a prospect, the more he's going to remember you, the more trust you're going to build up with the family. That's how we got Bo Jackson. That's at least part of why Johnny Damon signed that contract that Scott Boras thought was too small. That's how you separate yourself from the scouts of 29 other organizations that are all looking for the same thing.

Another important thing about the territorial scout is that he can see a player so many more times. He has the most complete picture of what a prospect is. A national cross-checker may only be able to see a particular kid once.

Well, what if the kid is playing through an injury? What if a ball takes a bad hop on him? What if he just has a bad day?

The territorial scout is the one who has to know what that prospect's body of work is, and what his full potential is. If the cross-checker just sees a bad day, the territorial scout has to have the trust of the organization that he's seen a more complete picture.

I've seen it in organizations around baseball, and I've seen it even within ours.

Organizations are usually as strong as their scouting departments, and scouting departments are almost always as strong or weak as their territorial scouts.

• • •

Most of the scouts are former professional players, many of them big leaguers. There may be fewer former big leaguers in it now than in the past, just because guys make so much more money now.

Sometimes guys try scouting after they've retired, but move to something else once they get a feel for the lifestyle and everything. George Brett was talking about being a hitting coach, not a scout, but it's the same lifestyle that made him give it up after a few months in 2013. If you've made enough money in your career that you can stay at home, play golf and avoid checking into hotels at 4 in the morning to begin another three-game road trip, most guys choose that option.

I can't blame them. Like I've said, it takes a different sort of person to not only scout, but to love scouting. That's why most of the scouts' section is full of former ballplayers, but not former stars.

For many scouts starting out who didn't play pro ball, that can be a tough world to crack. I played in high school, and those years in semipro ball with the Chicago Yankees, but I never signed a professional contract. I never played in a team's farm system, and certainly never made it to the big leagues.

That could've been a major obstacle, I suppose, but it wasn't for me. If you love the game and think you might want to scout, I don't think you should let that be a major obstacle for you, either.

The ways I made up for not having a background in professional baseball included being courteous and informative to all the scouts who came around when I was running that semipro team. I had a relationship with a lot of them, and they saw me as a coach who went out and got good players. There was a certain level of respect there, and they accepted me.

The biggest way I made up for it is that I was always willing to work. I loved it, and still do. I wanted to make that drive to see that game that may or may not include a professional prospect. I wanted to make that extra phone call, or follow up on one more tip. When word gets around that you were the first one on Rick Reichardt, or did so much to get the Royals Baseball Academy going, or what the organization did to draft Bo Jackson, people around the game hear about those things.

Being a scout is like being in a lot of professional fields, I think. Hard work gets you ahead, and hard work gets you respect.

It's not always like that, you know. Sometimes a guy will take up scouting, and if he doesn't have it, others will look at him and say, "he's never even put on a jockstrap."

I never had to deal with those kinds of things, because all the other scouts knew I was doing my job.

• • •

You have to scout ability, not production. Numbers are nice, and you need to know the numbers on every prospect you recommend for your organization. But you can't base your evaluations on those numbers, particularly when you're talking about high school kids.

You have to scout the ability. This is why scouts are always talking about tools. Bat speed and athleticism are the two most important *physical* tools I look for in a position player. I emphasize that word, *physical*, because this is only half of the equation. We'll talk about the other half soon.

But if all other things are equal, if a boy has tremendous bat speed but isn't putting up eye-popping numbers, give me that boy over one with a slower bat and great numbers against high school pitching.

There are a million things between drafting a player and making the big leagues that can hold a guy up, and most of them you can't predict. But if he doesn't have good bat speed, and doesn't have the physical potential to develop good bat speed, he's not going to hit professional pitching.

Athleticism goes along with that, to a certain extent, because it can make up for other flaws. If a player is a great athlete, he'll have an easier time switching positions later (which many players have to do) and an easier time translating instruction to production.

A good athlete can make adjustments in his swing, adjustments in his routes in the outfield, and should be better around the bases.

That's true with pitchers, too, which — just to give you an example — is part of what we all liked about Zack Greinke coming out of high school. Athletic pitchers usually do better with their balance on the mound, and can more effectively put on the right kind of weight and make the right kind of mechanical adjustments to throw a harder fastball or nastier curveball.

Physical tools aren't everything, of course. Dan Quisenberry slipped through the cracks because his fastball topped out at 82, but he turned into a great closer for so many years. Wade Boggs lasted longer in the draft than he should've, and probably didn't get called up to the big leagues as soon as he should've because he wasn't particularly fast, wasn't particularly powerful, and didn't have a particularly strong arm.

If you concentrate only on physical tools, you miss out on a guy who can overachieve with a feel for the game, or raw desire, or if he's a pitcher a real good idea on how to change speeds and keep hitters off balance.

But if you're going to take a chance on someone, history tells us you're better off taking that chance on the real good athlete. That's why teams are OK paying a premium for two-sport athletes coming out of high school who have a basketball or football scholarship offer.

But we'll talk more about the guys who don't stand out physically in a second.

• • •

Like Mr. K told us, scouts are salesmen. They are a lot of things, of course. They are detectives, weathermen, psychologists, negotiators, evaluators, psychics and usually under-rested.

But a critical part of what scouts do that you might not think about it is *sell*.

You have to sell yourself, and you have to sell the organization. You have to talk to the prospect and his parents about why *you* are different than the other scouts they've met, why *your* organization would be a better place than the other 29 in baseball.

And the most important part of this is honesty. You have to be completely honest with every prospect, coach, parent, friend and teacher you come across in the scouting process.

This is something Mr. K and his people from Marion always stressed to us. Don't let there be any surprises when a prospect signs that contract and starts his professional career. You must be honest about the bus rides, the living conditions and all of the things that go into what amounts as an apprenticeship to play major league baseball. Tell them the statistics on how many prospects make the big leagues, and how many of *those* prospects have long careers.

Tell them about the inconveniences of minor league travel, and that they will almost surely have doubts along the way. You should also tell them that you and the coaches he'll work with will do everything in their power to help them, but they should go into this with their eyes wide open.

That's best for you, it's best for the organization and it's best for the prospect. It doesn't take long to get a reputation in this business, and if you become known as the guy who glosses over the negative and only emphasizes the positive to a prospect, your ability to scout and earn trust is severely limited.

So always be honest. That's a good plan for scouting, and for life.

• • •

In the old days, we scouted through metaphors and similes and adjectives.

"This guy can run like a scared jackrabbit."

"This guy is faster than a meteorite."

"His arm can hang the clothesline."

"He's got that light tower power."

Like so many other innovations that have been good for our game, the change to a more modern, sophisticated,

**What scouts look for at each position**

Major-league scouts talk often of the "five tools" they look for in prospects. For position players, those tools are the ability to: hit, hit for power, field, throw and run. For pitchers, the strengths are: velocity, movement, a good breaking ball, control and a third pitch beyond a fast ball or a breaking ball.

The importance of a player's tools vary depending on what position he plays. Here is a breakdown of the strengths scouts look for at each position in order of importance.

| Pos | 1 | 2 | 3 | 4 | 5 |
|---|---|---|---|---|---|
| P | Velocity | Movement | Breaking ball | Control | Other pitch |
| C | Arm strength | Fielding | Hitting | Power | Speed |
| 1B | Power | Hitting | Fielding | Arm strength | Speed |
| 2B | Fielding | Hitting | Power | Arm strength | Speed |
| 3B | Hitting | Power | Fielding | Arm strength | Speed |
| SS | Fielding | Arm strength | Speed | Hitting | Power |
| LF | Power | Hitting | Fielding | Speed | Arm strength |
| CF | Fielding | Speed | Hitting | Arm strength | Power |
| RF | Power | Hitting | Arm strength | Fielding | Speed |

*This is a pretty good representation of what we look for when we're out in the field. It also gives you an idea of why guys who play shortstop in college, for instance, sometimes have to move to second base when they get into professional baseball. There are no-hard-and-fast rules, you know, but this is a good guide.*

organized scouting method came from Branch Rickey. That man was so far ahead of his time, in so many different ways. We all remember him for signing Jackie Robinson and breaking baseball's color barrier in 1947, which is one of the most important moments in baseball and recent American history. But Rickey also created the farm system and did so many other things that pushed our game along.

I remember sitting with him during a World Series game. This was back in the 1950s, when I was just starting out. It was like being in a classroom. He was talking about how baseball would eventually expand, beyond the 16 teams of the time all the way to 25, maybe even 30. He was talking about how night baseball would become a much bigger part of the sport, and television, too. His mind was on so many different levels. He's thinking the whole game, and testing me, too — trying to catch me off guard.

"Do you think that shortstop has the ability to go in the hole and make the play consistently?"

"Yes sir, because he has the great arm."

"That's what I want to hear."

Rickey was one of those rare men in baseball history to change our great game in so many different, and important ways.

But for scouts, we'll always remember him for the scouting scale.

• • •

Rickey's original scale went from 0 to 60. At some point in the last 25 years, it changed to 20 to 80. I don't know why the scale uses those numbers. I'm not sure anyone else does, either. But once you learn how it works, it's pretty simple to use and translate.

For a position player, you grade the prospect in five areas: hitting, hitting for power, arm strength, glove, and speed. You can use the scale for pitchers, too, grading their velocity, control and each of their pitches.

An 80 is the top of the scale. This is a Hall of Fame tool, the best there is. You can't give away too many 80s, or else the scale loses its importance. We're talking about Miguel Cabrera's hitting, or Justin Verlander's fastball.

A 20 is the worst possible grade, and if you're still high on the player, he better have something to make up for it. This would be like Cabrera's running speed, or Juan Pierre's power.

A 50 is an average attribute, like a 90 mph fastball or a .270 hitter.

Then you can fill it in between. For a position player, you add up all the grades, divide by five, and that should give you what they call his OFP number: Overall Future Potential.

If he's a 40, he has borderline major league potential. For a 50, he should be an everyday player in the big leagues, a No. 4 starter in the rotation, or an average middle relief pitcher. If he's a 60, he's above average, with some All-Star potential. A 70 is a true star, a perennial All-Star, and occasional MVP or Cy Young candidate, the kind of player you can build a franchise around.

Now, hitting is by far the most important of the tools — there's a reason designated hitters have the highest average salary of any position in baseball — so not all "50s" are equal.

If you have one prospect who's a 70 hitter with 70 power, but 50 speed, and a 30 glove and arm he's more valuable to a big league team than a prospect with a 70 glove and arm, but 50 speed and a 30 hitter with 30 power. There are some scouts who punch the hitting grades in twice, to give those tools more weight.

Scouts can be a quirky bunch, you know, and our jobs revolve so heavily around evaluating prospects with this scale that it can seep into our every day lives.

Like, for instance, Kansas City's barbecue is an 80. The traffic in Los Angeles is a 20. Maybe you see a friend at the ballpark, and his shirt's a little wrinkled. You might say to him, "You look like a 30 today, pick it up."

Feel free to use that in your every day life, but fair warning, if you tell your wife she's an 80 in that red dress you like, she's probably not going to understand what you're talking about.

• • •

No scouting scale can take away all the ambiguity, of course. We are fallible human beings judging other fallible human beings, and not only that, you're judging them at 17 years old based on what you think they'll be at 25.

So you have to know that you're just going to miss sometimes. You're going to be wrong. You don't want to accept that, because you always want to go back and try to find what you missed. But you can't make it in this business if you beat yourself up over every player you pass over who makes it to the big leagues, or every player you sign who doesn't.

I mean, look, seeing the finished product you'd think Nolan Ryan would've been the easiest evaluation of all-time, right? Big, strong frame. Powerful arm. Relentless drive. But he lasted all the way until the 12$^{th}$ round.

That was back in the early days of the draft — remember, he was part of the first-ever draft in 1965 — so as an industry we were still working out the kinks but the feeling from a lot of the scouts who covered Texas at the time was that they wanted more polish. They didn't think he had enough control, and it should be noted in those scouts' defense, it's not like he was throwing 100 mph in high school. That real good velocity came later, as Nolan got stronger, more mature, and cleaned up his mechanics a little bit.

None of us has all the answers, obviously. If we did, Greg Maddux wouldn't have lasted until the second round, Tony Gwynn until the third round, Rickey Henderson until the fourth round, Wade Boggs until the seventh, Albert Pujols until the 13$^{th}$ and Ryne Sandberg until the 20$^{th}$. You know, Mike Piazza went in the 62$^{nd}$ round of the 1988 draft — and only then as a favor from Tommy Lasorda to a family friend.

So you know going into this that you're going to be wrong at times. The key is to make sure that doesn't stop you from doing your best to be right, or keep you from continuing to be aggressive.

Because the benefits of being right can still provide drastic help to the big league team, which is the point of this whole thing.

• • •

I'll be honest. I didn't like Dustin Pedroia the first time I saw him play. Or the second time. Or even the third time.

The reason is, well, you look at him and he just doesn't look the part. He's short, and swings a bat that looks too big for him much harder than you think a guy that size can control. His arm is OK, but not great. He runs OK, but he's not a real speed guy. The first time or two you saw him at Arizona State, you sort of think, "What can he do in the big leagues?"

But that's why you always want to see a guy as often as possible.

The more you watched Dustin in college, the more you saw the potential. I never saw him swing and miss at a pitch. He had such great bat control, even with that big swing. He's as tough a competitor as you're likely to find. He's the first guy on the field. He's the one pumping up his teammates in the dugout, and if you watch closely you can tell it's genuine.

There's an old baseball term, false hustle, that we sometimes use on a guy who might just be rah-rahing his teammates to look good in the eyes of the coach or scouts. You try to sniff those guys out by seeing how the teammates react to him. If they don't reciprocate, sort of roll their eyes, or, worse, if they laugh behind his back, then you know you're looking at some false hustle.

But when you talk to him, and his teammates, and his coach, then you can usually get a good feel for that kind of thing. Pat Murphy, who was the coach at Arizona State for a long time, told me that Dustin had the best makeup of any player he'd ever coached, well, then you know it's legitimate.

Now, obviously, if as an organization we thought Dustin would turn into what he's become — an MVP, a Gold Glover, a perennial All-Star — then we wouldn't have let him fall to the Red Sox in the second round of the 2004 draft.

But there was something you could see in the way he played the game that stood out, that made you think he'd be a good player.

Which is why I always remember one other thing Krichell told me, that you should always ask yourself: Does he like to play? Does he love the game?

Just like athleticism, if a guy really likes to play, and really loves the game, it can make up for some other deficiencies. He's more likely to work on his weaknesses, to not break mentally when he's slumping, and to stay focused and committed when he's working his way up through the fast-food-and-slow-bus-ride life of the minor leagues.

If you look at the best players in the game, there aren't many you can look at and say they don't love the game. And baseball history is full of prospects who had all the tools but not enough heart and either gave up too soon or didn't work hard enough.

These are the players who are most likely to fall through the cracks, so you have to be aware of them, too. George Brett was a high second-round pick — the 29th overall pick, which today would be the first round — so it's not exactly right to say he fell through the cracks.

But there wasn't anyone I know of who expected him to have the kind of career he ended up having. And he'll be the first to tell you, he succeeded because he wanted it more than anyone else. Every day, he came to the complex or the ballpark with the sole focus of helping the Royals win. There were no wasted days with him, no wasted at-bats.

It's hard to criticize other players who don't approach the game that way, because it's not natural. It's not normal. It's a gift or a tool, just like great bat speed or a 95 mph fastball.

It's harder to see, especially in the beginning, but once a prospect becomes a professional it can often be the difference between him making it and not making it.

• • •

A lot of the rules of scouting involve never closing the door on a possibility. That's what those old mentors of mine were getting at when they said never leave a ballpark early, and to always follow up on letter writers.

That philosophy reaches all the way into the big leagues, when teams don't like to cut ties with a player until they absolutely have to, or a better and exclusive option materializes. But it also served me well back the 1960s, when I was the only scout in baseball I knew of to employ a woman as an associate scout.

Her name was Lois Brandenberg, and I met her in Marion, Wisc., at a legion game. She was the one with the lineup, so that's how we started talking and, boy, she really knew her stuff.

So I start bouncing things off her, and she's telling me about some other good players in the area. Turns out she sees something like 80 or 90 games a year. She told me about a guy over at Eau Claire Memorial High School.

"He's only a sophomore," she told me. "But really hard-nosed, impressive kid."

I saw him the next year, when he was a junior, and sure enough he was just as she described.

That player was Tom Poquette, who turned out to be the first player I got in the draft for the Royals.

It was the least I could do to put Lois on as an associate scout.

· · ·

One of the reasons we say that scouts need to be detectives is that there is often a story behind what you see on the field. I told you about the tip involving Kevin Seitzer's injury, which led to us drafting a guy who led the league in hits as a rookie in the 11th round.

But I'll give you another example. It's not always just a nagging injury that a guy doesn't want anyone to know about, but might be affecting his production.

Back in 1976, I went to scout the Brewers because we'd heard that Darrell Porter, their catcher, was available. Porter was having a pretty bad year. He ended up hitting just .208, with hardly any power at all, and it wasn't just that — he was a mess behind the plate, too.

Now, I'd seen him from high Class-A ball ball on, so I knew the kind of player he was. Porter was always such an intense competitor, the one you could tell was firing up his teammates, getting them going, being that rock you want out of your catcher.

Well, when I saw him, he looked lethargic. Like he was just going through the motions. The best way I can describe is that he was playing through a trance. I mean, this is a guy who made the All-Star team just two years earlier, at 22 years old, so there's got to be something going on here. Guys are supposed to get better from 22 to 24, and he was going backwards. There had to be a reason.

So I'm there watching the games, and start talking with some guys who've been around the Brewers all season. Coaches, scouts. And I'm asking about Porter, telling them what I'm seeing, and eventually I find out he's going through a divorce.

Well, that explains what I'm seeing. The talent is still there. The strength, the knowledge, the confidence, the charisma. But with something going on in his personal life, his focus isn't on the baseball field. And without that focus, it's taking away from a lot of what makes him such a good player — you can't be much of a leader when your mind and heart are somewhere else.

So I tell my bosses back in Kansas City what I found out, and over the offseason we trade Jamie Quirk (who would later come back to us and help us win the World Series in 1985), Jim Wohlford and Bob McClure (who would later become a very good pitching coach for us and other teams) to the Brewers for Porter and Jim Colborn.

Porter was our catcher from 1977 to 1980, some of the best teams in Royals history. He made the All-Star team three of those years, finished in the top 10 in MVP voting in 1979, and was our catcher for the Royals' first American League pennant winner in 1980.

And we got him by buying low in a trade, because we figured he'd come out of that trance.

• • •

I'll tell you one way *not* to scout.

Walter Millies was a catcher, a backup type, who got some time in the 1930s and 1940s with the Dodgers, Senators and Phillies. Later on, he became a scout for the Mets. I saw him once at Wing Park in Illinois and, before we start, it should be said that he was just starting out as a scout for the Mets, who themselves were just starting out as a big league team.

So you have to give the man a break for this, but it's still something I'd never seen before or since. We're watching this game and there's a second baseman by the name of Paige who we'd all seen throughout the years, before Walter started scouting. Paige could run like hell, but he just couldn't hit. He's a sand blower at the plate (this is before the 20-80 scale). He's about 21 or 22 years old by then, and we've seen enough of him to know he's not a prospect.

But Walter, he was new to all of this. So the first time he sees Paige, Paige ends up having one of the best games of his life. He gets a few hits, including a line drive, makes some really good plays in the field and of course he's flying down the line.

Now, we all know what we're seeing here, but Walter didn't. He wanted to get the jump on all of us so, and I swear this is true, he gets in his briefcase and goes into Paige's dugout in the fifth inning. Right there in the middle of the game.

We couldn't believe what we're seeing. Walter is in there with a standard contract for pro baseball, for Paige to become a Met, and not only is he signing a guy who's not a prospect — he can't even wait until the game is over to do it.

The next day, right there in the Elgin Courier is a big picture of Walter and Paige standing behind home plate after the game.

You know, at least the Courier waited until after the game to get them to pose together.

• • •

If there was a magic formula to scouting, I'd tell you about it, and this business would be a lot easier.

But basically, it's a combination of common sense and relentless work.

There are tips you'll pick up along the way, like being able to read a hitter's stance or a pitcher's arm slot and project how he might benefit from some mechanical tweaks. The more you get into it, the more connections you make, which can only broaden your resources and give you more information, which is the key to this whole thing.

The more information you have, the better. That's why we want to get to know not only the prospect and his family, but his coaches, his teammates, his girlfriend, even his priest. You never know when you'll pick something up that will either move a guy up your board or off of it. I told you how we got Kevin Seitzer. We never would've had him if not for my relationship with his college coach,

*I probably have this thing memorized. There's a copy of it framed and hanging on my wall at home. I really like this because it's a good way to picture what you can see with your eyes and measure (fastball velocity, speed on the bases, range in the field) against what you have to feel and find out over time (desire, intelligence, attitude). You really have to have both as a player, which means you have to find both as a scout.*

Tom McDevitt. There's a reason I was the one who got that call, and not someone we're competing against.

But the simplest, most helpful thing I can tell you, if you want to get into scouting, is what Greenwade told me so many years ago: keep your mouth shut, and your ears and eyes open.

You are an information gatherer, a detective, not some talking head on TV spouting off your opinions about everything. If you're more concerned with making friends in the stands than evaluating what's on the field, you will miss subtle things that might give you everything you need to know.

You might miss a hitter's body language after a strikeout, or how a pitcher reacts to giving up a home run. You might overlook the way the prospect interacts with his teammates and, more importantly, how they interact with him. You might just mindlessly write down his time to first base, downgrading him for being slow, while the more observant scout next to you knows the boy sprained his ankle the day before but doesn't want anyone to know.

You can also pick up on a player's personality, which can not only help position your club to be the one to draft him, but determine whether he's worthy of being drafted in the first place.

# Chapter

# *18*

# The owners and GMs

*Y*ou work so hard as a scout to find the best players possible, so those players can work so hard to make the best franchise possible. You work within your own world, making decisions and judgments and asking questions. The players do the same thing. They take extra swings in the cage, or concentrate on subtle-but-important tweaks to their deliveries in bullpen sessions.

Baseball is a team game, but it's a team game that requires each individual to max out their own little area. What I'm saying here is that it's a team game won and lost by individual battles, and if they're doing it right each man is so obsessed with his individual battle that he doesn't track the bigger picture.

That bigger picture is painted by the owner and general manager, though. The owner is everyone's boss, and sets the tone for the entire organization. Are you going to be loose, fun-loving, like the Athletics? Are you going to be serious, detail-obsessed, like the Cardinals? There are any number of ways to win, but that identity usually needs to be set by the owner and facilitated by the general manager.

Baseball is all about the players, and most of the attention justifiably goes to the stars.

But there's an important undercurrent here that's a direct result of the owner and general manager.

I've been fortunate to work for some great ones, and, of course, some not-so-great.

• • •

My first general manager might be the greatest of them all. George Weiss, a Hall of Famer and a legend in this business.

Weiss came on in 1932 when the Yankees were winning, but the farm system wasn't as strong as it should've been. Weiss's charge was to change that, and he did, with force.

He was like a god to the players. He was kind of aloof. He kept a distance from the players, never talking to them much. When the Yankees hit the road, Weiss stayed at a separate hotel.

He liked that distance, and it created this situation where the players were actually afraid of him. When he came into the ballpark, you'd see these big, strong Yankee ballplayers whispering to each other.

"George Weiss!"

"George Weiss is here!"

I always like to sit behind the plate, just like most scouts. You can see pitch movement and location, as well as a lot of other advantages. But when the Yankees were in Chicago, I sat behind the dugout, next to Weiss. Darnedest thing. He would come in, always, in the bottom of the first inning.

"Art, gimme your scorecard," he'd say.

He'd look it over.

"Siebern lined out to left," he'd say. "Did he hit a good pitch?"

"Fastball in, Mr. Weiss."

"What about Bauer?"

"Curveball up, Mr. Weiss."

From there, he'd keep his own scorecard. There had to be a reason he always came in late. I don't know what that reason was. I never asked. Weiss was just that type of guy.

He was probably the toughest general manager to get a raise out from, too. He treated the Yankee money like it was coming out of his own pocket. In 1950, Hank Bauer hit .320 for the Yankees and drove in 70 runs. Weiss sent him a contract to play the next year with no raise, not even a dollar.

"Can you believe that?" Bauer said. "I sent it back."

Well, shortly after that Bauer got another piece of mail. This time it was a letter, from Weiss.

"This is the last contract we're offering you," it read. "If you fail to sign it, we're suspending you."

That was that. Baseball players didn't have free agency back then. Clubs really controlled everything. So what was Hank going to do? He signed that contract.

One of the things I always appreciated about Weiss was the esteem in which he held the scouts. For all of those years, he might let manager Casey Stengel pick the 25th man but for the most part Weiss picked the roster on the advice of his top scouts.

The Yankees won five World Series in a row doing it like that, from 1949 to 1953. That had never been done before, and it won't ever be done again. It's such a different game now. Weiss was perfect for the time he was in charge.

• • •

The first owners I worked for were Del Webb and Dan Topping, with the Yankees. These guys were complete opposites, which made for an interesting time.

Dan was the flamboyant, Hollywood-type guy. Always dressed to kill, and usually with a beautiful woman on his arm. We're talking stars, like Lana Turner, the Hollywood star. In fact, his brother ended up marrying Lana Turner.

Topping had a lot of interests. He co-owned one of the early NFL teams, which he called the Brooklyn Dodgers, and was married six times to actresses, a model, and an Olympic figure skater.

He was a really nice man to work for. He didn't know too much about baseball, but he was a fan, and respected the work of the people he hired. As a scout, you can always live with that.

Del Webb was a construction guy, a businessman. In fact, he's the one who built Sun City West and Sun City Grand in the Phoenix area, where I have a home and live during the offseason and spring training. Del's mother lived in Chicago when I worked for the Yankees, so I got to know him better than Topping. I'd pick him up at the hotel, drop him off at his mother's house and take him to the game.

Webb loved baseball. He played as a boy, including on a semi-pro team. He was a self-made guy, who built an enormously successful construction company from the ground up. So much of what you see in the Phoenix area today with retirement living is because of what Del started.

The funny thing about Del, here's this guy who's worth all this money — a wealthy developer, and he owned the Yankees, for crying out loud — and you always saw him in the same clothes. Same navy suit, same gray tie, same straw hat. All the time.

Both owners did a good job of recognizing the work of their scouting and player development folks. When we made the World Series, they had a deal where they'd open the owners box to a different scout each game. They'd ask a lot of questions. Always respectful, always inquisitive.

"Why did Casey take the pitcher out there?"

"Why is this guy batting fifth?"

"What pitch is Mickey looking for here?"

As it happened, one of my turns in that World Series rotation was game seven in Milwaukee in 1958. That's the game where Bill Skowron hit the three-run bomb to right centerfield in the eighth inning and won the Series, avenging our loss to the Braves the year before. To this day, that's one of my great thrills in baseball.

I really don't know if I'd have ever left the Yankees with ownership like that, but the organization really took a turn for the worse when CBS bought it in 1965. They put an Englishman named Michael Burke in charge, and I believe he understood more about cricket than baseball.

It's not a coincidence that the CBS years are some of the worst in Yankee history. CBS took over and right away the Yankees went from the American League pennant to sixth place — our worst season since 1925. The next year, we finished dead last — the Yankees had *never* finished last, not since they were known as the Highlanders, anyway.

You just didn't feel like you were with the New York Yankees anymore. It was a factory, and you were just another guy on the assembly line. What we all worked so hard to build all those years, it was taken away.

So I don't regret leaving the Yankees when I did. Especially not for the opportunity in Kansas City, and the chance to meet so many wonderful people there — including my new bosses.

• • •

The first general manager I worked for in Kansas City was unlike any other I've been close to. Cedric Tallis was a wheeler and a dealer. That man would make a deal at the drop of a hat, if he felt good about it.

He was just a force of energy, all the time. He was always in the scouts' ears, getting the latest reports, and making judgments. And if a deal materialized, he was all over it. We did a lot of good drafting and developing, with George and Frank and Willie and all of that, but there's no way the Royals would've become the most successful expansion franchise up to that point without Cedric's aggressiveness in the trade market. Whether it was at a ballpark or the bar, Cedric was always ready to talk trade.

I mean, you talk about getting Lou Piniella for John Gelnar, or Amos Otis for Joe Foy, or John Mayberry for Jim York, or Hal McRae for Richie Scheinblum. These are building blocks for our best teams, and Cedric got them for what amounted to spare parts.

Cedric was a daredevil, too. If you got in the car with him, that was a ride you wouldn't forget. He was speeding down the highway, darting in and out of traffic. You felt like you were riding with Mario Andretti, like a road of Florida was the track in Indianapolis. Everything was fast with Cedric, in baseball and outside of baseball.

Cedric was the right person for the right time for those Royals. He was naturally aggressive, and he had the blessing of Mr. K to do whatever it took to be competitive quickly. And Cedric had guts. That's what you need to navigate the trade market when you're a general manager.

You need the best information — which Cedric had because he kept in constant contact with his scouts — and you need the guts to pull the trigger.

• • •

We talked about Ewing Kauffman earlier, but people don't typically talk as much about Avron Fogelman.

He was a very successful real estate developer from Memphis who bought in for 49 percent of the Royals. Mr. K had the controlling interest, and was the one ultimately responsible, but Fogelman was a tremendous baseball fan who was our co-owner from 1983 to 1991.

Fogelman owned our minor league team in Memphis, the Chicks, who at that time was our Double-A affiliate. Every time you'd go scout the Chicks, he'd have you out at his office for lunch and conversation. He was so proud of the players and franchise there, and he had private chefs who'd cook up the best food.

He was an avid collector of memorabilia. It was incredible. He had balls signed by Cy Young and Christy Mathewson. He had Joe DiMaggio's glove, Joe Louis' championship belt, Babe Ruth's last home run ball, and George Brett's uniform from the game he got his 3,000ᵗʰ hit.

Fogelman was such a fan, and really a good guy to work for because he appreciated the game and its rhythms and trusted everyone around him to do their jobs.

He only overruled his baseball people once, and that was with Bo Jackson. We didn't want to start Bo in Double A. He hadn't played baseball in months. We wanted to start him off slowly, get him used to live pitching again before challenging him with something like Double A — where you have a lot of guys who can jump straight to the big leagues.

*Photo Courtesy of Kansas City Royals*

*I don't know if there's an owner in baseball who knows more, and has a bigger passion for the game than David Glass. He'll pick your brain about prospects all the time, and not just the top guys. He wants to know all about the guys in A-ball, and he's always up for talking about the old days.*

But Fogelman owned the team in Memphis, and he wanted Bo there. That was a once in a lifetime deal, you know, when you're talking about a guy like Bo. And of course, Bo was so great he jumped into Double A and was a success after a slow start.

• • •

John Schuerholz took over as Royals general manager in 1981, after Joe Burke moved up to club president, and you knew he was going to be one of the best in the game right away.

John was so organized, so thoughtful, so good at gathering information and processing it and involving so many in the building of a good franchise. He had some George Weiss in him, with the way he involved his scouts and built up such a reservoir of information.

John might have the best vocabulary of anyone I've ever known, and he used it beautifully, to find exactly the right way to communicate what he was feeling and what he wanted. Whenever he was done talking — whether it was to a scout, a coach or a player — you'd be ready to run through a wall for him. That enthusiasm made its way through the whole organization.

There was a purpose to everything John did. You never saw a wrinkle in his clothes, and you never saw him present himself in anything other than the most professional way. That was an example he was setting, a message he was sending. That's how he expected everyone in the organization to act.

With ballplayers, sometimes there's the "look good, feel good, play good" motto. Well, with John, it was like that for the scouts and executives. You were to dress like the best professional, because you were to act like the best professional.

• • •

I don't know that there's an owner in all of baseball who knows as much about the sport as David Glass. It's not just me who thinks that, or people who work for the Royals. Scouts and people with other teams, men who know David, will talk to us about how much our owner knows.

He grew up a Cardinals fan, and has always been in love with baseball. He can talk to you about the old days, growing up watching

Stan Musial, and he can talk to you about the present day — who Eric Hosmer's swing reminds him of.

He knows the system, too. He'll talk to you about players down in the system, guys in A-ball, and not just the high-level prospects. He wants to know about all of those guys. It really is a rarity to have that in an owner, and you learn pretty quickly that when the boss is asking you about a prospect in A-ball you better have an answer — because he might know as much about the kid as you do.

The organization obviously ran on some tough times after Mr. Kauffman passed away. The franchise was run by a board of directors, and David was the chair. He ran the team per Mr. Kauffman's instructions, but those times were very tough. Spending was cut back, because they were trying to make the team as attractive as possible to a potential buyer.

When the buyer didn't surface and David ended up buying the team in 2000, he threw this wonderful reception for all the team employees, where we all got a Tiffany box with a gorgeous Royals key chain.

We still had some rough years there, with the exception of 2003, but the direction of the organization really started to change in 2006

*Photo Courtesy of Kansas City Royals*

*I've never enjoyed working for a GM as much as I do Dayton Moore. He's the best, most genuine family man I've worked for and he has all the good traits of the best GMs I've worked for: John Schuerholz's thoroughness, George Weiss' decisiveness and Cedric Tallis' guts.*

when David hired Dayton Moore as general manager. David knew the organization needed some changes, and Dayton convinced him that the best way to build it back up was through the farm system, and investing in both scouting and amateur talent. Now, we have the biggest scouting and player development staff in franchise history. It's not even close. I don't know the numbers for sure, but around baseball, Toronto is the only other team that might have more professional scouts.

The commitment that Dayton asked for when he was hired, David has lived up to it, and that's why you see our farm system built back up from the bottom to the top.

David has always been interested in the inner workings of the organization. There are times he'll come into our draft meetings, not to interrupt or interfere, but just to listen. Like all owners, I think he wants to get a feel for our thought processes, but I also think he enjoys seeing how everything works, and being a part of that.

One other thing about David: he has such a wonderful heart. He really cares about people. I bleed Royals blue now, as you know, but obviously I was a Yankee for all those years and David knew I hated to see old Yankee Stadium shut down. Someone must have mentioned that to him, because the last year of that stadium, when they had the All-Star game, I got a note saying they had plane tickets, hotel rooms and game tickets for me and my family. I took my daughter, her husband and my oldest grandson. We sat in the owner's box. Nobody ever knew about that. I don't think he told anyone. I don't think David wants that kind of publicity.

When my wife Donna passed, David and his family were there for me. Whatever I needed. You don't forget things like that. From the inside, trust me, the people who work for David know what kind of man he is.

• • •

Even all these years later, every once in a while, Dayton and I will talk about that summer day when I had him fill out an information card as a junior in high school at the Great Lakes Regional American Legion Tournament in Rapid City, South Dakota. He remembers everything about that day, but, you know, I'm glad he never asked me why I didn't offer him a contract.

Dayton has always impressed me. I don't know how many people know this, but he interviewed to be our scouting director when he was in Atlanta. We had a good shot with him, but Schuerholz gave him a promotion to stay in Atlanta.

Of all the general managers I've worked for, Dayton is, without a doubt, my favorite. And I'll tell you why. The first reason is that he learned from good people. Paul Snyder, a longtime scout for the Braves, was always one of the best in the game. And you know what I think of John Schuerholz.

Dayton has so many of the traits that John has, as far as organization, people skills, his ability to communicate and his ability to attract good people to work for him and to empower those people to do their jobs well. The advantage that Dayton has over John as a GM is, Dayton scouted a territory. He was out there and knows exactly what it is to beat the bushes and look for players. He's been in player development. He's a bit of a throwback to Weiss, too, in that he listens and listens and listens. He's very decisive once he has the information, but he wants to make sure he has the information first.

You know the way we scouts look at players, we're always trying to find a complete player. Someone who can run, but also hit for power. A pitcher with a great fastball, but also good command of his breaking pitches. Well, Dayton is that complete general manager. He's a terrific leader, who empowers and helps his people do the best work they can, but he's also the finest family man I've ever worked for. That's hard to balance as a general manager, and it's harder today than it ever has been before.

He also has the most sincere compassion for his people of anyone I've worked for, or with. There is no front with Dayton. When he asks you about your family, your wife, your children … he means it. In times of crisis, or sickness in your family, Dayton is there for his people like no individual I've ever worked for. He's just so sincere.

I'm not just saying this because he's my boss. I truly believe he has the potential to be one of the greats in this game.

# Chapter
# *19*
# Rosemary

*Y*ou know, I've actually known Rosemary, my wife now, for more than 50 years.

It was back in 1958, just after I signed Jim Bouton. I was really starting to come into my own as a scout, really feeling comfortable, making my way in the baseball world. You want someone to share that with, you know.

I met Rosemary at this small Lutheran church in Chicago. They say you meet a different kind of woman in church, and Rosemary was different. Right away, there was just a strong feeling between the two of us. Chemistry, is how they say it now.

I remember we went to *My Fair Lady* at the Schubert Theater in Chicago, right downtown. This was New Year's Eve, as 1958 was turning into 1959. I don't know what it was about her, or what it was about *us*, but I just felt so sure walking out of that show. That feeling we had, it was overpowering. I wanted to settle down, and she was worth settling down with.

So as we were walking out of that show, with everyone around us, into the Chicago night on New Year's Eve, I asked her if she'd be my wife.

She said yes.

We talked to our families, set a date, made invitations and everything. We even reserved the church, that small Lutheran church where we met. Looking back, I don't know that you'd say we weren't thinking straight. But it's probably true that we didn't think everything through. We were rushing. We both wanted this life. We both wanted the same thing.

But she was a lot younger than me. I was 31. She was 19. She deserved to be out in the world more. She probably needed that. She probably knew that, and I did, too. So one day, it was a month or so before the wedding date, we both felt the same thing. She was too young to be with a man who lived the life I lived, always on the road, always searching for the next Jim Bouton. Her being so young, that would've been really hard on her.

At first, we just told each other we would put the wedding off for a while. A new date. A little delay. But deep down, I think we both knew what was going on. This was it. We were breaking up.

Not too long after that, over another baseball summer, I was at Wing Park in Elgin, Ill., watching Ethan Blackaby play centerfield when Donna Wakely told Nick Kamzik, "There's only one club in baseball, and that's the New York Yankees."

Those years with Donna were such a thrill. Almost 50 years we were together. She protected me. She counseled me. She was everything to me — her and baseball.

I was so lucky that it happened the way it did.

After Donna passed away, that was so hard on me. She was such a constant in my life. She passed away in February, and I missed the start of spring training for the first time in all of my years in professional baseball.

And when I got back into my work, baseball helped me. I've always had baseball. I've always been attracted to baseball. The rhythms, the stories, the possibilities. It's something new every day, yet something so familiar. It can take you back to when you were a boy, and it can take you into the future.

So, if baseball is how I've lived my life, and how Donna and I met, baseball would be how I would move on and continue living my life when I no longer had Donna. She loved the game as much as I do. I know she'd want me to keep going, and I was lucky that I've made a lot of great friends in this great game. They helped me, too.

I was involved in a lot of things, like always. Seeing our minor leaguers, seeing draft prospects, preparing for the draft. There's a movement by some to put a scout's wing in the Hall of Fame. They have a temporary exhibit there now. Maybe we'll have that as a permanent fixture there in the museum.

So, eventually, I really felt like I was back into the swing of things, you know?

Anyway, after the baseball season one year I go to Chicago to see my daughter. When we're there, we went to that big, old Lutheran church. I'm telling you, I hadn't been there in 50 years.

I see Rosemary there.

Right away, I knew it was her. I hadn't seen this woman in 50 years. She looked different, of course. I know I looked different. You might think that after all that time you wouldn't recognize someone, you wouldn't remember what they looked like or you would've changed so much that they'd pass your eyes without a second thought. Not here. Not with Rosemary. I knew her right away, and she knew me right away, too.

We locked eyes, and started talking. I mean it. It felt like no time had passed at all. Here we'd gone off and moved on and lived our own lives. I'd been in professional baseball all these years, chasing talent all over the country, trying to build strong organizations with the Yankees and then the Royals. I'd met Donna, married Donna, we had our daughter. We'd moved to Kansas City, signed George Brett, opened the Royals Academy, seen the Royals go from an expansion team to a baseball power, won the World Series and fallen on harder times with the Royals. I mean, so much had happened in all of those decades.

But when I saw Rosemary, it was like time had stayed still. It was like I was 31 again, and like she was 19 again.

There's no way I could've imagined this, let alone expected it. Who finds love, again, at this point in their life? But we started talking, met for coffee and things like that a few times, heard about each other's lives, all of our successes and disappointments and funny stories along the way.

That chemistry we had 50 years before was still there. Somehow, we still had it. Maybe we got it again, or maybe it didn't leave. I don't know. People say it's the kind of thing they only see in the movies, but I guess in some ways my life has been like a movie. It's been better than anything I could've imagined. We got married, Rosemary and I, five years ago. I've felt the same way about her every day since. She's my companion, my counselor, my life.

I've worked in the game I fell in love with as a boy for more than 60 years. I've loved two franchises, and now I've loved two women. I couldn't have imagined this life.

*This is Rosemary and I on the lake near our house in the Kansas City area. Meeting her again and having the same feelings we had when we were younger after all these years has been more than I ever could have expected.*

# Chapter
# 20

# Seven decades
# aren't enough

*J*still do it because I still love it. That's really the answer to the
question I hear from people a lot, though it goes a little deeper.

I turned 87 years old this year. I'm in my seventh decade of
professional baseball. Phil Rogers, the great baseball writer still working
for the *Chicago Tribune*, once said I'd been scouting so long my first
report was done on a stone tablet.

There are guys who stick around a long time. Not a ton of them, but
there are some of us. Most of them want to slow down, though, at least
stay off the road. I've never felt that way. I've never wanted to scale back.

I do 81 home games a year, and when the big league club is on
the road I'm out watching either our minor league clubs or preparing
for the draft by watching the top amateur prospects. Basically, I do
whatever the front office asks of me. Dayton Moore and his assistants
have been very good to me, and they know I still have a passion for this.
Sometimes, they'll ask me to scout big league opponents, to stockpile
information that we can use for potential trades in the future.

That passion I have for this game is the same as when I started. I just
can't imagine doing anything else.

• • •

One of the things I love so much is representing the team at
the June draft. You probably know how they set it up now, with an
executive and former player representative for every big league club
to show on TV.

Frank White came with me the first year. We've also done it with John Wathan, Joe Randa, Willie Aikens, Dennis Leonard, Fred Patek, and Mike Sweeney — you should've seen it when Sweeney went, he became like the mayor of the whole place. George Brett was supposed to go last year, but he ended up taking the job as hitting coach.

One of the things I love about it is that having the former players there really enlightens them about what goes into scouting, signing players and the draft. They've been on one side of the draft, now they get to be on the other.

They invite some of the amateur players to be there, too, but for some reason the agents discourage it. I don't know exactly why that is, but back in 2009, there was only one amateur player to show up to the draft in person. Major League Baseball wants that camera moment, the kid shaking hands with the commissioner and getting his new jersey. It's the photo opportunity you always see in the NBA and NFL drafts.

Well, back in 2009, there's only one kid there, this outfielder from New Jersey. And the draft is going on, and on, and on, and nobody's picked him. He's sitting in this little dugout they made for the TV set with his parents, and they're on pins and needles waiting for this kid's big moment. This was the year Dennis Leonard was with me.

"I feel bad for that poor kid," Leonard says.

Well, right in front of us is Bill Stoneman, who has been a general manager and executive for the Angels for many years. Stoneman heard Leonard, and he turns around.

"Don't worry," Stoneman says. "We're taking him, and we're coming up next."

And that's how the Angels drafted Mike Trout 25th overall in 2009. Like most clubs we all missed on Trout. We just didn't see him enough, with him being in a cold weather state. He's the closest thing to Mickey Mantle that we've had in our game.

• • •

We fooled them in the 2013 draft. We were in on Hunter Dozier, the shortstop for Stephen F. Austin. We had a lot of really good reports on him, very positive stuff. We brought him into Kansas City before the draft, and he put on a tremendous show for us in a workout.

At some point we realized we were higher on him than most in the game. The way most of the other draft boards were, we'd probably be looked at as reaching too far if we took him eighth overall but we didn't think he'd be there for us when picked again at 34th overall.

Another kid we liked was Sean Manaea, a big left-handed pitcher out of Indiana State who tore up the Cape Cod league the year before. Manaea had everything you want in a starting pitcher. Velocity, control, a good feel for pitching. He was going to be a top-five pick in the draft, but he hurt his hip. As it happened, I was there the day he hurt his hip. And for the five innings before the injury, he was as dominant as any pitcher I've seen in a long time. You don't forget displays like that.

Well, the injury was fairly serious. He ended up having the same surgery Alex Gordon had on his hip. It's a serious injury, but the doctors are so good that you can be sure the player will come back from it at full strength. Good as new. But it takes time, and Manaea had tried to pitch through the injury and wasn't nearly as good. That turned off some clubs, but we'd seen him so good we never forgot.

So we had two players we really liked, but the way the draft boards were, we probably couldn't get them both.

So what our scouting director Lonnie Goldberg did was take a significant, but well-thought-out gamble. We took Dozier eighth overall, which at the time threw a lot of clubs (and fans) into confusion. We had "overdrafted" him, in the parlance of the game, but we did it for two very significant reasons.

First, we really believe he can play. We think he's going to be a very good big league player, and for a long time.

Second, the way that baseball's draft rules work now, each club has a certain amount of money they can spend signing their picks. Everybody has a different way of navigating this, but the way we tried it, we figured if we drafted Dozier first and signed him for less than the typical "slot" signing bonus that would give us the opportunity to spend more on a guy later.

The plan worked out for us when Manaea was still available when we picked 34th. When we took him, everyone who questioned us for drafting Dozier seemed to understand. It doesn't always work out like this, of course, and in baseball there are no sure things. There is a long way to go from being drafted with optimism to being a good big league player.

But we feel like we got two high-level first-round talents.

This is the kind of thing I just love, the reason I keep doing this.

• • •

One of the other movements in baseball that really has my attention is the possibility of a permanent way to recognize scouts in the Hall of Fame.

Birdie Tebbets was the first guy to bring this up. Birdie got 14 years in the big leagues as a catcher, even made some All-Star teams, despite losing three years to World War II. He later managed 11 years in Cincinnati, Milwaukee and Cleveland. He would propose a way to honor scouts at the Hall of Fame every year, starting when he was selected to the Veterans' Committee in 1981, and every year (starting in 1981) he was turned down without hearing a reason.

Well, that started to change in recent years. Two people in particular have been instrumental in this. Roberta Mazur, who serves as the president for the Scout of the Year Program, and Jeff Idelson, the president of the Baseball Hall of Fame.

A few years ago, Idelson said he'd consider a way to recognize scouts if we could get enough information, display art, artifacts, that kind of thing. Well, Mazur was the perfect person because she had ways of getting all of that, and now they have an exhibit called "Diamond Mines" right there in Cooperstown.

It really is something. They have old stopwatches, old straw hats worn by great scouts like Tony Lucadello. I sent them some old reports, like the ones we had on George Brett and Bo Jackson. They've honored all the past winners of the Scout of the Year Award, including me. I was so humbled to receive the award in 2008. A truly great honor.

The opening of the exhibit really was something. They had panel discussions, where baseball fans could come in and learn about scouting.

Scouts have always been the faceless men of baseball. Nobody can picture a scout. Not even a guy like Tom Greenwade, who found Mickey Mantle in a small Oklahoma town before anyone had even heard of Mickey Mantle.

Nobody knows a scout. To a fan, if anything, scouts are the guys behind home plate with the radar gun. For the most part, we like it that way. It's a beautiful game, and the focus should always be on the fans and the players. Without the fans, we'd all be out of work. And without the players, none of us would have anything to watch.

So scouts are happy to stay anonymous, which is part of why you'll rarely see us named in stories in newspapers or magazines or websites. But we love to talk about the great game, which is why we talk to a lot of reporters.

The thing that's so encouraging to me about the momentum around a scouts exhibit at the Hall of Fame is that it will help fans understand the job. It will put some names and faces on what to this point is a largely untold story that's behind every great player or moment in baseball history. For every player in Major League Baseball, there's a scout and a story behind them. There are bad apples in any bunch, but for the most part, scouts have a tremendous love and passion for the game. They better, anyway. They'll never become millionaires.

You hear hitters say the hardest thing in sports is to hit a baseball, and that's absolutely true. Putting a round bat on a round ball thrown by wildly talented pitchers intent on you not being able to hit it is one of the great achievements in sports. But the success rate of a big league hitter against a big league pitcher is higher than the success rate of being able to project an amateur prospect to the big leagues.

That's why I say the hardest job in baseball is to project what the 17- or 18-year-old youngster will be when he's 21 or 25

*Photo Courtesy of Kansas City Royals*

*Baseball is the most important thing to me besides family. And when I play my cards right, I can have both together. This is me and my grandson David, keeping score and scouting a spring training game in Arizona.*

and a major league player. You put all your time and knowledge and experience into making those projections, and your name is on those projections. Your reputation.

You just can't buy the self-satisfaction you feel when you go out on a limb for a prospect, and then you see him prove you right. That's a bond that can't be broken.

And a feeling you never forget, and at least for me, never stop chasing.

• • •

There has never been a single day in more than 60 years of doing this that I've woken up and not wanted to work. Never a day that I haven't wanted to see a player, watch a game, try to find the next great player. I love this game more than anything in life, except family.

I never look at a clock — except to see if I have the right game time.

It's not the kind of work that a lot of people would love. Or, rather, it's not the kind of work that a lot of people would love for a long time. Watching baseball is great. Who wouldn't want to do that? But a lot of guys get into scouting and get worn down by the long hours in the car, or the long days watching another game with nobody you think is worth signing, or even the disappointment of being wrong on a guy you thought had that special quality.

That's never been an issue with me. This life keeps me going. Being around these young players with stars in their eyes, before they're big leaguers and all share the same dream, it really keeps me going. Keeps me young. I knock on wood, but my health has been good. I'm a little slower now getting around with a bum knee, but that's OK. It doesn't hold me back.

If I couldn't contribute anymore, or didn't have the passion to do this, I wouldn't want to do it. I don't want to do it just to do it. But to still be able to go on the road, I love that. I still love to drive. I love that feeling of getting in the car and wondering if you're going to see the next great thing. It's the same feeling I had back when I had a territory.

It's the same feeling I had all those years ago. There's just something that happens in your gut when you see these players and what they might be. Maybe there's another Bo Jackson out there. I'd love to see another George Brett come into our organization with that kind of fire, to work so hard to get every bit of production out of his talent. Maybe there's another Carlos Beltran out there I can see. I'd love to see another player with the tools of Rick Reichardt.

As long as I have that feeling, and as long as the Royals think I'm valuable, I never want to give it up. I've never wanted to do anything else, and every day I understand how lucky I am that I've never had to do anything else.

Maybe that's part of why I'm still doing this.

If you're living your dream, why would you want to wake up?

*Photo Courtesy of Kansas City Royals*

*I've never woken up without wanting to spend some of the day at the ballpark, and the opportunity to do that is part of what keeps me young at heart.*

# Acknowledgements

*I*'ve been so fortunate, not only to be able to make my way in the game I love so much for all these years, but to have come across so many who've helped me along the way.

George Weiss, my first general manager with the Yankees, was as good as anyone who's been in this game. I learned so much from Branch Rickey, those one-on-one conversations about the game were an invaluable learning experience for me. Lee McPhail was one of the first general managers I worked for directly, and helped me in a lot of ways. I have to give thanks, of course, to John Schuerholz for recognizing me and hiring me as scouting director. And to Mr. Kauffman, the father I never had.

Tom Greenwade, one of the greatest scouts of all-time, shared tips that I've held onto. Same with Lou Maguolo. I learned about the business, both on and off the field, from both of those men. They were instrumental in helping me get into the scouting business at a very young age, when most of the scouts were former big leaguers. And Dayton Moore for being able to work under him in such a great scouting environment.

Also, Linda Smith, my right arm in preparing for drafts all those years as scouting director, and who is still a huge help, not just to me, but all of us in baseball operations. For as many tireless days she works for the Royals, if we ever tried to pay her back she'd be off for a few years.

My uncle Clarence, for taking me to my first major league game, helping solidify that baseball was it for me.

Of course my dear wife Donna, who put up with this for 47 years. She was my wife, my friend, my partner, my co-scout for all those years. My daughter Dawn was always supportive as well, even when I was traveling all those summers when she was out of school.

Rosemary for her love and support over these past five years of our marriage.

The Glass family for their support through the years.

A very special thanks to Sam Mellinger who has helped tell my story so accurately.

# Author Bios

**Art Stewart:** The only scout ever inducted to the Royals' Hall of Fame, Art has been an integral part of the franchise since 1969. He grew up on the North Side of Chicago, walking distance from Wrigley Field, and ran his own semipro team before his 13<sup>th</sup> birthday.

He was a good enough high school player that the Hall of Famer George Sisler offered him a pro contract with the Dodgers, but Art was making too much money hustling his semipro games to take the paycut. Instead, he kept the team and started scouting for the New York Yankees — going full-time in 1958.

Stewart left the Yankees to help start the Royals, and was a key component in everything the franchise did from the innovative Royals Academy to building an organizational strength that was the envy of the entire industry.

One of the best-known scouts in baseball, Art is considered the model for generations of scouts who've come up after him. He signed more than 70 players who made the big leagues, including Bo Jackson, Johnny Damon and Carlos Beltran. The Royals were named major league baseball organization of the year four times by various publications during Art's 13 years as director of scouting.

**Sam Mellinger** has worked at The Kansas City Star since 2000, the last four years as sports columnist. His work has been recognized by the Associated Press Sports Editors, Kansas and Missouri Press Associations, and Best American Sports Writing. He lives in Kansas City with his wife Katie and son Samuel.

Visit www.ascendbooks.com for more great titles
on your favorite teams and athletes.